PLURAL OFFICE-HOLDING IN MASSACHUSETTS

PLURAL OFFICE-HOLDING

in Massachusetts

1760-1780

Its Relation to the "Separation" of
Departments of Government

By Ellen E. Brennan

CHAPEL HILL
THE UNIVERSITY OF NORTH CAROLINA PRESS
1945

COPYRIGHT, 1945, BY
THE UNIVERSITY OF NORTH CAROLINA PRESS

To the Memory of

ANASTASIA E. BRENNAN

PREFACE

PLURAL OFFICE-HOLDING is a practice conspicuously absent from modern American government. While an American Governor today may determine that certain bills must pass the state legislature and it seems by party pressure may secure their passage, yet it is not possible for him to reduce legislature and courts to continued compliance through distribution of numerous offices among the members of those bodies. The absence of plural office-holding is so much taken for granted in our modern political life that very little inquiry has been made as to how it was eradicated from American political institutions. For plural office-holding was not only a prevalent but an almost universal custom in the American colonies before the Revolution. Transplanted from England, it was a custom which beset the colonies as well as the mother country throughout most of the eighteenth century.

The present study, however, does not aim at an examination of the problem and its eradication from American political institutions. No survey of plural office-holding is here attempted even for a single one of the American colonies. The purpose of the present study is rather to show the relation of the custom of plural office-holding to the movement for a separation of the departments of government in Massachusetts in the latter part of the colonial period, as that movement culminated in unmistakable provisions in the Massachusetts Constitution of 1780. Interest here centers about the custom of plural office-holding as one of the chief factors which led to the adoption of provisions for a separation of departments of government in the Massachusetts Constitution.

At the same time, an interpretation of the purpose of the Massachusetts provision for a separation of departments and its meaning is sought in contemporary opinion of the period of the adoption of the Constitution of 1780. The conclusion is here reached that the provision for a separation of the departments of government in Article XXX of the Declaration of Rights of the Massachusetts Constitution was to be made concrete by the provisions of Chapter VI, Article II, which called for a detailed separation in office-holding. By so providing, the Massachusetts constitutional fathers hoped to put an end to the abuses of plural office-holding, following the common law and numerous English "place bills" of the eighteenth century. The evidence indicates, however, that the Massachusetts constitutional statesmen did not intend to establish a hard and fast separation of departments of government on the basis of different types of power.

An interesting conclusion for American governmental development emerges in that the Massachusetts constitution framers, under the English influence, not intending definitely to separate the executive and legislative departments, did not attempt, in fact, to exclude the Governor from a seat in the legislature. On the contrary, the clause designating officers to be excluded from the legislature (Chapter VI, Article II) expressly omitted the Governor and the Lieutenant-Governor.

That it was not intended that the Lieutenant-Governor should be independent of the legislature is also obvious from the method of election provided for that officer, for he was to be chosen by the two houses of the legislature meeting in joint session. That the Governor's Council was to be in close relationship with the legislature is likewise obvious from the fact that members of the Council were to be chosen from the members of the Senate.

Colonial practice left its mark in the concept of the office of Governor and his relationship to the legislature. The Governor's independence of the legislature apparently should be ascribed rather to the independent method of his selection than to the provision for a separation of departments in the Constitution. Previously the Governor's independence of the two houses of the legislature through his appointment by and representation of the Crown had been a source of endless strife under the province Charter. The Governor's independence of the two houses in selection and responsibility was perpetuated by the provision for popular election of the Governor in the new Constitution. That the significance of popular election of the Governor in his relationship to the legislature was not well understood at the time is indicated by the omission of the Governor from the list of officers in Chapter VI, Article II, who were to be excluded from the two houses after the manner of the English place bills.

The fact that the separation between executive and legislative departments was only relative in its nature has heretofore been overlooked. This conclusion results particularly from a consideration of Chapter VI, Article II of the Constitution of 1780, and it deserves some emphasis, in that it has generally been assumed that the separation between executive and legislature was intended to be definite in early American state constitutions. Quite otherwise, however, a far-reaching separation of courts and legislature in personnel was effected by Article II of Chapter VI. These conclusions are the more important since cross-references reveal a similar treatment of the problem of the separation of departments in various other colonies. Indeed, the English backgound of the principle is undoubtedly significant in all of them.

It has been deemed essential to set out at considerable length the original materials on which these conclusions are based. Much of this material has not been previously published and the extracts in their original form may serve to call attention to these little known sources of Massachusetts history. Furthermore, many of the quoted sources show first hand the political ferment of the American Revolution as it extended into the far reaches of Massachusetts towns and as it involved constructive political thinking on the part of the citizen body. Another object in using the original sources extensively is to show that the abuse of plural office-holding made the movement for a separation of departments a popular one, so that there was widespread discussion and expression of opinion on the subject not only by political leaders but also from the pulpit, and from the people at large including even those who were not strictly literate. Thus the achievement of a separation of departments of government in Massachusetts was not a theoretical matter, but it incorporated a practical reform of a long-standing grievance. It was a step in the direction of popular control of government.

The opportunity afforded by way of preface is all too brief to express adequately my appreciation of the contributions of others which have gone into this study. Many of these are referred to in the footnotes and bibliography but there are more direct obligations too numerous to mention. Among my college professors in Radcliffe College whose teaching formed the background for this study, I should mention Professor William Bennett Munro and Professor Frederick Merk, and especially Professor C. H. McIlwain, in whose class in "Colonial Charters" at Radcliffe College I first became interested in the subject of American colonial institutions. Professor Roscoe Pound made a number of helpful suggestions at the beginning of the study, one of which was that Coke's *Institutes* should be looked into, and actually the *Institutes* proved to be the source to which the researches led in the final instance.

Mr. Stewart Mitchell, former editor of the Massachusetts Historical Society, and of the *New England Quarterly*, carefully read the manuscript, and made a number of helpful suggestions, particularly as to style. Professor Julius Goebel,

Preface

Jr., of the Columbia University Law School, very kindly read the introduction and last chapters of the manuscript and made discerning suggestions, particularly that the records of the General Court following the adoption of the Constitution of 1780 should be examined. Professor Robert L. Schuyler of the History Department of Columbia University has also read parts of the manuscript, and made a number of valuable suggestions looking toward greater accuracy and clarity in treatment of the material. The scholars who have thus contributed to the study are of course in no way responsible for the conclusions reached, nor for factual errors of which no doubt some have escaped the author.

The Library of the Massachusetts Historical Society has been relied upon to a very great extent, the staff there having with great courtesy expended considerable time and energy in making available a large amount of the source material which went into the research involved in the study. The original documents in the Massachusetts State Archives were also with great courtesy and patience made available for the study, particularly by Miss Marie Hession, and by other willing assistants in that department. Mr. Robert H. Haynes has also graciously given access to the facilities of the Harvard University Libraries in connection with the research during several summer vacations. Lastly, some materials have also been helpfully made available in the Essex Institute of Salem, Massachusetts, and in the libraries of Columbia University, New York City. Miss Lisle John and Miss Marjorie M. Bruce have given generous and painstaking assistance with the proofs.

To the many other persons too numerous to mention by name who have helped otherwise and contributed to the present study, I gratefully express my appreciation and thanks.
            ELLEN E. BRENNAN

Rockport, Massachusetts
June, 1944

CONTENTS

CHAPTER	PAGE
PREFACE	vii
INTRODUCTION	3
1. THE GRIEVANCE OF PLURAL OFFICE-HOLDING	25
2. AGITATION AGAINST OLIGARCHY	41
3. OVERTHROW OF EXECUTIVE CONTROL	74
4. PLURAL OFFICE-HOLDING BY PATRIOTS, 1775-1778	107
5. ACHIEVEMENT OF A "SEPARATION" OF DEPARTMENTS	136
APPENDICES	179
BIBLIOGRAPHY	191
INDEX	205

Plural Office-Holding in Massachusetts

INTRODUCTION

IN POINT OF IMPORTANCE, the "separation of departments," commonly interpreted as a "separation of powers," ranks among the one or two leading principles of American government, but as a source of obstruction and rigidity in governmental organization, it is second to no other principle. The principle of organization of government on the basis of "separate" departments is not only fundamental in the structure of American Federal government, but it has been written into every one of our state constitutions in one form or another. American governmental development, not only in the past but for the future, will undoubtedly be shaped by this principle. It is one which comes before American courts constantly, and particularly in its application to the establishment and organization of administrative agencies and commissions its interpretation has formed an embarrassing obstacle in government, the provision appearing as an expression of political theory too unrealistic to be taken literally, and too important to be disregarded.

It seems generally agreed among political scientists that the principle is to be treated as a theory, and the practical background of English and American experience has been neglected. The historical background of the principle has generally been assumed to be too evident to merit much consideration—the principle appearing so obviously to be taken from the theories of the French writer, Baron de Montesquieu. Most writers on the subject have chosen to analyze the meaning of Montesquieu's theory, and then have applied their findings to American institutions with anything but helpful results. They have concluded that the theory defines a separation of the "powers" of government into three separate departments according to type of power as a method of securing liberty under government. Indeed, American constitutional theorists have long regarded the incorporation in American constitutions of Montesquieu's suggested method of attaining liberty as the institutionalizing of an unfortunate oversight. For many of the best American authorities in the field have found that Montesquieu, in drawing his theory from observation of the English government, was mistaken in his conclusion, and that there was little basis in fact to be found in English institutions for his theory.[1]

Writers have frequently pointed out that at the very time (1748) when Montesquieu published his famous principle in his *L'Esprit des Lois* the Cabinet principle of government, which unites rather than separates legislative and executive powers, was in process of development in England. A less critical and a more accurate view of Montesquieu's formula

[1]. C. E. Merriam, *A History of American Political Theories*, p. 91: "But many of the features admired in Montesquieu were derived from his study of the English Constitution and the English political system. This was eminently true of his celebrated doctrine of the tripartite division of governmental powers, which he had found or thought he found in the English Constitution." See also p. 79.

W. S. Carpenter, *The Development of American Political Thought*, p. 49: "It was supposed that the writings of the Frenchman depicted the political situation in England at the time he wrote, but the assumption had little basis in fact. At the precise moment when Montesquieu was formulating his principles, the British government was assuming a form inconsistent with the doctrine of the separation of powers."

Henry M. Bates, "Trends in American Government," *Proc. 5th Ann. Meeting Calif. State Bar* (1932), p. 58: "But it is familiar learning today that the theory of a completely tripartite distribution of the powers of government, and the setting up of airtight compartments between them, grew out of the idealistic and abstract theorizing of French political philosophy of the eighteenth century, and a very serious misinterpretation by Montesquieu and other Frenchmen of the constitution and functioning of the British government, and particularly of its allocation of governmental powers. There is not now and never has been in England anything like the trinitarian separation and distribution of the powers of government which Montesquieu supposed." Quoted in a collection of materials on the Separation of Powers in Walter Gellhorn, *Administrative Law, Cases and Comments*, p. 35.

for securing liberty, that he did not mistake the English Constitution but merely exaggerated the sharpness of the separation of powers therein, has been set forth by the English constitutionalist Holdsworth.[2]

Even in the eighteenth century it was observed, and in modern times the French scholar Dedieu has pointed out, that Montesquieu was not original in his theory of a "separation of powers" but that he followed Locke and other English theorists of an earlier period in his philosophy of political institutions.[3] Dedieu also has demonstrated that Montesquieu wrote *L'Esprit des Lois* for propaganda purposes against the absolutism of the French monarchy of his time. In fact, the theory of organizing government on the basis of different distinct branches or departments was used long before the publication of *L'Esprit des Lois*, on the Continent, in England, and in the American colonies in the long struggles of the seventeenth and eighteenth centuries to secure power to the popular branch of government. It is also a fact that in England and in the American colonies the theory of separation was a weapon wielded against the King or his representative, and for the purpose of attaining more effective popular participation in government.

An attempt will be made in this study to show that the chief problem of the eighteenth century in connection with the subject of "separation" in government was an elementary one: the separation of the personnel of the departments in order that the departments might use their powers independently effectively to check each other. The separation of departments was insisted upon in order to make the independence of the departments effective, and was to be attained primarily by a separation in office-holding, and not by a separation of abstract powers of government. While the

---
2. "The Conventions of the Eighteenth-Century Constitution," *Iowa Law Review*, XVII, 164-5.
3. *Montesquieu et la tradition politique anglaise en France*, pp. 99-191.

principle will be referred to in this study as a separation of departments rather than as a separation of "powers," since the latter was not an eighteenth-century problem, the use of "separation" here is inaccurate in implying too great differentiation.

A distinguished scholar has recently considered the theory of separation under its aspect of "balanced" government, and has shown that most of the literature on the subject of balance was English.[4] It is a fact, however, that eighteenth-century advocates of a distribution of powers among separate departments of government or of balanced government were intent in England as well as in Massachusetts upon upsetting the existing "balance of power," in favor of increased power to the branch of government which represented the people. The concept of balanced government therefore does not seem to be useful as a practical expression of the purpose which the early constitutionalists, at least those in Massachusetts, had in mind. Also it would seem that the checks, particularly those upon the executive, were more important than the balances among the departments. As to the impact of the theory, Pargellis finds it incorporated in the Federal Constitution: "their practical plan was also a deliberate monument to a theory,"[5] a conclusion not applicable in Massachusetts.

Quite at variance with this view is that of another author who, skeptical of the influence of Montesquieu, undertakes to prove that adoption of the theory of a separation of powers in early American state constitutions was the result alone of the "indigenous experience" of the colonists. "It is in the history of the colonial governments that one finds the reasons for the acceptance of the general theory of separation of powers," he states, and yet he concludes that the theory written into American constitutions is the one generally ascribed to Montesquieu: a separation of "powers" of govern-

---

4. Stanley Pargellis, "The Theory of Balanced Government," *The Constitution Reconsidered* (Conyers Read, Ed.), p. 39.
5. *Ibid.*

ment. However, the essential question in the problem is considered mistakenly to be: *why* did the colonists adopt the theory of a separation of powers?[6] The problem is, rather, *what* theory did they adopt, and *why*?

As to the practical result in American government, modern authorities are well agreed, in a way which imports little respect for the framers of early American constitutions, that the separation of powers which they earnestly provided for is impossible of execution. The separation of powers has thus come to be regarded by political scientists as a handicap in government, its recent history being a matter of criticism and disparagement. Representative comments on the principle run like the following: "In recent years the triad has been much attacked by theoretical writers, and has been proved by actual experience to be impossible," and: "There is no longer any virtue in the triad, except as a provisional scheme. We must discover some other rough differentiation of the functions and organs of government."[7]

There is general agreement with this present-day evaluation of a fundamental principle of American government, which is supposed to have had its origin in error, and which must be admitted to cause serious obstruction in governmental practice. The title of the contribution of one of Montesquieu's own countrymen exemplifies recent disposition of the principle: "La fin du principe de séparation des pouvoirs."[8]

6. B. F. Wright, Jr., "The Origins of the Separation of Powers in America," *Economica*, XIII (May, 1933), 170.

7. Herman Finer, *The Theory and Practice of Modern Government*, I, 170, 171. See also C. A. and Wm. Beard, *The American Leviathan*, pp. 68 and 70: "In their view the separation of powers creates friction in government, divides responsibility . . . and altogether works for confusion and obscurity instead of simplicity and public scrutiny."

Henry M. Bates, "Trends in American Government," *Proc. 5th Ann. Meeting Calif. State Bar* (1932), p. 58: ". . . it is idle to hope that we can confine governmental bodies of this age to functions which are either strictly legislative, strictly executive or strictly judicial, as an absolute theory. The complete differentiation of the powers of government was never sound."

8. Marcel de la Bigne de Villeneuve: "De l'étude que nous venons de

Confronted with such a problem so basic to administrative organization, clarification may well begin with a closer examination of the origins of the theory, rather than with further attempts at theoretical interpretation of the principle of a separation of powers.

A study of the historical background and interpretation of this most characteristic of American governmental principles should determine, therefore, whether or not the early constitution makers followed Montesquieu, or at any rate what principle they adopted, what their interpretation of the principle was, and their purpose in adopting it. If modern constitutionalists have misapprehended the provision, that fact should become clear from a study of the events leading up to the adoption of the principle and the constitutional articles comprehending it.

An organization of government on the basis of "separate" departments was provided for in the early American state constitutions some years before it was incorporated in the Federal Constitution, and approach to an interpretation of the principle should historically be made, therefore, from its use in the states. Since the Massachusetts Constitution of 1780 adopted the principle in unmistakable form, a study of its history and interpretation in Massachusetts should therefore be of especial profit. In examining the historical background of the organization of government in separate departments in Massachusetts, an attempt will be made to show that the principle was adopted as the result of extended experience in England and in Massachusetts colonial history, and not merely to achieve escape from a general and remote tyranny described by the French writer, Montesquieu. It would be a serious error, however, to neglect the influence

---

terminer, nous retirons cette conclusion que la théorie de la séparation des pouvoirs, strictement prise dans les termes employés par Montesquieu, est rationnellement et pratiquement inacceptable."

of English experience in accounting for the principle in this country, as at least one writer has done.⁹

The separation of departments had a well-understood meaning to Massachusetts constitution makers, and it was incorporated in the Constitution of 1780 for a practical purpose. This study seeks to show that the primary purpose of the constitutional statesmen in adopting the principle was in reality not a "differentiation of the functions and organs of government," for discussion of differentiation of the functions of government was negligible at the time. What they actually sought to ensure was the independence of action of the various branches of government or departments: they did not have in mind a separation of powers into different types of power in the modern sense, nor any absolute separation of departments. In the eighteenth century the chief problem in connection with the separation of departments was a separation in office-holding, for which they went back to the common-law rule against the holding of incompatible offices and the English place bills. Neither was the separation of departments, as modern students have supposed, an end in itself.

The examination made in this study of the meaning and purpose of the organization of powers in separate departments in Massachusetts in the colonial period has shown that not only was the principle possible of execution in terms of the colonial understanding of it, but that its execution became so universal in the early Massachusetts state government that it was then very much taken for granted. Today political scientists for lack of consecutive discussion have lost sight of the ends which the constitutional framers had in view, their reasons for adopting the principle, and their interpretation of it.

It will also be seen that the separation of departments, far

9. B. F. Wright, Jr., "The Origins of the Separation of Powers in America," *Economica*, XIII (May, 1933), 176.

from being a check to the majority as is sometimes said,[10] actually was looked upon by the constitutional fathers of Massachusetts as their most important protection against an oligarchy and as a guarantee of government for the benefit of all groups in the state, although not, of course, for the benefit of the majority alone. This study, it is believed, will show that the purpose which the constitutional statesmen of Massachusetts had in mind was to establish a "government of laws and not of men," that is, a government which would function in the public interest. This end they sought to achieve through a separation of departments.

English constitutional experience and theory and the common-law rule against incompatabile offices have hitherto been much neglected as an influence in American constitution making. Actually, for decades prior to the Revolution, the separation of departments was something more than a theory to the Massachusetts colonists. That the principle was necessary to insure effective checks and balances in the public interest was demonstrated to them, not only by their own experience, but also by the statutes and common law of England. In the mother country, the Revolution of 1688 with its constitutional changes was conceived to have furthered greatly the separation, or independence, of the departments[11] and to have resulted in provisions for this purpose not only in the Act of Settlement (since important provisions in that Act were never enforced) but also in a long series of subsequent statutes. In adopting the principle, therefore, the Massa-

---

10. W. R. Sharp, "The Classical American Doctrine of 'The Separation of Powers,'" II *U. of Chicago Law Review*, 436 (1935): "A limit on the many in the interests of the few was the first purpose of the principle as it appeared in American constitutions." The same rationale for the theory in American government is given in Finer, *Theory and Practice of Modern Government*, I, 165.

11. Act of Settlement, 12 and 13 Wm. III, C. 2: "That no Person who has an Office or Place of Profit under the King, or received a Pension from the Crown, shall be capable of serving as a Member of the House of Commons." Statutes at Large (English), IV, 58.

chusetts constitution makers looked upon it as something which had already been achieved in England by the common law, by the Act of Settlement and by the various place bills, the passage of a series of which began in 1693 and continued for the greater part of the eighteenth century.

In her first state constitution, Massachusetts adopted a threefold statement of the principle of a separation of departments. The experience which called for such a thrice-certain guarantee went back not only to the beginnings of Massachusetts government, but also to the constitutional struggles of the mother country. The "government of men," which the Constitution of 1780 provided against, had flourished in Massachusetts from the earliest days of the colony, but the practice of combining important offices of state in the hands of a few men was a custom of long standing in England before it was transplanted to Massachusetts. From the colony period (1629-1692), the "government of men" was carried down in Massachusetts (but with some differences) into the province government set up by the Charter of 1691.

The Trading Company Charter of 1629 had given the Massachusetts Bay Company a Governor annually elective by the General Court, which was a body made up of all the members of the Company. During this colony period, the annually elective Governor was merely *primus inter pares*,[12] his fellow magistrates (the Assistants) like him acting in an administrative and judicial body of the company known as the Court of Assistants, and constituting also the County Courts and the Council of the Magistrates. They also were members of the General Court. Quite otherwise under the Charter of 1691, the Governor was removed from popular influence by being made appointive by the Crown, while new powers given by the Charter established him as the chief magistrate of the province. In the colony period, the Gen-

---

12. Thomas Hutchinson, *History of Massachusetts Bay*, III, 299. "Colony" is used to designate the period 1629-92; "province," the period 1692-1776.

eral Court, under the influence of the English parliamentary development, had been made the "cheife civill power" of the "commonwealth."[13] Important powers, which had been previously exercised by the General Court or Assembly, were, by the Charter of 1691, placed in the hands of the Governor.

Despite the fact that the terms of the Charter of 1691 saved a General Court for Massachusetts Bay, it was a General Court curtailed in legislative and judicial powers, and shorn of all important executive powers. By the new Charter, the General Court was made to consist of three branches, the House of Representatives, the Council, and the Governor, instead of only two houses as formerly. A radical change in the power of law making was that the houses of the Assembly were for the first time subject to the negative of a Governor appointed by the Crown in all their Acts, while within a period of three years Acts of the General Court might be disallowed by the Privy Council.[14]

Nor was the upper house of the General Court (the Council) for the future dependent upon the two houses of the General Court alone for its election, since the province Governor was given a veto over the election of the Council, as over other acts of the Assembly. The colony Court of Assistants (the same in membership as the Council and second house) had been elective by the General Court. Though the product of evolution and quite unknown to the colony Charter, the Council of Magistrates of the colony government had been set up with the general power of acting "for provision and protection" of the "commonwealth" in the "vacancy" of the General Court.[15] In practice it had exercised a variety of powers. By the new Charter, the *province*

---

13. *Records of the Governor and Company of the Massachusetts Bay, in New England*, II, 95-96.
14. *Acts and Resolves of the Province of the Massachusetts Bay* (hereafter cited as *Acts and Resolves*), I, 17.
15. See Ellen E. Brennan, "The Massachusetts Council of the Magistrates," *New England Quarterly*, IV, 1 (Jan., 1931), 54.

Council functioned in several official capacities: as executive council, as legislative upper house, and as a judicial court.

The province Council was limited to advisory action in its capacity as part of the executive branch of the government. The Council was to give advice and assistance to the Governor, and powers were granted to it for the "directing and ordering the Affaires"[16] of the province in Council (except in the case of military powers). The Governor was not obliged to take the advice of the Council, however, and one Governor who fell back upon the advice of the Council to shield himself from popular fury in enforcing unpopular measures was informed by the Secretary of State that he alone was responsible for the exercise of power delegated by the Crown: ". . . the Admission of a Right in the Council to be consulted on all Occasions would be to establish in that Body a Power & Authority, inconsistent with the Spirit of the Constitution, as it is You, to whom the Crown has delegated its Authority, and You alone are responsible for the due Exercise of it."[17]

Likewise, the judicial power given to the Council by the province Charter was inconsiderable. Only the power to probate wills and the power to grant administration of any interest or estate survived to the Governor and Council in the province Charter.[18] By statute, the Governor and Council were given jurisdiction over one or two other judicial subjects.[19]

16. *Acts and Resolves*, I, 10.
17. Bernard Papers, XI, 192 (June 11, 1768). From Hillsborough.
18. *Acts and Resolves*, I, 15.
19. H. R. Spencer, *Constitutional Conflict in Provincial Massachusetts*, p. 28.
Late in the province period, an opinion of the Privy Council was given that in "proving Wills and Administration and deciding Controversies concerning Marriage and Divorce," the majority of the councillors present should make the decision, and that the Governor should acquiesce in such decision, even though he should differ from the majority. *Journals of the House of Representatives*, 1773-74, pp. 102-3 (Jan. 26, 1774).

In legislation, the Charter of 1691 gave coequal powers to the Council and House of Representatives. The General Court, which was to consist of the Governor and "Council of Assistants," and of elected freeholders, was obviously not a body of enumerated legislative powers, for it was given the broad grant of power ". . . to make ordaine and establish all manner of wholsome and reasonable Orders Laws Statutes and Ordinances Directions and Instructions . . . (soe as the same be not repugnant or contrary to the Lawes of this our Realme of England) . . ."[20] But laws so made were subject to the veto of the Governor, as well as to possible disallowance by the Privy Council. In practice, the House sought to reduce the part of the Council in legislation, particularly in the case of money bills, to a subordinate position.[21]

Considering the fact that the colony government of Massachusetts had "approached very near to an independent commonwealth" (at least from 1640 to 1660),[22] that the colony Governor had been scarcely more than the colleague of the other magistrates, while the General Court had acted as "the chiefe civill power of the commonwealth," without doubt the new charter provisions would bring with them difficulties of execution. It might have been predicted that the province Charter would effect considerably less than it set out to in the matter of the powers conferred upon the royal Governor. The powers actually exercised by the Governor were by no means so complete as the Charter specified. Conflict between the previous constitutional development and the new attempts at royal control was continuous.

Hutchinson remarked of the incidence of the Charter of 1691, "They came off by degrees from their practice under the old charter,"[23] but Hutchinson, when he wrote this (the

---

20. *Acts and Resolves*, I, 15-16.
21. Spencer, *Constitutional Conflict in Provincial Massachusetts*, p. 96.
22. Hutchinson, *History*, II, 10.
23. Spencer, *Constitutional Conflict in Provincial Massachusetts*, p. 96.

date of publication was 1767), had not seen the province government in collapse. It would be more just to state that Massachusetts never "came off" entirely from the practice of the colony period. The representatives of the people fought consistently against the powers given to the Governor by the province Charter.

Like the early house under the province Charter, the Council in the first years of the new Charter was largely composed of men with parliamentary experience under the colony government. Practically all the Council members for the Massachusetts territory in 1691 had served in the colony General Court, for the most part as magistrates, and of the twenty-five members making up the whole Council (including those from territory not before represented), all but eight had experience in the General Court under the colony Charter.[24] Also in the Council of 1693, practically all the members from Massachusetts had served as magistrates under the colony regime, and of the whole Council, two-thirds of the twenty-seven councillors had served in the colony General Court. Even twelve years later, fourteen out of eighteen members of the Council from the old Massachusetts territory had sat in the colony General Court, and of the whole number of twenty-eight councillors, twenty-one had served in the colony General Court.

But in spite of the colony tradition, in the struggles which took place regarding the executive powers transferred from the General Court of the colony period to the Governor, the Council almost uniformly aligned itself with the Governor, until the end of Bernard's administration in the province period. Why the Council was thus identified with the prerogative until 1766, in contrast with the House of Representatives, is not obvious from the method of its selection.

24. List of Representatives for 1689-92 in *Mass. Hist. Soc. Coll.*, 3rd Series, IV, 289; Council lists in *Acts and Resolves*, VII, 5-6, and VIII; and Council lists in the General Court Records (Mass. State Archives), 1689-98. Hutchinson, *History*, II, 20-21.

Greene calls the method of election of the Council under the province Charter a concession to the "old republican traditions," and speaks of it as a survival of the colony principle of popular control of the executive.[25] Instead of being appointed by the Crown, as was the ordinary royal Council, or of being elected exclusively by the two houses of the General Court, as was the case with the colony Council of the Magistrates, the province Council (twenty-eight in number) was elected by the General Court.[26]

The question of whether the power of electing the Council rested with the Council as well as the House was not clear from the Charter. It was decided in the affirmative by the two houses in 1693, but the decision that the election was to be a joint one turned out to be a point of great political importance. Not only was election by both houses required, but also approval by the Governor was necessary, since "in all elections and Acts of Government," according to the Charter, the Governor was to have "the negative voice." The election of the Council by the two houses was a survival of the colony custom in electing magistrates, as is pointed out by Greene; but the negative of the Governor over the elections was an unpopular innovation. As such it was opposed by the agents of Massachusetts at the time of the framing of the Charter.[27] By an instruction, the Governor was cautioned in using his negative to take care that the councillors were men of property and of good standing in the province.

In the election of the Council, the votes of the House greatly outnumbered those of the Council—more so as time went on, and the number of towns returning representatives increased.[28] The negative of the Governor was not always

---

25. Evarts B. Greene, *The Provincial Governor in the English Colonies of North America*, p. 76.   26. *Acts and Resolves*, I, 12.

27. Spencer, *Constitutional Conflict in Provincial Massachusetts*, p. 16.

28. "In the year 1718 there were but 91 Writs issued, in 1692 when the Charter was opened probably not above 84, Now there is near 170 And yet the Council keeps its old Number of 28, So that the Assembly

an effective weapon, since he could not take the initiative in nominating candidates for the Council. He could only negative the candidates named by the House, and the House might leave vacancies where the Governor had used his negative.[29] Yet John Adams recorded his impression in 1775 that, from the date of the Charter to the Stamp Act, "the council of this province have been generally on the side of the Governor and the prerogative."[30] And Hutchinson wrote in the spring of 1769, "I do not know that there has been an instance since the Charter until now of the Councils combining against the G."[31] The explanation, however, of the long identification of the Council with the prerogative is to be found in methods of influence less outright than those resulting from its election.

One source of the Governor's influence over the Council derived from his right of presiding over executive sessions of the Council, and from his presence in legislative sessions of the Council, since he was forbidden to preside over the legislative sessions by a rule adopted under Governor Shirley.[32] The independence of action of a councillor whose election had to be approved by the Governor obviously might not be very real when he acted under the surveillance of the same Governor. At least one Governor, although he did not presume to preside over legislative sessions of the

---

were to the Council at the time of their first meeting as 3 to 1 now they are 6 to 1 and consequently the Councils share in elections is diminished by half." Governor Bernard to Lords of Trade, Aug. 3, 1701. Quoted in H. A. Cushing, *History of the Transition from Provincial to Commonwealth Government*, p. 23. A great many towns made default in sending representatives, however. Bernard Papers, II, 75.

29. Massachusetts State Archives, XXVI, 306: Hutchinson Correspondence.
30. "Novanglus" (John Adams) in the *Boston Gazette*, Feb. 20, 1775.
31. Massachusetts State Archives, XXVI, 350: Hutchinson Correspondence (to Jackson, Apr. 16, 1769).
32. An opinion of the law officers of the Crown to this effect was given. Greene, *The Provincial Governor*, p. 43. Hutchinson, *History*, II, 15, 107.

Council, explained why he found his presence in the legislative sessions very helpful to his policies. Writing to England on his practice in this respect, Governor Bernard said:

> I . . . neither have desired to preside or interfere with their debates as a Legislative: but I have claimed a right to be present at these debates whenever I please, & to give them such informations & as should seem to me to be necessary to a right Judgement to the Questions before them, without entring into Arguments or making conclusions therefrom. I have also when I have had doubts concerning Matters which have been laid before me for my consent & were passed in Council in my absence stated my doubts to the Council & desired to be informed of the reasons they proceeded upon for directing my Judgement. This has generally been the means of satisfying me, but sometimes has occasioned the Council to reconsider the business & alter their Vote.[33]

The presence of Governor Bernard in the legislative sessions of the Council, on the basis explained above, raised at least one complaint by the popular party of "Undue influence."[34]

But what strengthened the influence of the Governor even more than his presiding in the Council was the fact that the ancient custom of plural office-holding was carried over into the province government. In keeping with the custom of a plurality of offices, councillors frequently filled other offices in the government, such as those of judge, secretary, attorney-general. It was almost an unbroken practice to fill the judicial offices, particularly those of the Superior Court, with leading members of the Council. In fact, on the bench of the Superior Court from 1692 to the Revolution there appears to have been but one justice who did not sit in the Council for all or a part of his term of office, and that one justice was on the bench for one year only.[35]

33. Bernard Papers, VI, 187-188.
34. *Ibid.*
35. Thomas Graves, who was on the Superior Court bench in 1738-9. Emory Washburn, *Sketches of the Judicial History of Massachusetts from*

Introduction

The appointment of judges was in the hands of the Governor, with the advice of the Council, and hence the office of councillor was more frequently an introduction to the bench, than the bench to the Council. The first bench under the province Charter was named from members of the appointed Council (in the same year), and in the naming of the second bench the politic Dudley did not neglect his opportunity to establish a hold over the Council by judicial appointments. The practice of giving judicial commissions to councillors was continued by subsequent governors. The judicial tenure in the province abetted the practice, since it was defined neither by the Charter nor by the commissions of the judges. In practice, it was at the will of the Governor and Council as John Adams pointed out, rather than *quam diu se bene gesserit*, and a judge might be removed by the Governor and seven members of the Council, without a hearing.[36]

The influence over the Council—and the courts—which the Governor would gain from the distribution of remunerative judicial posts among the councillors is obvious. Frequently, however, several offices, instead of two, even of widely varying powers, were combined in the hands of one councillor. A formidable combination of offices thus was vested in the leading councillors, built up through the agency of and usually under the control of the Governor. Influence by the Governor over the Council as the second legislative

---

1630 to the Revolution in 1775, p. 242; and *Acts and Resolves*, XII, 475-6, 1738-9, and I-V.

36. *Boston Gazette*, Feb. 22, 1773. *Ibid.*, Feb. 15: "Our Judges commissions, have neither the clause quam diu se bene gesserit, nor the clause durante beneplacito, in them. . . . Thus the argument arising from the omission of the clause in our Judges commissions of durante beneplacito, seems to have no weight in it, because the same clause is omitted from the commission of the peace both at home and here, and yet the commission has been settled at home to be determinable, at the pleasure of the King, and here at the pleasure of the Governor and Council, particularly in a late instance. . . ."

chamber, and over the council members as judicial officers, and direction of the councillors in their capacity of executive officers, gave the Governor a lever in both courts and legislature, in addition to control over the executive department.

Yet the governors of Massachusetts, from Dudley to Hutchinson, complained to the home government of the method of selecting the Council: they found it a serious hardship to be left to the mercy of indirect methods to gain the support of the Council. Upon the Council hinged control of the government, and a wholly appointive Council was the goal of the Governor in the struggle to enforce royal policy.

It was obvious, even to non-political observers, that control of the Council was an unstable factor in the government. Andrew Eliot explained the position of the Council thus:

> Sometimes they are intimidated by the House of Representatives. At other times they are under the awe of a negative. This precarious situation makes their conduct fickle, uncertain and inconsistent. At one time this motive preponderates; at another, that. A few years since, when some interesting point was depending, the Council were menaced by the Governor on one hand, and the House on the other. An honest old Councillor broke out in that homely language, "In short, we are like a turnip, squeezed between two trenchers." Besides, they often hold places, or have expectations for themselves and their friends, which renders them still more dependent. At present there are but few men of abilities among them. One or two changing sides, the rest follow.[37]

To a less extent, the Governor used the patronage to maintain support in the House of Representatives. Here inferior court commissions and military and customs commissions were used for the purpose.

37. Hollis Papers, pp. 154, 4, and 179, 2 (Jan. 29, 1769). Eliot goes on to say: "It is by no means a well constituted body, chosen annually by the representatives and *by themselves!* subject to a negative from the King's Governor." The letter is published in *Mass. Hist. Soc. Coll.*, 4th Series, IV, 438.

The Governor therefore was not solely dependent upon his veto of council elections or of legislation for control of the General Court. It is apparent that with a compliant body of twenty-eight councillors and a substantial number of "placemen" from the House of Representatives the election of Council members could be carried for the administration in a poorly attended General Court, generally of around one hundred and fifty members. The Governor's veto over the election of councillors was therefore reserved for extreme cases.

But when a serious breach came between British policy, which the Governor represented, and the province interest, upheld by the House of Representatives, the popular party found that by organization, which they extended even to the use of intimidation, they could dominate the election of the Council. Executive and judicial officers could be dropped from the Council then and the Governor thus deprived of the close control which he had maintained, not only over the Council as an advisory body, but as upper house of the legislature as well. The Governor's veto was then found to be an ineffective weapon, since candidates were named by the houses jointly and they could refuse to fill the seats of negatived councillors, thus leaving the Governor with an ineffective Council. Thereby the hold of the Governor over the province government would be broken. Bernard was involved in this extremity, which he had foreseen: ". . . if the Faction once gets possession of the Council . . . the Governor has nothing to do but to Strike his Colours."[38]

The system of control which the royal Governors maintained in the province of Massachusetts Bay reflected on a smaller and provincial scale the system of Crown influence in the House of Commons which was the chief subject of constitutional controversy in England during the greater part

38. Bernard Papers, IV, 237. To Lords of Trade, July 7, 1766.

of the eighteenth century. In England, however, that influence had been limited by a long series of place bills. One of the advocates of the "successful expedient of influence" who defended the system as essential to the practical functioning of the British government, attributed the loss of the American colonies to the lack of such a system in the colony governments. William Paley, the English philosopher, writing shortly after the American Revolution, ascribed to popular assemblies certain reprehensible characteristics which led them ever to extend their power: "the secret pleasure of mortifying the great, or the hope of dispossessing them; a constant willingness to question and thwart whatever is dictated or even proposed by another; a disposition common to all bodies of men to extend the claims and authority of their order; above all, that love of power, and of showing it, which resides in every human breast." Such characteristics might lead the majority of an assembly to try "to draw to themselves the whole government of the state,"[39] whence it was necessary for the government to possess "an influence to counteract these motives" . . . "it must have some weight to cast into the scale, to set the balance even."

In the American colonies, however, Paley concluded that the drive to power on the part of the popular assemblies was left without a bridle. Paley found that the British colonies of North America had assemblies which possessed "much of the power and constitution of our house of commons," yet he discerned this difference: "The king and government of Great Britain held no patronage in the country, which could create attachment and influence, sufficient to counteract that restless, arrogating spirit, which in popular assemblies when left to itself, will never brook an authority, that checks and interferes with its own."

39. William Paley, *The Principles of Moral and Political Philosophy*, p. 492.

Hence the loss of the colonies: "To this cause, excited perhaps by some unreasonable provocations, we may attribute, as to their true and proper original, we will not say the misfortunes, but the changes that have taken place in the British Empire."[40]

This study undertakes to show that Massachusetts was subject to such a system of "influence" as Paley advocated, but that it failed as a method of control in Massachusetts as it did in England in the face of the movement for popular government. The account of how the Governor came to lose control of the province government and had the groundwork of a revolution laid before his eyes will explain how the principle of a separation of departments was used for propaganda purposes against the administration, and how Montesquieu's theory was applied to the political situation in Massachusetts. It will also explain the purpose and importance of the principle as it was understood by the Massachusetts of that time. That purpose was stated in Article XXX of the Declaration of Rights of the Massachusetts Constitution to be the achievement of "a government of laws, and not of men." In another article the same purpose was stated more fully in the following words: "Government is instituted for the common good;—and not for the profit, honor, or private interest of any one man, family, or class of men."[41]

While Montesquieu was quoted more than any other theorist on the separation of departments in Massachusetts, when the constitution makers came to write a provision on the subject into their Constitution, their concept differed in important respects from that of Montesquieu. For the practical organization of their government into "separate" departments they leaned heavily on English constitutional

40. *Ibid.*, pp. 493-4.
41. Article VII, Declaration of Rights, Massachusetts Constitution of 1780.

experience, as well as their own experience in Massachusetts. In other words, in the Constitution of 1780, the departments of government were only as "separate" as the experience of the mother country and of the province had shown they should be.

CHAPTER I

THE GRIEVANCE OF PLURAL OFFICE-HOLDING

LATE IN THE AFTERNOON of September 15, 1760, a man on horseback riding across Dorchester-Neck passed a carriage proceeding in the opposite direction. The carriage was returning from Castle Island, from the summer home of Francis Bernard,[1] recently appointed Governor of the province of Massachusetts Bay. The plump, round-faced rider on horseback was traveling toward that same place.[2] The rider was later to understand that a similar motive brought the occupants of the carriage and himself to Castle Island that day—to proffer a candidate for the vacancy on the Superior Court bench of Massachusetts, left by the death of Chief Justice Sewall on the previous Wednesday, September 10.

The man on horseback was James Otis, Acting Advocate-General in the King's Court of Admiralty, and he was approaching the Governor with an application for an appointment to the Superior Court for his father, Colonel James Otis, a prominent lawyer of Barnstable County. The occupants of the carriage were Thomas Hutchinson, Lieutenant-Governor of the Province, and Charles Paxton, recently appointed surveyor of the customs in Boston, and something of a political "boss" in Massachusetts.[3]

---

1. There was a difference in the accounts of the episode, as given by Hutchinson and Otis, as to whether the occupants of the carriage had dined, or had been at tea in the home of Governor Bernard.
2. *Boston Gazette,* April 11, 1763. Also Thomas Hutchinson in *Boston News-Letter,* April 7, 1763.
3. *Ibid.* See also Mass. Hist. Soc. *Proceedings,* LVI, 347; Mass. Hist. Soc. MSS.: Paxton to Townshend, Jan. 12, 1760; *Boston Gazette,* April

The Governor, in his interview with Otis, did not commit himself in the matter of the appointment, and Otis was later to believe that a promise of the vacancy had been given by the Governor to the Lieutenant-Governor shortly before his arrival. From the disposition of this appointment, immeasurable animosity and political controversy was to rise in Massachusetts. It was also to contribute to a sharpening of the issues in the revolt of this, the British King's most valuable maritime province, which formed a link in that wider insurrection on the part of the thirteen colonies—the American Revolution. The appointment turned out to be of so unfortunate a nature, that it brought to a climax feeling against the long-standing custom of plural office-holding, frequently a violation of the common-law rule against the holding of incompatible offices, making of it a grievance and rallying-point against the administration.

When Governor Bernard addressed the two houses of the General Court, shortly after his arrival, he alluded to the remarkable harmony existing in the British government: "Very singular," he said, "is the Happiness of the present Times, beyond all other known in our History: When all Parties are united, and even the Voice of Faction is silenced; When the Sovereign is acknowledged to be the Maintainer of the Privileges of His Subjects, and the People are become the Supporters of the Prerogative of the Crown."[4] But the longer Governor Bernard dwelt in Massachusetts, the less occasion did he have to refer to the remarkable harmony which he noted on his arrival, and the more at length did he complain of the evils of faction in the government. More and more turbulent did his administration become, until finally the preliminary conflicts of a revolution were to drive him from the province. One of the chief factors in

---

4, 1763; and John Adams, *The Works of John Adams, with a Life of the Author by his Grandson, Charles Francis Adams*, X, 298. Hereafter cited as *Life and Works*.

4. *Boston Evening-Post*, Aug. 18, 1760.

these conflicts was the grievance of plural office-holding, an account of the significance of which can be given only in its setting of political controversy in the province.

Party divisions had required the attention of many Massachusetts governors before the time of Governor Bernard. The split into popular and prerogative parties in Massachusetts had appeared more than once in the history of the province, on occasions when the policy of the Crown, represented by the Governor, was not accepted by the popular party, which had its foothold for the most part in the House of Representatives. The origin of patriot and prerogative parties has been found by one historian to stem from the difference of opinion in the colony as to whether the original charter should be defended against the Crown, when its abrogation was threatened by Charles II.[5]

Political factions (if not parties) characterized the colony period in Massachusetts, and division into parties may be observed in the beginning of the province government. Differences of opinion stirred up by the inflammatory issue of the currency under Governor Belcher still persisted. Various of the party leaders were lined up in their respective positions before the arrival of Governor Bernard.

At the beginning of the controversy in 1760, Thomas Hutchinson was already a well-identified political leader in Massachusetts. Starting his political career as selectman for the town of Boston in 1737, Hutchinson had served in the Council since 1749,[6] had held the office of Judge of Probate

5. George Richards Minot, *Continuation of the History of the Province of Massachusetts-Bay*, I, 51: "From this period we may date the origin of two parties, the patriots and prerogative men, between whom controversy scarcely intermitted, and was never ended until the separation of the two countries. Such as were for adhering to their patent naturally won the feelings of the people, and received their confidence in proportion to their zeal; whilst such as hoped to assuage a power which, in their opinion, could not at this period be overcome, were subject to the reproach of cowardice, or self-interested motives."

6. Wm. H. Whitmore, *The Massachusetts Civil List for the Colonial and Provincial Periods, 1630-1774*, pp. 58-60.

for Suffolk County, "inherited" from his uncle, and had been Lieutenant-Governor during Governor Pownall's short administration. Hutchinson had projected the sound currency bill of 1749, which substituted a currency based upon silver for the paper money of Massachusetts. Its passage was an achievement for which Hutchinson said he "had the thanks of many persons," but for which, one may observe, he had none from the popular party. The cause of paper money, thought to inure to the benefit of the provincial merchants in transactions with British merchants,[7] Hutchinson continued to oppose after the passage of his sound currency bill. Much of the unpopularity which he later acquired Hutchinson attributed to his position as "the father of the present fixed medium."[8]

A growing opposition to Hutchinson was already evident at the time. To his friend Israel Williams, Hutchinson gave an account of its appearance in the General Court in 1759.[9] Samuel Adams was one of those who opposed Hutchinson over the currency issue. Adams had suffered from the invasion of provincial property holdings by an Act of Parliament dissolving the "Land Bank." The "Land Bank" had been an attempt on the part of provincial businessmen to add to the currency in circulation by mortgaging their estates, or by giving bonds as security for the issue of notes.[10] Samuel Adams had been able also to observe the efficacy of direct action in preventing the execution of an attachment against

[7]. Mass. State Archives, XXVI, 87: Hutchinson Correspondence; Wm. V. Wells, *Life and Public Services of Samuel Adams*, I, 7.

[8]. Mass. State Archives, XXVI, 3, 155: Hutchinson Correspondence.

[9]. Israel Williams, Letters, II, 150: Hutchinson to Williams, June 14, 1759, Mass. Hist. Soc. MSS.: "Some of my Friends moved for some notice to be taken of me, the answer was they never paid the L G for what he did while the Gov. was in the Province. You can guess what quarter this must come from. Its an interest that has prevailed some time & I think rather increases than otherwise & I know its very agreeable to more persons than I could wish but after two or three hours mortification I have got over it."

[10]. Wells, *Samuel Adams*, I, 8, 10, 26.

his estate, which had been issued as a result of the Act of Parliament dissolving the "Land Bank."

While the Act of Parliament brought the Land Bank to an end, the province passed a law of its own which was regarded as directly conflicting with it.[11] Of this Act of Parliament, John Adams said that it raised "a greater ferment" in the province than the Stamp Act did, and that the unrest "was appeased only by passing provincial laws directly in opposition to it."[12] Not only did the conflict serve as a precedent for the later controversy over parliamentary legislation, therefore, but it aroused Samuel Adams into vigilance against "unwarrantable encroachment on the charter rights of the people, and an illegal interference in their local concerns."[13]

For lack of information, it is impossible to say when Oxenbridge Thacher joined the opposition to the administration, but in 1761 he argued with James Otis against the writs of assistance. James Bowdoin took up his course only after later events: Hutchinson claimed that Bowdoin's opposition stemmed from the quarrel between his son-in-law, William Temple, the Surveyor of the Customs, and Governor Bernard, over forfeitures in the customs. How James Otis came to oppose the administration requires narration at greater length.

Governor Bernard had been in the province only a few weeks when the portentous vacancy on the Superior Court bench occurred.[14] For the place on the Superior Court, the Governor had to decide between Colonel James Otis, father of James Otis, later referred to as *"the* Otis," and Lieutenant

---
11. *Ibid.,* I, 29.
12. John Adams, *History of the Dispute with America,* p. 46.
13. Wells, *Samuel Adams,* I, 26, 29.
14. On Aug. 2, 1760. Mass. Hist. Soc. MSS.: Benjamin Bangs, Diary, II, Aug. 2, 1760.

Governor Hutchinson.[15] Both were "government" men.[16] Colonel Otis practiced law, while Hutchinson had been trained to be a merchant.[17] The expectation of judicial office in the Otis family was of long standing.[18] According to Governor Bernard, neither Colonel Otis nor his son showed marked reticence in regard to the father's candidacy. Colonel Otis, he wrote, "proposed himself for a seat on the Bench in Case one of the Judges was made chief. Both these proposals could not be complied with; & there was no ballancing between the two Candidates. But Mr Otis Senr urged his pretensions, by telling me & the Lt Govr, that if he (the L^t. G^r.) was appointed, we should both of us repent of it. Otis jun^r did not confine himself to Hints; but declared publickly with oaths, that 'if his Father was not appointed Judge, he would set the whole Province in a flame, tho' he perished in the Attempt.'"[19]

Otis published a qualified denial of having made such a threat: "I think myself obliged in my own Vindication thus publickly to declare, that I have not the least Remembrance of my having ever used such Expressions in my Life; nor do I believe I ever did."[20] However, after he was answered by Hutchinson in the *Boston News-Letter*,[21] Otis made the further explanation:

15. Colonel Brattle also had some hopes of the office. *Mass. Hist. Soc. Coll.*, LXXIV, 66: Edmund Trowbridge to Wm. Bollan, July 15, 1762.
16. Wm. Gordon, *History of the Rise, Progress, and Establishment of the Independence of the United States*, I, 100; Hutchinson, *History*, III, 88.
17. Wm. Gordon, *History*, I, 100. *Mass. Hist. Soc. Coll.*, LXXIV, 77. James Otis to Mauduit, Oct. 28, 1762.
18. Wm. Gordon, *History*, I, 100: "Colonel *James Otis* . . . had been promised by Mr. Shirley, when in the chair, to be made judge of the superior court, upon an opportunity's offering." After being passed over in a following appointment, he received new assurance of the next vacancy. No further vacancy occurred until the one discussed, in Governor Bernard's term.
19. Bernard Papers, IV, 275-6: To Shelburne, Dec. 22, 1766.
20. *Boston Gazette*, April 4, 1763.
21. *The Mass. Gazette* and *Boston News-Letter*, April 7, 1763: ". . . I was informed by Gentlemen of undoubted veracity, that Mr. *Otis* the

'Tis probable enough that I might say about the time refer'd to that I fear'd his Honour would never cease engrossing places of power & profit for himself, his family, and dependents, 'till he had set the province in a flame. . . . After all, if the pretended threats were uttered, which I am satisfied never were, every unprejudiced man of common humanity would excuse them as rash unadvised words of heat and passion, especially, when uttered in the cause of an injured father, and, as there has been nothing done by me to disturb the quiet of the province. . . .[22]

Bernard said that the threat had been proved by "two Gentlemen of Credit" under oath, and that their depositions were in the "public Offices at home."[23] Otis strove to clear himself in part by saying that *"a real, or imaginary cause of offence given my Father, ought not to be considered as the sole spring and motive of all my public conduct."*[24]

Hutchinson was more politic in his candidacy. He did not put himself forward at all, but was proposed for the office "by the best Men in the Government."[25] His qualifications for the office were not put in the foreground of discussion. On November 13, Bernard gave the appointment to Hutchinson. The new Chief Justice was not commissioned until December 30, however. Thereupon James Otis resigned his office of Advocate-General.[26] There is some evidence that Bernard would have found it difficult to have resisted the appointment of Hutchinson, such was his support.[27] In fact,

---

son had declared . . . that he would do all the mischief he could to the Government, and would set the Province in a flame, etc. if his father should not be appointed (the town was full of the talk of it). . . ."

22. *Boston Gazette*, April 11, 1763.
23. Bernard Papers, IV, 276.
24. *Boston Gazette*, April 11, 1763.
25. Bernard Papers, IV, 275.
26. Josiah Quincy, Jr., *Reports of Cases Argued and Adjudged in the Superior Court of Judicature of the Province of Massachusetts Bay between 1761 and 1772*, p. 411, note. Hereafter cited as Quincy, *Reports*.
27. Otis in the *Boston Gazette*, April 4, 1763: "His Excellency has more than once intimated, that the Lieutenant Governor's Connections were too formidable to be disobliged. . . ."

Hutchinson had been in the Council, which was the "inner circle" from the point of view of political advancement, from 1749, while Otis was not even a member of the Council.

Yet from the point of view of policy, the appointment of Hutchinson to the Chief Justiceship was disastrous. Hutchinson already held the office of Lieutenant-Governor of the province; he was Commander of the Castle (the fort on Castle Island), a member of the Council, Judge of Probate for Suffolk County, and now Chief Justice of the Superior Court.[28] As John Adams later remarked, Hutchinson had obviously "too many offices for the greatest and best man in the world to hold."[29] Some of them were decidedly incompatible with each other.[30]

Although the custom of plural office-holding was of long standing in Massachusetts,[31] Hutchinson's contemporaries began to observe that he carried self-interest very far indeed.[32] While the office of Lieutenant-Governor as such had no salary attached to it,[33] Hutchinson had been receiving from time to time, in almost every year, commissions from the General Court to perform special services for the province, for which he received a grant varying from £30 to £80.[34] Although the seat of councillor, it was said, was not very profitable to Hutchinson, yet it gave him an opportunity of promoting relatives and friends to other profitable offices, "an opportunity which the country saw he most religiously

---

28. Wm. Gordon, *History*, I, 100.
29. John Adams, *Life and Works*, IV, 63.
30. Jasper Mauduit, *Mass. Hist. Soc. Coll.*, LXXIV, 77: James Otis to Jasper Mauduit, Oct. 28, 1762.
31. Some of the county and local offices also descended in the same family, from father to son. *Boston Evening-Post*, Oct. 27, 1763; John Adams, *Life and Works*, IV, 393.
32. *Ibid.*, IV, 63.
33. Jasper Mauduit, *Mass. Hist. Soc. Coll.*, LXXIV, 144: Hutchinson to Bollan, Feb. 6, 1764: ". . . my post had neither business nor emolument annexed to it."
34. *Acts and Resolves*, XVI, 320, 463; XVII, 268, 361, 570.

The Grievance of Plural Office-Holding   33

improved."[35] The members of the General Court voted their own allowances for the time they were engaged in public service.[36] In 1762, the allowance for a councillor would have added up to over £30 for the time the General Court was in session, exclusive of the travel allowance.[37]

The Chief Justiceship carried with it, in 1760, a regular grant of £150.[38] An extraordinary grant of £40 was customarily allowed to the Chief Justice, in addition. There were fees, also, which accrued to the Superior Court justices, but the amount of these, Hutchinson wrote, did not cover traveling expenses.[39] The net income from the post of Chief Justice amounted to about £100, without the extraordinary grant; about £140 when it was received. The Probate Judgeship for Suffolk County was estimated by Hutchinson to be worth £60 annually.[40] As Commander of the Castle, Hutchinson received around £100 per year.[41] Hutchinson's

---

35. John Adams, *History of the Dispute with America*, p. 73. Wm. Gordon, *History*, I, 100: "Mr. Hutchinson . . . got himself appointed chief justice, by which he gratified both his ambition and covetousness, his two ruling passions."

36. Mass. State Archives, L, 154, 183. In 1761, the councillors received 5/4 s. per day; in 1762, 6/4 s. per day.

37. The total warrants for Council pay, 1762, came to £572/17s. The number of days for which Council pay was voted came to ninety-eight; the greatest number present at any Council in that year was twenty-two; the smallest number seven, which was the number constituting a quorum. *Ibid., Council Records*, XV, 111, 144, 159, 221.

38. £750 was granted to the Court as a whole. It was made up of five justices.

39. Mass. State Archives, XXV, 23. Dec. 27, 1765 (?). See Appendix I, sec. 1, *infra*.

40. Mass. State Archives, XXVI, 189: Hutchinson Correspondence.

41. ". . . if he should be allowed (as has been usual for all Lieutenant Governors) to hold the command of the castle, that would be another £100." *Letters of Governor Hutchinson and Lieut. Governor Oliver*, p. 42 (to Nathaniel Rogers, Dec. 12, 1766).

"The lieutenant governor has no appointments as such: The captaincy of Castle William, which may be worth 120 £ sterling [a] year, is looked upon indeed as an appendage to his commission, and the late lieutenant governor enjoyed no other appointment." Andrew Oliver, in the *Mass. Spy*, Aug. 5, 1773.

offices therefore added up to at least £400 sterling per year.[42] While the salaries in provincial offices at the time were admittedly small, the offices described did not require full-time service.[43] Hutchinson had a sufficient private estate, furthermore, to make him independent of his governmental income.[44]

If the union of so many offices in Hutchinson's hands alarmed his enemies, the fact that he showed an inveterate facility for filling other high places in the government with his relatives and friends made his appointment to the Chief Justiceship even less tolerable. Andrew Oliver, a brother-in-law of Hutchinson's, was Secretary of the Province, Judge of the Inferior Court of Common Pleas of Essex County, and a member of the Council. His son sat in the House of Representatives for Salem. Two other justices of the Superior Court (also councillors) were related to Hutchinson by marriage: one, the brother of the Secretary, Peter Oliver; the other, Benjamin Lynde.[45] A half-brother of Hutchinson's took the seat on the Inferior Court of Common Pleas for Suffolk County which the Lieutenant-Governor had given up shortly before he received his appointment to the Superior Court.[46]

Hutchinson was not the sole example of an "engrosser" of offices at the time. There were other councillors—Superior Court justices at the same time—who held additional

42. Bernard Papers, III, 279, Jan. 25, 1765. To Jackson.
43. John Adams, *History of the Dispute with America*, p. 72.
44. Mass. State Archives, XXVI, 103.
45. Hutchinson's daughter was married to Peter Oliver's son; Benjamin Lynde's daughter was married to the son of Andrew Oliver. The family ties in public office became even closer and more involved after Hutchinson became Governor (1771). See H. A. Cushing, *Writings of Samuel Adams*, II, 265-6. S. Adams to A. Lee, Oct. 31, 1771.
46. This was Foster Hutchinson, who also received the Probate Judgeship for Suffolk County when Hutchinson found it prudent to vacate it in 1769, and was appointed to the Superior Court in 1771. Whitmore, *Mass. Civil List*, p. 78.

The Grievance of Plural Office-Holding

judicial appointments as well, such as Chambers Russell, who was a Judge of Admiralty and a Superior Court justice; and John Cushing, who was also Judge of Probate for the County of Plymouth.[47] Actually the Superior Court at the time was entirely made up of councillors.[48] Those members of the Council who were not on the Superior Court generally held county or local judicial appointments: Israel Williams, for example, was Chief Justice of the Inferior Court of Common Pleas and Judge of Probate for Hampshire County;[49] Samuel Danforth was Chief Justice of Common Pleas and Judge of Probate for Middlesex County; John Choate and John Chandler were Chief Justices of the Inferior Court of Common Pleas and Judges of Probate for their respective counties.[50]

The most important executive offices of the province were encompassed in the Council: Andrew Oliver, the Province Secretary, sat as a councillor; Edmund Trowbridge, Attorney-General, was in the Council from 1764; Harrison Gray,[51] Treasurer and Receiver-General, was also of the Council; Thomas Hubbard was Commissary-General and a member of the Council; James Russell, Commissioner of Impost and Excise, also sat there. Other councillors held executive offices in their counties. John Choate, for example, was Treasurer of Essex County as well as a councillor.

The decentralized methods of administration which prevailed in Massachusetts at the time brought out the incompatibility of judicial office and that of councillor. The responsibility of farming out the excise upon tea, coffee, and

47. Wm. T. Davis, *History of the Judiciary of Massachusetts*, p. 77; John Adams, *History of the Dispute with America*, p. 73; *Life and Works*, VI, 62.
48. Whitmore, *Mass. Civil List*, pp. 59-62, 70. Chambers Russell sat in the Council only in 1759 and 1760.
49. *Ibid.*, pp. 92-94.   50. *Ibid.*, pp. 84, 86, 118-19.
51. The offices of Treasurer, Commissary-General, and Commissioner of Impost and Excise were annually elective by the General Court.

chinaware in the various counties, for example, was not that of the Province Treasurer, but was divided among the numerous members of the Council. There was no exception even of those who sat on the Superior Court,[52] they reporting back to the General Court the amount for which the excise was sold, and receiving an allowance for their "charge and expences."[53]

Other administrative functions which in modern governments would be provided for by contract were undertaken by members of the Council acting with a "Committee" and in such a connection frequently large sums of money passed through their hands. In the year 1761, for example, it was the undertaking of Thomas Hutchinson, acting with a committee, to provide for repairing the Province ship *King George* and to procure supplies for the ship. For this purpose he received a warrant for £500 at each of two meetings of the Council in July, 1761,[54] and the same amount in December of that year.[55] Construction and repair on province buildings, forts, and other undertakings were taken care of in the same informal way. For their "extraordinary services" the members of the Council commonly received considerable grants from the General Court, many times without any enumeration of the services rendered, except a reference to the petition asking the grant.

Multiple office-holding easily spelled oligarchy in Massachusetts, with the Governor and Hutchinson and Andrew Oliver at the head, indicating ability to control the government more closely than might any modern "ring."[56] Massa-

---

52. *Acts and Resolves*, XVII, 58-59. Executive Records of the Council, XV, 60, 65, 66, Mass. State Archives MSS.
53. *Acts and Resolves*, XVII, 56.
54. Executive Records of the Council, XV, 23, 26, Mass. State Archives MSS.
55. *Ibid.*, p. 73.
56. John Adams, *Life and Works*, II, 150-1. Appendix I, section 2, *infra*.

chusetts, however, was not unique in the oligarchical character of its government. The governmental organization of Massachusetts on the basis of a small governing class merely paralleled the organization in the mother country, where government centered in the House of Lords.[57] The danger to the province interest of such a monopoly of public offices was shortly to become apparent.

Before the beginning of Governor Bernard's term of office, the Acts of Trade were believed to conflict with the commercial interests of Massachusetts merchants. Some of the regulations amounted in practice to a prohibition of trade (the heavy duty upon molasses, for example), and their avoidance was openly connived at by merchants and customs officers. On the other hand, the failure to enforce the Trade and Navigation Laws in Massachusetts had resulted in an increased volume of emphatic instructions to each successive Governor. By the time of Bernard's appointment, the failure had become notorious, and Bernard was given the most extensive instructions on the subject that had yet been framed.[58]

One article in Governor Bernard's instructions directed him to aid and assist the collectors and other officers of the admiralty and customs in enforcing the Acts of Trade.[59] Bernard also had special instructions from Pitt, Secretary of State, to "take every Step, authorized by Law," to suppress the illegal trade with the French. This branch of trade involved wholesale evasion of the Sugar Act.[60]

Bernard was not long in encountering difficulties in carrying out his instructions regarding the customs laws. It was to his financial interest to carry out the laws, inasmuch as the

---

57. W. S. Holdsworth, "The House of Lords, 1689-1783," XLV, *Law Quarterly Review*, 307-42.
58. Bernard Papers, XIII, 149 *et seq.*
59. *Ibid.*, pp. 196, 199.
60. Mass. State Archives, XXII, 163-5.

Governor received one-third the amount of forfeitures made under the Acts of Trade.[61] His profits from forfeitures Governor Bernard estimated to be about £340 per year.[62] Since the "certain income" (salary and fees) of the Governor from the province came to about £1400 per year, the forfeitures, it will be seen, formed a not inconsiderable addition to the Governor's income.[63]

Unconcealed antagonism on the part of the Boston merchants was the reaction to the efforts of Bernard to enforce the customs laws. The merchants felt that the Governor was using more rigor than was shown in other provinces.[64] In 1763, Hutchinson wrote that there were seizures every day, which were to the advantage of the Governor, but to the discomfiture of the merchants.[65] An open clash broke out between the Governor and the Collector of Customs in Boston, who was supported by the popular party. From Bernard's point of view, the merchants were organized against his honest enforcement of the laws.[66]

Under the leadership of Otis, the merchants brought sev-

61. Bernard Papers, III, 131: To Jackson, Feb. 13, 1764: "I sent to M^r. Pownall a Defence of the right of the American Governors to a third of Seizures made under the 12 Ch, 2. 15 Cha, 2 & 7 & 8 Will, 3. notwithstanding the 2 of Geo, 3." Hutchinson, *History*, III, 89. 6 Geo. II.

62. Bernard Papers, V, 40. To Barrington, Nov. 15, 1765.

63. Temple, Surveyor-General of the Customs in 1764, came to controversy with Bernard over the forfeitures. Temple accused Bernard of avarice: "M^r. Bernard's insatiable avarice has led him to draw an income from all quarters & from all departments in this Province in such a manner as it is a shame to his appointment." Bowdoin and Temple Papers, *Mass. Hist. Soc. Coll.*, 6th Series, IX, 28. John Temple to Thos. Whately, Sept. 10, 1764. *Ibid.*, p. 40. Temple to Whately, Dec. 1, 1764.

64. *Boston Gazette*, Dec. 7, 1761. "Is it not notorious that the Acts of Trade are no where executed *with Rigor* but in this Province?"

65. Israel Williams Papers, II, 158. Nov. 17, 1763: ". . . which make well for the governor &ca. but there is a great rumpus among the merchants, who are ready to say with Horace Militia est potior. . . ."

66. Bernard Papers, III, 218: "Upon my coming into the Government, immediately begun the confederacy against the Customhouse & Admiralty which was accompanied with much popular Commotion. At the beginning of this The then acting advocate general deserted his post & put himself at the head of the attack of the Kings Officers."

The Grievance of Plural Office-Holding 39

eral actions at common law, directed against irregularities in the forfeitures allowed in the Court of Admiralty.[67] The case of Gray vs. Paxton, if successful, would have diminished the portion customarily allowed the Governor in forfeitures.[68]

One of the cases brought at this time was to test the legality of the issuance of writs of assistance by the Superior Court. Writs of assistance apparently had issued from the Superior Court since 1755.[69] It is uncertain whether the question of the legality of the writs of assistance was pending when Hutchinson received his appointment, but it is possible that it was. John Adams said emphatically that the appointment of Chief Justice Hutchinson had been made with a design to influence the decision in the case of the writs but does not cite his proof of the point.[70]

There is also doubt as to the manner in which the case on the legality of the writs came up. There is no trace of a written application for the writ in the fall of 1760.[71] Hutchinson said that the application for the writ was made by one of the customhouse officers, and that exception was taken to it.[72] Bernard wrote that the case on the writs of assistance was brought about by reason of the death of George II, in October, 1760: that the writs having thus come to an end,

67. Quincy, *Reports*, p. 541, note.
68. Hutchinson, *History*, III, 89. *The Boston Gazette*, Dec. 7, 1761: "Private Informers, the Disgrace of Civil Society, are multiplied and well paid at *our own* Cost. . . ."
69. Quincy, *Reports*, Appendix I, p. 404. Bernard Papers, V, 261, March 24, 1768: "I must observe that Writs of Assistance were first granted in this Province by Chief Justice Sewell many Years ago." Also Executive Records of the Council, Mass. State Archives MSS., XV, 111.
70. *Life and Works*, VII, 267. Also, X, 183, where it is said that Bernard "appointed Hutchinson, for the very purpose of deciding the fate of the writs of assistance."
71. Quincy, *Reports*, p. 418, note; 409, note; 423, note.
72. Hutchinson, *History*, III, 93: ". . . and Mr. Otis desired that a time might be assigned for an argument upon it." Quincy, *Reports*, p. 409, note; 423, note. Cockle, Collector of the Customs in Salem, who had been recently appointed, is said to have made the application in Nov., 1760, by John Adams. This may be an inaccuracy.

the merchants determined to have a hearing on the legality of the issue of new writs. Hutchinson, in spite of the effective arguments of Otis and Thacher in February, 1761, was able to prevail upon his colleagues to continue the case until the practice of the exchequer could be ascertained.[73] By then writing to Mr. Bollan, the colony agent in England, and procuring a copy of the writ as it issued out of the exchequer,[74] Hutchinson incurred the opprobrium of the popular party.

In the following term, after further argument, the Superior Court gave judgment in favor of the writs, and the writs were thereafter granted, though there is doubt whether they were executed, so great was popular hostility to them.[75] The importance of the case of the writs of assistance consisted therefore not in the decision, but in the effect of the case upon public opinion.

73. Quincy, *Reports*, p. 415, note, quotes Hutchinson to Secretary Conway, Oct. 1, 1765. Hutchinson, *History*, III, 94: "Some of the judges, notwithstanding, from a doubt whether such writs were still in use in England, seemed to favour the exception, and, if judgment had been then given, it is uncertain on which side it would have been." Also, Mr. Bollan's Memorandum, British Museum, Additional MSS. 32,974, fo. 368, a copy of which is in the Mass. Hist. Soc. Misc. MSS. for this period.
74. Mass. State Archives, XXVI, 155.
75. Quincy, *Reports*, Appendix I, 414, 417, note. Wm. Tudor, *Life of James Otis*, p. 86, footnote, giving John Adams as authority.

CHAPTER II

AGITATION AGAINST OLIGARCHY

THE GREAT DANGER to the province interest from executive domination, maintained through a union of executive and judicial offices in the same persons, became evident as a result of the case of the writs of assistance. Gathering opposition to the "Junto," more clearly drawn party lines followed the defeat of the merchants' case in the matter of the issuance of the writs.[1] Whereas Hutchinson's course "disgusted the people exceedingly,"[2] James Otis became the popular hero through his part in opposing the writs, and at the following election in May, 1761, his choice as a representative to the General Court from Boston was almost unanimous. Otis, with the collaboration of Oxenbridge Thacher, conducted the ensuing tactics of the opposition against the administration.

An attack on plural office-holding by members of the Council was launched in the spring of 1761. A skilful pamphlet, "Considerations on the Election of Councellors humbly offered to the Electors," by "a good subject in private life," was undoubtedly Oxenbridge Thacher's contribution to the agitation. The pamphlet was anonymous, and has been hitherto unidentified, but evidence points to Thacher as author.[3] The subject matter of the pamphlet

---

1. Tudor, *Life of James Otis*, pp. 89-90.
2. Wm. Gordon, *History*, I, 125.
3. See the Supplement to the *Boston Evening-Post* of Dec. 1, 1766, in which a note says that Mr. Thacher "in a judicious pamphlet written by him, has left his testimony against a union of the two powers in the same persons, as being unconstitutional, and tending to the destruction of the liberties of his country." The pamphlet above referred to is the only one

was the expediency of having judges of the highest court of law serve as members of the Council. The author first demonstrated the incompatibility of a political office, such as that of a councillor, with judicial office. He pointed out that attendance on both the circuit and the Council was incompatible, even if the Court and the Council were sitting in Boston at the same time, while when the Court was on the circuit, attendance upon both was impossible, and the public was deprived of either a councillor or a judge.[4]

The work of the courts was so important, Thacher went on, that the judges should give full-time attention to it: they were paid by the province to leave all other business, and to devote themselves wholly to the law.[5] It was too much to expect, Thacher wrote, that any one man could be an able judge and a successful politician at the same time:

> The gaining a skill in the laws sufficient to qualify a man for the important station of Judge, where the properties, the liberties, and often the lives of the King's subjects are nearly concerned. And the rightly discharging so important a function, when a man is vested with the office, is as much as can be expected from any one man, unless his powers and capacities greatly exceed those of all other mortals. The rightly understanding the political interest of a people, and pursuing it in the various matters which come under the consideration of a General Court, this is another branch of skill quite distinct from the former, and no meer man since the fall, ever excelled in both.[6]

The writer emphasized that the very nature of a judicial office was incompatible with a political office: "Moreover, a

---

that can be found, and is the only one that is mentioned in the discussions of the time. The style is that of Thacher. See the irony of one of the last paragraphs, which is typical of Thacher: "I guess it would have puzzled the ablest casuist, to determine what is duty and propriety in this instance, [i.e., a union of the councillor and judicial offices], if the honorable gentlemen themselves had not the last winter decided it."

4. Appendix II, section 1, *infra*.   5. Appendix II, section 2, *infra*.
6. Pages 4-5. Reprinted in the *Boston Gazette*, April 26, 1762.

Judge should be ever unmixed with all those political quarrels, that in such a State as ours, must be expected to arise. He ought to stand indifferent to all parties, as one whose business is alike to distribute justice to all." The practice of the mother country, in excluding judges of the common law courts from the House of Commons, and in allowing no voice of their own in the House of Lords to those judges who were present to give their advice on questions of law, was cited by Thacher: "This policy of our mother country is perhaps the very thing that hath saved our liberties, and is highly commended by all good writers on the subject of politics."

Montesquieu's maxim for securing liberty by a "separation of the powers" of government was then stated and applied. Thacher's solution is "the due adjustment of the several powers of the community" which follows his statement of Montesquieu's principle, and is apparently identified with it. The struggles of the mother country constituted an attempt to bring about such an "adjustment" of the powers of the government, which was finally achieved in the settlement following the revolution of 1688:

The essence of liberty in any state is preserved by the due adjustment of the several powers of the community. Where this is lost, where the powers loose their checks, run into one another, or one branch of powers swallows up other branches, it becomes a tyranny, be the external form of government what it will. This hath always been obvious enough with respect to the regal power. Hence the frequent struggles in our mother country to prevent its becoming exorbitant. . . . Hence the constant jealousy exercised over it. Hence the glorious revolution, where at last the true basis of English liberties was firmly fixed.

It is worthy of note that Thacher, who was learned in English constitutional law, did not find that Montesquieu was wrong in his theories about the English government. On the other hand, Thacher understood the "separation of departments" as an "adjustment" of powers resulting from one branch of government checking the action of another. Thacher did not go into an analysis of the nature of the various "powers" of government, nor, for that matter, did the other writers of the time in Massachusetts.

Thacher's exposition of Montesquieu's theory elucidated another point. Applying Montesquieu's theory to a "democratical" government, Thacher wrote that if the offices of government, usually delegated to many persons, were centered in a few, the substance of liberty was gone, and those few persons became tyrants although the form of liberty should be preserved. If the whole legislative and executive powers were vested in the same individuals, their power would be uncontrollable. However, Thacher ironically said this was not the case in Massachusetts, because the province judges had many equals in the legislature, but he did find that the whole executive power was vested in them. Thus he felt it should be considered whether the Massachusetts example "verges toward that fatal point."[7]

In this passage, Thacher makes it clear in what a union of the "whole" legislative and executive powers consists: it is an identity of the personnel holding the legislative and executive offices of government. If the personnel differs in part, then the "whole" powers are not united. Accordingly judges in Massachusetts did not exercise the "whole" legislative power but they did have the "whole" executive power: "This it is confessed is not the case in the instance before us, for-as-much as the judges have many their equals in the legislative, while the whole executive may be said to be lodged in them." There was no question here of a separation of the abstract powers of government according to type; the contemporary problem was that of a separation in office-holding.

7. Appendix II, section 3, *infra*.

Agitation Against Oligarchy

Thacher then argued the incompatibility of the nature of judicial office and a seat in the legislature. A judge, he said, should receive no information except in court. If he heard one party out of court, he would not be acting as an upright judge. Nevertheless, it frequently happened that prosecutions in cases of revenue frauds were ordered by the General Court, which necessarily discussed the question of the frauds. The judges who were members of the Court were put in a dilemma, because if they entered into the discussion and gave an opinion whether an action lay, they violated their judicial trust, while if they withdrew from the discussion, the province was deprived of its five ablest councillors in an important matter.[8]

Thacher's final recommendation was that a year of release from political pursuits be given the judges: ". . . that all the leisure the circuit gives them, may be religiously employed in the manner most agreeable to their own inclination, in the study of that science wherein they most excel." Of the two offices (obviously incompatible), Thacher was of the opinion that councillors should retain the judicial, since the places on the Council might be more readily filled. The last passage, like many others in the pamphlet, seemed to contain ironical allusion to Hutchinson, who although untrained in the law, had been made Chief Justice of the province, and who, though on the bench, continued to engage in political intrigues.

To Thacher, it is evident, the point of attack was lack of independence of the departments which resulted from a union of offices. His argument was for a separation in office-holding, as a means of attaining the essential condition—liberty.[9] Thacher had a sound basis for his argument in the

8. Appendix II, section 4, *infra*.
9. The synonymous use of the phrases, "powers" and "persons holding powers" was more explicit in a writing of an earlier date. It is an essay on "Liberty," seemingly by Samuel Adams. He defines "powers" as fol-

well-settled rule of the common law against holding incompatible offices. His pamphlet was later reprinted as a whole,[10] as well as quoted in part. Events in the following winter proved that widespread opposition was gathering to executive domination maintained through a combination of plural offices.

Previous to the Council elections of May, 1761, there appeared an article in the *Boston Evening-Post*[11] urging that instructions should be given the representatives at the coming elections to "dry up the first springs" of the detriment arising to the province from the union of executive and legislative powers in the councillors. Montesquieu was quoted on the necessity of separating the powers of government to secure liberty, and freeholders were counselled to advise their representatives: "to *pass over* such gentlemen, as by experience have been found less useful at the Council-Board. And such also, as by reason of *divers great employments in the State,* cannot so constantly attend their duty at the Board, without great inconvenience to his Majesty's subjects." Plurality in office-holding, which had long been complained of in the Church, was perhaps no less to be avoided in the State: it was as detrimental to the civil interest in the one instance, as to the ecclesiastical, in the other.

A discussion of multiple office-holding also came up in connection with another popular issue: the question of the monetary standard in the province, a particular interest of Hutchinson's. Hutchinson, in the *Boston Evening-Post,* published a short series of articles demonstrating the advan-

---

lows: "It [i.e., Liberty] is *then* enjoyed, when neither *legislative* nor *executive* Powers (by which I mean, those Men with whom are intrusted the Power of making Laws and of executing them) are disturbed by any internal Passion, or hindered by an external Force from making the wisest Laws and executing them in the best Manner. . . ." *The Independent Advertiser,* Boston, April 10, 1749. Wells, *Samuel Adams,* I, 18, attributed this essay to Adams.

10. In the *Boston Gazette,* April 26, 1762.
11. April 27, 1761. "T. B.," Salem.

tages of a "fixed invariable standard." For this expression of opinion on a political issue, the Chief Justice was rebuked by Oxenbridge Thacher (who contributed a pamphlet to the discussion) with characteristic irony: "And I have too much confidence in the justice of the honourable gentleman himself, to suppose the extra-judicial opinion, he hath given in the news paper, would influence even his own judgement; when the matter came before him in tryal. At the same time, I must say it is great pity that the honourable gentleman should publicly in such peremptory and strong terms, declare his opinion on a question, which in all probability unless some new law be made will one day or other come judicially before him."[12]

Hutchinson's articles on the currency were answered by James Otis in the *Boston Gazette*. Otis here digressed from his discussion of the monetary standard to attack Hutchinson on multiple office-holding.[13] Otis applied Montesquieu's theory that tyranny was the result of a union of the powers of government to the province government, and particularly to the case of Hutchinson. Otis set forth a familiar doctrine, that the British Constitution established "a mixed monarchy," which was a composite of three orders ". . . of *monarchy*, supplied by the King, *aristocracy*, supplied by the lords, and of *democracy*, supplied by the commons." Otis gave his opinion that when the checks and balances were preserved, this was perhaps the most perfect form of government that "depraved human nature" was capable of devising. But, he said, it was a fundamental maxim in such a government to keep the legislative and executive powers separate. Should these powers be in the same hands, "such government is hastening fast to its ruin."[14] Otis on these various points was faithfully reproducing the conclusions of English theorists.

12. *Considerations on Lowering the Value of Gold Coins, Within the Province of the Massachusetts Bay*, p. 22.
13. *Boston Gazette*, Jan. 11, 1762.   14. Appendix II, section 5, *infra*.

Then, lest the reader should fail to apply his conclusion to the provincial situation, Otis went on to be more explicit, in appropriate phrases:

> It may happen in governments formed after this model that in consequence of art and corruption, half a dozen, or half a score men will form an oligarchy, in favour of themselves; and an aristocracy in favour of their families and friends. Instances may be found, where a man of abilities, shall monopolize a power proportionate to all those of lord chief baron of the exchequer, lord chief justice of both benches, lord high treasurer, and lord high chancellor of Great Britain, united in one single person. There is no axiom in the mathematicks clearer than that no man ought to be sole legislator of his country, and supreme judge of his fellow citizens.

And, sarcastically, he added:

> Should it be objected, that in making these political reflections, I have wandered; my apology is, I went out of the way, for the sake of his Honor's company, whose observation upon the democratical *byass*, led me astray if I have erred.

Otis then quoted from the *Spirit of the Laws* Montesquieu's well-known definition of liberty:

> ". . . the political liberty of the subject, is a tranquillity of mind, arising from the opinion each person has of his own safety. In order to have this liberty, it is requisite the government be so constituted, as one man need not be *afraid* of another."[15]

An explanation of the danger of a union of powers followed, which seemed to show that a union of powers was looked upon as arising from an identity of the personnel exercising those powers:

> When the legislative and executive powers are united in the same person, or in the same body of magistrates, (or nearly so) there can be no liberty, because (just and great) apprehensions

15. From Vol. I, Book XI, Ch. VI.

may arise lest the same Monarch or Senate, (or Junto) should enact *tyrannical* laws to execute them in a *tyrannical* manner.

Otis then quoted another well-known extract from Montesquieu, on the necessity of separating the powers of government. He concluded with over generous acclamation of the wisdom of Montesquieu:

> O *Secondat!* thou wast surely inspired, or you could never have so exactly described the *state* of provinces, perhaps unpeopled, and of people unborn, when you first felt their miseries.

More direct measures than writing were employed to attack the executive-legislative-judicial combination which ruled the province. The province agent, Bollan, who had sent the copy of the writ of assistance to Hutchinson, was dismissed. His dismissal was calculated to cause chagrin to Hutchinson.[16] A bill to prevent the issue of writs of assistance passed both houses of the Assembly, but was negatived by the Governor.[17]

Popular disapproval also found a way to retaliate against the Superior Court. A reduction in the annual salary grant to the justices of the Court from £750 to £700 was effected in February, 1762, while the customary additional grant to the Chief Justice of £40 was omitted altogether. It was not again restored to Hutchinson until 1765, and then with difficulty.[18]

As a further step toward reducing the Court to provincial usefulness, a committee was appointed to inquire into the law of the province establishing the Superior Court, and "to examine into the Jurisdictions and Powers exercis'd by said Court." The committee was particularly instructed to consider "the Utility of the Judges of the Superior Court hold-

---

16. Jasper Mauduit, *Mass. Hist. Soc. Coll.*, pp. 74, 77 (Oct. 28, 1762); Bollan's Memorandum, British Museum, Addit. MSS. 32,974, fo. 368. Copy in Mass. Hist. Soc. Misc. MSS. for this period.
17. Bernard Papers, II, 188.
18. *Acts and Resolves*, XVII, 161, 313, 456, 599.

ing their Commissions during good Behaviour," and the question of a fixed salary for the judges. The report of the committee was unanimous that it would be of "great utility" for the judges to hold commissions during good behaviour, instead of during the pleasure of the Governor and Council, and against the fixing of salaries: "at present it will not be of publick Utility to fix them."[19] But the House found a more effective way of attacking the position of the judges, and it never acted upon the report.

The more drastic method, for which there was many an English precedent in the place bills, was hit upon of bringing a bill into the House to exclude judges of the Superior Court from a seat in the Council.[20] The bill as drafted would have excluded the Judges of the Superior Court from either branch of the Assembly. The text of this bill has been lost. Otis was one of three members who drew up the bill.[21] It failed of passage by six votes only, "in a very full House."[22] Apparently the argument was used against the bill that it was superfluous, inasmuch as the judges could be dropped from the Council at the elections, if that were desirable.[23] Such action, however, was not taken, and the opposition failed to exclude the judges from the Council, either by legislative act or at the elections. The opposition at this time lacked a majority in the House,[24] and

19. Mass. State Archives, XLIV, 502-4.
20. Minot, *Continuation of the History of the Province*, II, 111; J. G. Palfrey, *History of New England*, V, 248.
21. *Journal of the House of Representatives*, 1762, p. 311. April 17, 1762.
22. *Boston Gazette*, April 26, 1762. "Z. X." Mass. State Archives, XXVI, 12. Hutchinson to Bollan, April 24, 1762: ". . . upon a second reading in a full house would have carried a vote for it if the party could have brought four or five more over to them."
23. *Boston Gazette*, May 24, 1762.
24. Bernard had somewhat previously estimated the opposition in the Assembly at one third of their number. Bernard Papers, I, 323, July 6, 1761: "The Assembly keeps in very good temper; all necessary business is properly done, notwithstanding an opposition is kept up (seldom raising the minority to one-third)."

plurality of office-holding was only disturbed, and not dislodged, in Massachusetts in this early attempt.

However, after this experience with the storm of controversy that was brewed and set loose by James Otis, Bernard attempted to reconcile the opposition. The Governor himself wrote of his attempts at reconciliation of the "confederacy": "I have the strongest assurances that the persons that have given me the most trouble intend to act a different part for the future. In short, I have now the fairest prospect I have had yet, that I shall accomplish my purpose of founding my administration on the broad bottom of a Collation [*sic* Coalition]...."[25] Bernard attempted to disengage himself from the factions in the government, and to set up a coalition of parties.[26] He wrote as if this had been his policy from the beginning: "It has been the principal object of my politicks, since I arrived here to place myself on a bottom of my own. I had no other choice: When I came here I found the province divided into parties so nearly equal, that it would have been Madness for me to have put myself at the head of either of them. I had therefore nothing to do but to keep to myself & maintain my own Dignity."[27] However, he was obliged to admit that a "violent Spirit of Disunion" still prevailed, and that he found some of his friends merely "profest" ones.[28] As a

25. Bernard Papers, I, 316. To J. Pownall, April 28, 1761. *Ibid.*, II, 9. To T. Pownall, Aug. 28, 1761: "M^r. Otis Junr. is at the head of the Confederacy." *Ibid.*, I, 323, July 6, 1761: "M^r. Otis Junr. who hase been M^r. Barrons faithful Councellour from the first begining [*sic*] of these commotions to the hour of this present writing."
26. Bernard Papers, I, 317: "I am now assured that I shall be free from this trouble for the future & upon my own terms a coalition of parties & not my engaging in them."
27. *Ibid.*, II, 189. To Barrington, May 1, 1762.
28. *Ibid.*, II, 30, Feb. 13, 1762: "The Flame that Barons and his People lighted this time twelve month still continues having taken several different turns in the course of which I have got clear of the disputes in the General Court & am now only a spectator of & sometimes a moderator in them. But there is such a violent Spirit of Disunion still prevails...."

matter of fact, the merchants persisted in their hostility to Bernard, and they were preparing to make representations to the home government which could scarcely fail to undermine his standing.[29]

In his *History*, Hutchinson recorded the "appearance of reconciliation" between the Otises and Governor Bernard.[30] Hutchinson implied that Bernard made his peace with the Otises by using his patronage for the purpose. By the death of George II, Hutchinson said, Bernard was afforded the opportunity of making nominations for all the various civil and military commissions which thereupon required renewal. He allowed Colonel Otis to "settle" the County of Barnstable to his liking: offering him the principal offices in the county for himself, and allowing him to name relatives and friends to other offices. Hutchinson said that Otis became Chief Justice of the Court of Common Pleas, and also Judge of Probate in Barnstable County, thus attaining great weight and influence.[31]

Hutchinson went on to say that James Otis, the son, soon afterward appeared in favor of the grant of Mount Desert to the Governor by the Assembly. But the reconciliation was short-lived, for the reason, Hutchinson seemed to imply, that offices once granted by a Massachusetts Governor could not be taken away at his pleasure, except appointments to the militia, which, once the title and rank that went with the appointment were acquired, were not much valued anyhow.[32]

Hutchinson's statement is not in all ways consistent with the facts. Colonel Otis did not receive his appointments with the renewal of commissions on the death of George II.

At present I stand entirely upon my own bottom. & have some real friends & a great many profest ones on both sides: and I have the strongest assurances from the most active, that care shall be taken not to embarras me: but I trust to nothing but my own discretion & Integrity."

29. *Ibid.*, II, 27. To Barrington, Feb. 20, 1762.
30. III, 95-96.
31. Appendix II, section 6, *infra*.   32. *Ibid.*

Agitation Against Oligarchy

Rather, at that time, Sylvanus Bourne had his commissions as Chief Justice of the Court of Common Pleas, and as Judge and Register of Probate for Barnstable County renewed, which renewal took place on January 21, 1762.[33] Colonel Otis did indeed receive the offices named at a later date, on February 1, 1764, but then as a consequence of the death of Sylvanus Bourne.[34]

However, in 1762 Colonel Otis was elected to the Council, and was approved by the Governor.[35] At the elections in the General Court of 1762, Colonel Otis declined the office of Speaker of the House, which he had hitherto held, for the reason, he said, that "his living at such a Distance rendered his constant Attendance very uncertain."[36] He nevertheless accepted the seat in the Council, and continued to sit there until 1766, when he was negatived by Bernard. Also, in 1762, Joseph Otis, a son of Colonel Otis, was appointed as sheriff for Barnstable County.

According to Hutchinson, the grant of Mount Desert to the Governor came after the appointment of Colonel Otis to the judicial posts in Barnstable County.[37] But the resolve granting Mount Desert to the Governor passed on February 27, 1762, about two years *before* the appointments of Colonel Otis were made.

Also, Hutchinson's comment in regard to the reasons for the grant of Mount Desert to Governor Bernard is not altogether explicit. The grant passed the General Court unan-

33. Whitmore, *Mass. Civil List*, p. 106.
34. *Ibid.*, p. 104, and footnote.
35. Mass. State Archives, Commissions, Proclamations, etc., 1756-67, pp. 264-5; *Journal of the House of Representatives*, 1762, p. 5. *Mass. Civil List*, pp. 106, 61. Whitmore indicates that Joseph Otis was appointed sheriff for Barnstable County in 1762, while Joseph Otis, Jr., was made Justice of the Peace and of the Quorum for the county in 1764.
36. *Journal of the House of Representatives*, 1762, p. 5.
37. *History*, III, 95-96: "Mr. Otis, the son, soon after appeared in favour of a grant, made by the assembly to the governor, of the island of Mount Desert; and there was the appearance of reconciliation."

imously. It was made with an understood purpose of obtaining Bernard's influence in securing validation of other province grants in the region, which the Assembly did not have a clear right to make. Bernard acknowledged this condition himself.[38] Otis announced in the *Boston Gazette* of March 28, 1762, that he would write a "full and true Account of the Grant of Mount Desert Island to his Excellency," but the account apparently never appeared.[39]

Hutchinson's statement that there was the "appearance of reconciliation" is in accord with the facts; but the reconciliation was fleeting. With the meeting of the new Assembly in May, 1762, the Governor saw results from his policy of detachment, and coalition of parties: "There never was a greater Harmony in the Government than at present. For proof of which I send your Lordship the address of the lower house, the expressions of which do not exceed their deeds."[40] There is also a comment of Oxenbridge Thacher's of this time which testifies to the success of the administration in securing harmony, and suggests even that the opposition of the press had been silenced.[41]

38. Bernard Papers, II, 32. To Wm. Bollan, March 2, 1762: "However, there is also a tacit consideration, that I should give my utmost assistance towards obtaining the Kings approbation of the grants of the Townships, which I should have thought it my duty to do if I had not been paid for it." For an account of the grant of Mount Desert to Governor Bernard, see Sawtelle Otis, "Mount Desert Island to Governor Bernard," *Pub. of the Col. Soc. of Mass.*, XXIV; *Boston Evening-Post*, Dec. 29, 1766.

39. At the same time, Otis also promised "An Impartial History of the last Session of the Great and General Court or Assembly . . . ," and "The present political State of the Province of the Massachusetts-Bay, . . . to which will be added, by Way of Supplement, a View of Provincial Administration for about three years past, interspersed with Strictures upon the Conduct of some eminent Personages in former years." It is possible that these items were contained in the book of which Otis was said to have burned the copy, upon being told by one of his colleagues that it might be considered seditious. *Boston Evening-Post*, July 11, 1763; March 31, 1766.

40. Bernard Papers, II, 194, June 7, 1762. To Barrington.

41. "I want now to give you a little sketch of y^e. present state of our

The fall of 1762 proved that Bernard's "coalition" of parties was very unsteady. Through the efforts of Otis, a reprimand was given to the Governor by the House for encroachment by the Governor and Council upon "their most darling Priviledge; the Right of Originating all Taxes."[42] It is probable that Bernard was attacked in this instance for following a policy advised by Hutchinson, because Otis, in his *Vindication of the Conduct of the House of Representatives*, published in November, 1762, advised the Governor of his conviction:

... that if his Excellency will in all cases take the advice of the general assembly, (which however contemptably some may affect to speak of it, is the great council of this province, as the British parliament is of the kingdom) that his administration will be crowned with all the success he can desire.[43]

Otis also warned the Governor:

... if instead of this, the advice of half a dozen or half a score, who among their fellow citizens may be chiefly distinguished by their avarice, ignorance, pride or insolence, should at any time obtain too much weight at court, the consequences will be very unfortunate on all sides.[44]

At the same time there was comment in the *Boston Gazette* on the threatened renewal of party antagonisms, which

---

domestic politics, but . . . who can penetrate into y^e. politics of a country y^t. hath no politics. We seem to be in y^t. deep sleep or stupor y^t. Cicero describes his country to be in a year or two before y^e. civil wars broke out. The sea is perfectly calm & unagitated. Whether this profound quiet be the forerunner of a storm I leave to your judgment. . . . I even hear y^t. y^e. press now is under y^e. dominion of our great men, and y^t. those printers who owe their first subsistence & present greatness to y^e. freedom of their press refuse to admit anything t^y. suspect is not pleasing to our sovereign lords." Mass. Hist. Soc. *Proceedings*, 1st Series, XX, 46-7. To Benjamin Prat, 1762.

42. *Journal of the House of Representatives*, 1762, p. 104.
43. *Ibid.*, p. 52.   44. *Ibid.*

had been "so dexterously *removed out of this small province....*"⁴⁵

In the spring of 1763, public opinion had apparently turned against the opposition. Now Hutchinson was able to say of Otis: "I have the satisfaction that people in general are very angry with him." Hutchinson also indicated that he thought Otis was changing his course.⁴⁶ Otis was in fact discouraged about the state of the government. His opinion about this time shows that he blamed Hutchinson as the source of the divisions in political life in Massachusetts:

> I really fear that this poor Province will be undone under the present administration, which is the weakest and most arbitrary that we have known since the Revolution. If either the Governor could be removed to some better place, and a wiser man sent in his room, that would act for himself, or if the Lieut. Governor could be confined to any one or two great posts, as Chief Justice or anything but Governor in Chief, we might doe well enough. But while he has all the real power of the Province in his hands but the militia a much wiser Governor than I have yet seen must submit to him or live in perpetual broils.⁴⁷

If Otis had been able to peruse the contents of a letter which his political opponent wrote shortly afterward, he might have taken heart. Hutchinson complained as follows to his fellow conservative, Israel Williams: ". . . between you & I notwithstanding outward appearances I am sometimes

---

45. ". . . how sorry we should be, if *party divisions*, so dexterously *removed out of this small province*, should again break out into a flame. . . ." Nov. 29, 1762.

46. *Mass. State Archives*, XXVI, 46. To Col. Cushing, Feb. 14, 1763: ". . . you are less of a politician than I always before took you to be . . . as soon as a character is attacked wch you really are not obliged to defend you lose your temper & grow quite angry. I differ from you toto caelo. I think O is a clever fellow. He was so unfortunate as to mistake before [*sic?*] but he certainly has ye right scent now. Pray do not stop him in his course."

47. *Mass. Hist. Soc. Coll.*, LXXIV, 96-7. To Jasper Mauduit, Feb. 14, 1763.

discouraged. I never met with two such men as the father & son. The latter professes to have buried the hatchet every three or four months...."[48] Hutchinson went on to describe the inimical attitude of Otis toward him, in spite of gestures in the direction of reconciliation.[49] That there had been no effective understanding between the administration and the Otises up to February, 1763, is established by an article written by James Otis at this time.[50]

In this article, Otis explains why the attempts at reconciliation had not been successful. Speaking of the "Junto," whom he sarcastically called the "benefactors," he wrote:

The way to their caresses and favours, is known to be broad, smooth and easy; and many there are that find it.

As the war was occasioned by the Benefactors, so early terms of peace and alliance have been offered unask'd. The capital article upon which all negociations have hitherto split, is, that certain gentlemen should, be treated worse than being given as hostages, in plain English, become the Tools to a few in power. Those who have attempted to bring a bout this submission . . . have hitherto found themselves mistaken.

While this article is not signed, evidence indicates that it was written by Otis.[51]

48. Israel Williams, Letters, MSS., II, 157. To Williams, April 15, 1763.
49. "As soon as ever anybody affronts him be it who it will instead of returning the affront to the person from whom he received it he wreaks all his malice & revenge upon me. The former just before the Court rose desired to speak with me in the Lobby & mentioned that we used to think alike etc. I told him he could not be insensible of the injurious treatment I had received from his son & that the Monday before he had published the most virulent piece which had ever appeared, but if he would desist & only treat me with common justice & civility I would forgive & forget everything that was past. He replied it was generous and yet his son has gone on in the same way ever since and I have no reason to think the father dislikes it." Israel Williams, Letters, MSS., II, 157. To Williams, April 15, 1763.
50. *Boston Gazette*, Feb. 28, 1763.
51. *Boston Gazette*, Feb. 28, 1763. There is internal evidence that the article was written by Otis. See the offer that "Bluster" (one of the

Otis was answered by Hutchinson himself in the *Boston News-Letter* of April 7, 1763, and by a writer who was probably John Worthington,[52] and by other administration writers. Otis and Hutchinson now made newspaper "confessions" of the actual role which each had played in the naming of the Chief Justice in 1760. Otis proceeded, in self-justification, to condemn the holding of multiple offices, insisting at least on the English practice of re-election, if compromise were necessary. Otis stated his opinion that any member who accepted an office while he was a representative deserved to be branded with infamy and that he should be disqualified from serving afterwards; or at the least, he should have to stand for re-election, as in the Commons in England, that the constituency might have a chance to pass on the election of a man who had probably "carried them to market." There would be less selling of votes and of the country, Otis predicted, if the restriction were adopted.[53]

In an article on April 11, Otis explained his attitude on the offices held by Hutchinson. He would not object that Hutchinson should retain his commissions as Lieutenant Governor and Chief Justice, but they were "enough for any gentleman to hold"; and it was illegal that he should at the same time act as Judge of Probate. In fact, the commission as Chief Justice was legally a supersedeas of the commission as Judge of Probate. Likewise, the commission of a Superior Court judge was a supersedeas of the commission as Judge of Admiralty. Any acts made in the inferior capacity were by law null and void, after the superior commission

---

names given to Otis by his enemies), on security for the good behavior of the Junto, "shall never seek or accept of any office during life but shall devote all his leisure, to the detecting and exposing state crooks and robbers." The Essex Institute copy of this issue has a note (by Benjamin Pickman), saying: "This Piece was written by James Otis, jun Esq."

52. *Boston Evening-Post*, May 23, 1763.
53. *Boston Gazette*, April 4, 1763, Appendix II, section 7, *infra*.

issued. It was a great grievance, also, that the Chief Justice should continue to sit in the Council, and have a great share in making the laws he would apply in court. Otis here relied upon the common-law rule against the holding of incompatible offices which were defined as those which either "from the multiplicity of business" or "from their being subordinate" could not be exercised at the same time by the same person consistently with the public welfare.⁵⁴

While Otis and Hutchinson were disclosing informal details of political life in Massachusetts, other writers joined in the discussion of the necessity of distributing the offices of government. Prior to the elections in 1763, a more moderate writer than Otis under the pseudonym of "T. Q.," who, however, was no more tolerant of the practice of plural office-holding, took up the subject in the *Boston Gazette*. While there does not seem to be direct evidence to identify "T. Q.," he was very probably Oxenbridge Thacher.⁵⁵

In the *Boston Gazette* for April 18, "T. Q." wrote on the incompatibility of the office of judge and that of councillor, quoting Montesquieu's definition of liberty and the necessity of a separation of the powers of government to secure it. While the author considered that a "multiplicity" of offices might have been justified in the infancy of the country, "as it may easily be suppos'd, that gentlemen of education and ability could not be found at that time to fill up every place in government," that necessity had long since ceased to exist.

The reason for the opposition to plural office-holding was here clearly stated. It was an objection to *too much power* on the part of the officers concerned, which might constitute danger for the safety of the state.

---

54. Matthew Bacon, *A New Abridgment of the Law*, III, (K), 736. *Boston Gazette*, April 11, 1763; Appendix II, section 8, *infra*. Otis, in the midst of this literary controversy, counselled moderation before the Boston town-meeting of March 21, 1763. *Boston Post-Boy*, March 21, 1763; *Boston Gazette*, March 21, 1763.

55. In the *Boston Evening-Post*, June 13, 1763, a letter from his opponent, "J.," states: ". . . from . . . some peculiar formalities of expression . . . some *obsolete*, and some *new-coin'd* words contained in this obscure piece, I am induced to think, *another Politician* is the true author." Thacher had just been elected to the General Court for the first time.

All men will allow, that it is possible for *one* gentleman to be possess'd of *more* power than is consistent with the *safety* of a community. The enquiry ought not to be how much he may possess with *safety*, but with prudence. . . .

The time may come [wrote the author] when an *ill use* may be made of precedents which we are *now* establishing; when *others* by being invested with the *same offices* . . . may have an *inclination* as well as *power*, not barely to "disturb the peace," but to destroy the liberties of a province. This then may be as happy a season to put a stop to such precedents as we may ever expect to have; since the *only* reason assigned for lessening the powers of any gentlemen *at present* is, that they possess rather too much.

It was not a question of envying these men the profits of their offices, and it was a matter of indifference whether the offices were lucrative or not. The only ground of "jealousy and uneasiness" was their uniting in their persons the "several branches of magistracy" and the great offices of state.

A writer on the administration side, who signed himself "J.,"[56] undertook to answer this "moderate piece," in the *Boston Evening-Post* Supplement of May 23, 1763, giving a searching exposition and interpretation of Montesquieu's theory. The debate between these contemporaries of Montesquieu who were learned in the English constitution of which Montesquieu wrote elucidates understanding of Montesquieu's principle from the point of view of eighteenth-century Massachusetts.

Both writers praised and admired Montesquieu; both writers agreed that a separation of "powers" was necessary to the attainment of liberty; both writers found such a principle in the Constitution of their mother country, but neither regarded it there as a complete separation of powers. The

---

56. Very probably John Worthington. "J." came from Springfield. *Boston Gazette*, March 24, 1766; *Boston Evening-Post*, April 18, 1763.

two writers were agreed that a separation of powers involved a separation in office-holding, but neither thought a complete separation of all the offices included in the different departments necessary. "J." interpreted Montesquieu to mean that a separation in holding of the majority of offices in the different departments was necessary; "T. Q." that the necessity of separation depended upon the importance of the offices concerned, and the danger to liberty which their union might constitute. Neither writer suggested any separation of the powers of government according to abstract type of power. The danger would consist in too much power on the part of certain persons, not in a mixture of types of power derived from various departments.

"J." undertook to argue that Montesquieu's doctrine did not require that the powers of government should be so *"entirely* separate" as that liberty would be in danger, or lost, "whenever any *one member* of that *body* which exerciseth the *judiciary power,* is a *member* also of that *body* which exerciseth the *legislative power*," but rather that his meaning was: ". . . that the *body* which exerciseth the *legislative* power should be composed of *members,* a *majority* (or if it be more agreeable to T. Q.) a *large* majority of whom should have *no share* in the exercise of the *judiciary* power."

"J." found his authority in the English government, which had furnished Montesquieu with his example, and the English practice of allowing judges and chancellors to sit in the House of Lords. It was not an uncommon thing, according to "J.," that chancellors and lord chief justices of King's Bench and Common Pleas were created peers (as had been the then Chief Justice, Lord Mansfield), with a seat and a voice in the House of Lords; and the House of Lords was the supreme court of judicature of the nation. "Now can it be supposed that the great Montesquieu, who had just before observed, that the English nation, 'has for the *direct end* of its *constitution*, political liberty,' and was now professedly describing the *constitution* of *England*, should yet, lay it down as a maxim, that, 'there is no liberty where the legislative and judiciary powers are not *entirely* separated . . . ?'"

On the separation of *executive* and *legislative* powers, "J." also interpreted Montesquieu. The King, he said, who has the sole exercise of the executive power, also has an essential share in the legislative power, namely, the power of rejecting. Montesquieu's meaning in saying that "the executive and legislative ought not to be *united*," must therefore be understood to be that: "the *whole* executive, and the *whole* legislative powers ought not to be united"; or, in other words: ". . . a *majority* of the *body* which exerciseth the *legislative* power, should have no *share* in the *executive* . . . and so long as the *legislative* and *executive* powers are kept thus separate, they are an effectual check upon each other. . . ." Thus "J." made it clear that he understood Montesquieu's "separation of powers" to signify a separation of the personnel of the different departments of government; and he was of the opinion that the theory of Montesquieu would not require a *complete* separation in the personnel of the different departments, but only of a majority of the members.

But "T. Q.," in his answer in the *Boston Gazette* of June 6, 1763, would not allow that it was a common thing for lord chief justices to be created peers of the realm, or that the practice of allowing judges to sit in the House of Lords was consistent with a separation of powers: ". . . the author of the spirit of the laws, no where says that I know of, that it is not inconsistent with liberty that it should be so; or that it is reconcileable with his maxim . . . a practice may sometimes take place, which may interfere with and obstruct the direct end of the constitution. Mr. J's inference that it

Agitation Against Oligarchy 63

is *constitutional* because it has sometimes been a *fact*, I take to be inconclusive."

To "J.'s" point that the King had a veto on legislation, and so a part in the legislative power, "T. Q." answered, following Montesquieu's words, that a negative in the executive differed from a power of resolving in council: "By the power of *rejecting*, the author of the spirit of the laws tells us, he means not the right of ordaining by their own authority, or of mending what has been ordain'd by others; for this is the power of *resolving*; if a prince says that he should have a share in legislation by the power of *resolving*, liberty would be at an end."

He explained the difference further: ". . . the whole share which the executive power has in legislation is barely *negative*; it may or may not *annul* the resolutions of the legislative body as it pleases; but a councellor has a *positive* share in those resolutions. . . ." Hence the two offices (that of chief executive and councillor) could not be united in the same person, or ". . . if the commander in chief should be a councellor at the same time, the two powers being invested in the same person . . . unavoidably, in a certain degree, there would fall in the scale of executive power too much weight of *influence:* or in other words the person possess'd of the *whole* executive power, would have an *undue* weight in the legislative body, and the ballance would be *disadjusted.*"

This discussion, which went farther than any other of the time in Massachusetts, in analyzing the meaning of Montesquieu's theory, is important also because "T. Q." makes it clear that Montesquieu was not understood to prohibit the executive any share whatsoever in the making of the laws, but to prohibit his exercise of the power of a legislator; hence, in this instance, he might not act as a councillor; the reason being that in so acting, the executive might exercise undue influence over the council. "T. Q." and his opponent, it is clear, were basing their theories of executive and legislative relations upon the British Constitution.

Opposing "J.'s" understanding that Montesquieu's meaning was ". . . that the *body* which exerciseth the *legislative* power should be composed of *members,* a *majority* . . . a *large* majority of whom should have *no share* in the exercise of the *judiciary* power . . ." and also that Montesquieu merely meant that ". . . the *whole* executive, and the *whole* legislative powers ought not to be *united*," no such compromise would be admitted by "T. Q." "If a single member of the one body, may also be a member of the other, why may not more?" he asked.

If a large majority of the legislators should have no share in the judicial, or in the executive department, it must arise from the danger to liberty. But the weight of influence in one man (a judge) might be greater than that in a number of men. "Mr. *J* may easily see that it is the weight of *influence,* we are all along speaking of as alarming; and he himself is aware, when he speaks of a *large majority,* of the certain destruction of liberty, if the weight of *influence,* in the legislative, should be in *those* members of it, who are also members of the *judiciary* body." Reasoning from Montesquieu's definition of liberty, "T. Q." explained how the presence of a single member of the judiciary in the legislative body might endanger the liberty of the subject, and that in proportion to his influence:

Political liberty is a tranquility of mind, arising from the opinion each person has of his own safety . . . it needs no great stretch of understanding to conclude, that whatsoever has a tendency to destroy the opinion which each man has of his own safety, and the tranquility of mind arising therefrom, is inconsistent with political liberty. The aforesaid author tells us, that when the Judge is the maker of the law, the life and liberty of the Subject is exposed to arbitrary controul: Now this arbitrary controul destroys the subjects opinion of his own safety, and the tranquility of mind arising therefrom; and is consequently inconsistent with political liberty, according to the above definition of it . . . according to the aforesaid maxim, liberty must be in danger in *proportion* to the degree of *influence* which a *single* member of *one* body may have in the *other*. . . .

From this exposition of Montesquieu's theory, it appears that the influence of a single judge sitting in the legislative body might constitute the "arbitrary control" which would endanger liberty. In another article, "T. Q." pointed out that the danger to liberty from a union of offices would depend upon the importance of the offices concerned.[57] A writer in the *Boston Evening-Post* had remarked that "T. Q.'s" principle would lead even to the exclusion of the justices of the peace from the General Court.[58] To this, "T. Q." answered: ". . . when *their* holding a seat shall appear to be in any considerable degree dangerous, we shall be for excluding *them*. . . ." The necessity of separation in office-holding would depend upon the importance of the offices concerned. Not so great danger was to be apprehended from justices of the peace, whose jurisdiction was confined to matters of little importance within their own county and "whose influence therefore must be *inconsiderable*." But it was otherwise with "judges of the land whose authority runs from county to county, whose influence spreads over the whole province, and upon whose decisions depend fortune, liberty and life."[59] The underlying reason for the opposition to influence by a member or members of one branch of the government over those of another not clearly expressed here would seem to be that such domination would

---

57. *Boston Gazette*, May 23, 1763.
58. *Boston Evening-Post*, May 16, 1763. "A. Z."
59. Appendix II, section 9, *infra*.

destroy the independence from control of one branch of the government over another, which was necessary to prevent tyranny. "J." retreated from the discussion with excuses, apparently outdone in his arguments for a losing cause.

Other writers made contributions to the subject. One "S. A." quoted Thacher's pamphlet *Considerations on the Election of Counsellors*.[60] "L. Q."[61] (probably also Thacher) wrote on the incompatibility of the office of judge and legislator in the *Boston Gazette* of May 16, basing his discussion to some extent upon Montesquieu's doctrine.

In spite of the newspaper campaign, the opposition was submerged in the General Court which met on May 25, 1763. The Governor claimed for the administration a predominance of two to one.[62] Probably the newspaper disclosures of Otis and Hutchinson had not helped Otis, and no doubt Bernard's patronage was used to good advantage in undermining the opposition. Very important, also, in promoting satisfaction with the administration was the news of the Peace of Paris, which came in the spring of 1763.

Congratulatory addresses were exchanged between the Governor and the two houses of the Assembly in Massachusetts, and the great benefits which were derived from the tie with Great Britain occupied the public mind. The loyal address of the two houses was forwarded to the Ministry by Bernard who prayed that the peace which prevailed in the Empire might also pervade the province of Massachusetts Bay: "As we are delivered from foreign War," he said to the two houses of the Assembly, "let us be equally free from intestine Divisions: And now that Peace is diffused throughout the vast Circle of the *British* Dominions, let it

---

60. By "S. A." in the *Boston Evening-Post* of May 23, 1763.
61. A typographical error, Spurlin says. Paul M. Spurlin, *Montesquieu in America, 1760-1801*, p. 107.
62. Bernard Papers, III, 77, June 8, 1763. To R. Jackson.

prevail, in an especial Manner, in the Councils of this Province."[63]

At this low point in the struggles of the opposition, James Otis felt driven to resign his seat in the General Court. Just previously, Bernard thought that he was making "an overture for a reconciliation."[64] In this session of the Court also, the printer and the chaplain, who were friends of James Otis, were dismissed, and his father, Colonel Otis, narrowly escaped being dropped from the Council. With the turn of events, the Governor was delighted: ". . . there never was," he wrote, "in the opinion of those who know the Country, an assembly better Composed than the present."[65] While the Governor hoped for the termination of the differences which had prevailed between the factions in the government, there is no account of a permanent agreement made. But the evidence would seem to point to some reconciliation.

In the fall of 1763, Colonel Otis was accusing Hutchinson of holding up "his appointment," subsequent to the death of Sylvanus Bourne, which left the two judicial vacancies in Barnstable County to which Colonel Otis was appointed. Evidence on this point is given by Hutchinson.[66] Bernard's account of these appointments seems worth quoting:

[Otis] still continued in a constant opposition to Government, except during an interval when his father was solliciting for two offices which put him at the head of his County. These I gave

63. May 26, 1763. *Journal of the House*, 1763, 10; *Boston Gazette*, May 30, 1763.
64. Bernard Papers, III, 77. To John Pownall.
65. *Ibid.*
66. "I have been charged by Col°. Otis with hindering his appointment. He had no other grounds for it than his own imagination of the consequence of such injurious treatment as I have received from him & his son. I do not intend in the least to oppose the appointment, nor do I wish that he should fail of it. The Governor keeps it off and both he & his son keep themselves silent. I have no doubt that he will be finally nominated and approved." Israel Williams, Letters, MSS., II, 158, Nov. 17, 1763.

him together with a good place to one of his Sons, & was assured that this would wipe away all the ill humours which his former disappointment had occasioned. But no sooner were these patents sealed than Otis renewed his hostilities against governm^t, with fresh Vigour; but to no purpose, as the Council & House was then filled with Men of Worth & Ability, who greatly outweighed & outnumbered the Opposers of Governm^t. . . .[67]

On February 1, 1764, Colonel Otis, who already sat in the Council and held a commission as Colonel in the militia, was appointed Chief Justice of the Court of Common Pleas of Barnstable County, and Judge of Probate as well.[68] The danger of uniting civil and military offices had been pointed out a short time before to the people of the province by James Otis.[69] A writer from Barnstable, apparently when it became known that the judicial appointments were going to the elder Otis, facetiously called on James Otis ". . . to pour forth all his zeal and eloquence to prevent any persons being commission'd for more than one department. . ." especially if the person came from the native town of Otis. A reference was here made to Cromwell, in connection with the danger of uniting civil and military powers.[70]

About the same time, Hutchinson seemed to prevail in the General Court. To the surprise of the public, Hutchinson was elected agent to represent Massachusetts in London by the two houses of the Assembly in February, 1764.[71] His views were publicly known to be at variance with those of the popular party. Hutchinson received all the votes of the General Court except eight, three of which were those of the Boston members.[72] But Hutchinson's acceptance of the

67. Bernard Papers, IV, 277. To Shelburne, Dec. 22, 1766.
68. Whitmore, *Mass. Civil List*, p. 104, and footnote, p. 106.
69. *Boston Gazette*, Feb. 28, 1763.
70. *Boston Evening-Post*, Oct. 24, 1763. "Philo-Politiae."
71. Tudor, *Life of James Otis*, I, 170.
72. Mass. State Archives, XXVI, 76-77. Hutchinson to Bollan, Feb. 6, 1764. The General Court was meeting in Cambridge when this vote was

agency was delayed by Governor Bernard, who suggested that he should have the permission of the Ministry to be absent from the Lieutenant-Governorship.[73]

When the question of allowing Hutchinson time to obtain leave from the Ministry came up, Oxenbridge Thacher was present in court. He spoke against Hutchinson's election and was given credit for defeating him by Hutchinson.[74] Thacher thus kept alive the opposition to the British policy when practically all others had abandoned it.

When the Sugar Act[75] was re-enacted, the House felt it was largely because the objections to it had not been adequately represented. The Governor had hampered their representations by postponing the General Court from time to time until late in the fall of 1763. Again, when the warning of impending "inland taxation" was given by the agent, the Governor twice prorogued the General Court in the face of petitions from the Boston members. The consequence was, as it was said, that instructions could not be sent to the agent, "tho sollicited by him, till the Evil had got beyond an Easy Remedy."[76]

---

taken. Thacher, one of the Boston representatives, was not present at the time. Otis could not have voted for Hutchinson, it should be noted.

73. *Boston Gazette*, Feb. 6, 1764. "L." His enemies were so unkind as to say that Bernard's motive was fear that Hutchinson would obtain the post of Governor when he got to court. Bernard Papers, III, 124, Feb. 2, 1764. Otis wrote somewhat earlier of the possible agency of Hutchinson: "In short he thinks going home agent would enable him to get the Government which event would be as terrible to the honest part of this Province as a Volcano or an Earthquake. . . . Mr. Bernard was and I believe now is against Mr. Hutchinson . . . from the motive of fear, lest he might thereby obtain the Government." Jasper Mauduit, 77-78. Otis to Mauduit, Oct. 28, 1762; *ibid.*, 143-4; Hutchinson, *History*, III, 106.

74. Hutchinson, *History*, III, 106.

75. 6 George II.

76. *Report of the Boston Record Commissioners*, XVI, 121, *Boston Town Records, 1758-69*. Instructions from the Town of Boston. See also H. A. Cushing, *Writings of Samuel Adams*, I, 4. The General Court was prorogued from July 25 to Sept. 5 to Oct. 10 to Oct. 18. *Journal of the House, 1764*, p. 91; *Boston Gazette*, Aug. 20, 1764; Oct. 1, 1764.

The petition of Massachusetts to the House of Commons for repeal of the Sugar Act and against parliamentary "inland taxation," was "pared down & enfeebled" through the influence of Hutchinson, and the word "Rights" was not used.[77] There were great differences between the House and the Council before the petition was prepared by Hutchinson and one or two others, and finally accepted with very little change.[78] Otis was a member of the committee of the House to prepare the petition. Instead of asserting "their exemption from parliamentary taxes in positive Terms as a right," under the lead of Hutchinson, the petition was phrased to "only insinuate it in the way of praying a continuance of that favour & indulgence which they had hitherto experienced."[79] The result was brought about by the political management of Hutchinson: ". . . the Lieut. Governor acted a principal part, & by judiciously giving way to the popular party at first, at lenghth [sic] got the lead in his hands."[80] The efforts of Oxenbridge Thacher at this point were unavailing. The position taken in the petition was not the one taken by Otis in his *Rights of the British Colonies Asserted and Proved*, which was published in the summer of 1764; nor was it the position taken in the letter of instructions to the agent, of June 13, 1764.

The Governor succeeded in having a friend of his, Richard Jackson, chosen at this critical time, first to be counsel to the agent of Massachusetts at court, and in 1765 as joint agent for the province. To achieve the election of Jackson, Governor Bernard had to use openly political methods.[81] Hutch-

---

77. Hutchinson, *History*, III, 113-14. *Boston Gazette*, May 5, 1766. "A." *Ibid.*, May 14, 1764. "Nov-Anglicanus," accusing the representatives of being in a "sound sleep."
78. Bernard Papers, III, 262. To R. Jackson, Nov. 17, 1764.
79. *Ibid.*, p. 263.
80. Bernard Papers, III, 263. *Journal of the House*, 1764, pp. 97, 111, 112, 133, Oct. 19, 1764.
81. *Boston Gazette*, Dec. 22, 1766. "A." ". . . was it not given out, that if any other beside Mr. J—n was chosen, were they a D—t or

inson observed that the Governor used "more zeal than he would have done for anybody else & more than I ever knew him use on any other occasion. . . ." If he had not done so, Hutchinson thought, "the other side would have prevailed."[82] Thus did the Governor use influence to bring about the election of a man who was his own personal friend and the secretary to Lord Grenville (who had devised the Stamp Act) as agent of the province. When the Stamp Act became a reality, the political interference in the election of the agent added to the popular distrust of Governor Bernard and helped to undermine his administration.[83]

Apparently the Governor did not neglect to build up support in the House of Representatives by means of commissions; for hostility to prerogative placemen, previously directed against their presence in the Council, in 1764 had been extended to the House, by the instructions of Boston to its representatives. A provision like that of the English disqualifying Act of 1705[84] which excluded certain officers absolutely and required a precept to issue for a new election upon appointment of a member of the House of Commons to any "Office of Profit from the Crown" was advocated. The instructions of Boston made it clear that the object, like that of the English measure, was to secure the independence of the popular House of the legislature. While the instruction discoursed of the "critical Ballance" of the Constitution, it was directed against executive influence in the House:

That you will endeavor as far as you shall be able to preserve that independence in the House of Representatives, which char-

---

M—d—t, they would be certainly negatived? And did not the G—r by closeting almost every member, actually influence to that choice. . . ."

82. Mass. State Archives, XXVI, 131.

83. John Adams, *Life and Works*, II, 151: "Was not all this . . . enough to excite suspicions among the vulgar that all these gentlemen were in a combination to favor the measures of the Ministry, at least to prevent anything from being done here to discourage the Minister from his rash, mad, and dogmatical proceedings?"

84. 4 and 5 Anne, c. 20.

acterizes a Free People . . . guarding against any undue weight which may tend to disadjust that critical Ballance upon which our happy Constitution, and the Blessings of it do depend. . . . And for this purpose we particularly recommend it to you to use your endeavors to have a Law passed whereby the Seats of such Gentlemen as shall accept Posts of Profit from the Crown or the Governor while they are Members of the House shall be vacated agreable to an Act of the British Parliament, till their Constituents shall have y^e. Opportunity of Re-electing them if they please . . . or of returning others in their room. . . .[85]

The English provision requiring re-election upon the acceptance of any "Office of Profit from the Crown"[86] was looked upon in the province as disclaiming executive influence in the House of Commons. It was referred to from time to time as a precedent for the provincial attempt to bring about independence of the departments of government.[87] The Boston instruction was no doubt directed against military and civil officers (including some of the customs officers) who sat in the House, although holding executive commissions. There is some evidence to show that military commissions were used to advantage by the administration to gain supporters.[88] The House Journal shows that out of

85. *Report of the Boston Record Commissioners*, XVI, 120. Cushing, *Writings of Samuel Adams*, I, 2. Wells, *Samuel Adams*, I, 46: "The original autograph still exists among his papers."

86. The provision in 12 Wm. III, Cap. II, 3 (Act of Settlement) was uncompromising: "That no Person who has an Office or Place of Profit under the King, or receives a Pension from the Crown, shall be capable of serving as a Member of the House of Commons." This provision was repealed by 4 Anne Cap. VIII, 25, and a designated list of officers was set up for exclusion from the House, and a provision was added requiring open appointment and re-election to offices which did not disqualify. The Place Act of 1742 (15 George II, Cap. XXII) disqualified certain commissioners, and deputies and clerks in a long list of government departments, whose status might render them subservient as members of the Commons. The Statutes at Large, IV, VI. E. and A. G. Porritt, *The Unreformed House of Commons*, I, 210-11.

87. *Mass. Spy*, May 18, 1776. "O. P. Q."

88. *Boston Gazette*, April 14, 1766. "B. W." "There is a refined

113 representatives in 1764, fourteen captains were returned. The number of Inferior Court of Common Pleas judges in the House in 1764 appears to have been fifteen, while the number bearing appointments as justices of the peace ran over sixty; three sheriffs and four registers of probate, all executive appointees, were members of the House.

English legislation of the year 1372 had excluded sheriffs from the House of Commons of the mother country,[89] while officers concerned in farming or collecting any tax had been excluded in 1695, the prohibition being extended to all customs officers and commissioners in 1701.[90] Long lists of other officers were excluded by the Place Acts of 1705 and 1742 while the provision for re-election in the Act of 1705 required that those offices which did not disqualify should be accepted by the Commons openly and with the approval of their constituents. The exclusion policy which Boston advocated was therefore of long historical development in England. The rule of the common law made incompatible in the hands of the same person the offices which "from the Multiplicity of Business in them cannot be executed with Care and Ability; or when their being subordinate and interfering with each other, it induces a Presumption they cannot be executed with Impartiality and Honesty."[91] There was no question but that the rule was being flagrantly violated in Massachusetts.

Sort of Policy practised in a certain Province I could mention, of giving Commissions previous to Elections, to certain Court Sycophants, to be Field Officers, with full Power to nominate the Captains and Subalterns thro' the Bounds of the Regiment."

Mass. State Archives, XXV, 262. Hutchinson to Gov. Pownall, June 7, 1768. Hutchinson speaks of the election to the Council of "one Ward a very sulky fellow who I thought I could bring over by giving him a Lt. Col Commission in the Provincial forces after you left the government but I was mistaken." The "sulky" Artemas Ward was found acceptable for the Council by Hutchinson in 1770, after having been rejected in 1768 and 1769 by Governor Bernard.

89. 46 Edward III. Re-enacted 23 Henry VIII.
90. 5 and 6 Will. and Mar., Cap. VII.
91. Bacon, *A New Abridgment*, III, (K), 736. Sir Edward Coke, *The Fourth Part of the Institutes of the Laws of England*, cap. 78, p. 310; 12 and 13 Will. III, Cap. II and X.

CHAPTER III

OVERTHROW OF EXECUTIVE CONTROL

THE ATTEMPT to enforce the Stamp Act furnished a final demonstration of the danger to the province interest which the union of executive, judicial, and legislative offices under executive domination might present. Popular resistance to the Act not only furnished impetus for the reorganization of the defunct opposition, and incidentally returned James Otis to political favor, but it also brought about such conflict between the popular party and the administration as resulted in the overthrow of the "Junto." When the Council and the Superior Court played all too readily the prerogative part in supporting the detested Act, the opposition gained such cohesion as enabled it to attack the prerogative domination, which was held responsible for the intolerable policy of enforcement, in defiance of the popular will.

Great was the chagrin of the people of Massachusetts at their acquiescence when the independent assertions of rights from other colonies against the Stamp Act manifesting an attitude of resistance found their way into Massachusetts. The effect of the New York address was described by Hutchinson. The proceedings of the General Court of Massachusetts, which had considered the power of taxation as an "indulgence," of which they prayed the continuance, had been approved by the people, until one of the Boston members[1] brought the New York address into the town. The effect was observed by Hutchinson: "This was so high, that the heroes of liberty among us were ashamed of their own

1. William Bayard.

conduct and would have recalled what had been done here if it had not been too late." Later, Hutchinson, who had promoted the Massachusetts petition for "favour & indulgence," rather than "rights," was charged with "treachery & from his dependence on the crown betraying his country."[2] The Governor incurred the odium of the people by advising "Submission to the Act, as the readiest Way to get rid of it."[3]

The efforts of the popular party to drop Hutchinson and Secretary Andrew Oliver, the Stamp agent in Massachusetts, from the Council, failed by only a few votes in 1765.[4] Bernard noted the lack of scruples in the methods used by the popular party in an attempt to influence the elections, "tampering" with the members: "Some of the factious People of this Town therefore made it their business to tamper with the Members as they came to Town and incense them against Mr Oliver for accepting this Office; in which, Misrepresentations & downright Falsehoods, as it appeared afterwards, were not spared . . . it was so successful that Mr Oliver gained his Election but by three Voices out of upwards of 120."[5] Soon the opposition gathered momentum, not without influence from other provinces.

Following the appearance of the Virginia Resolves, a new spirit was observed to take hold in Massachusetts.[6] The Massachusetts petition against the Stamp Act was reviled as a "tame, pusilanimous, daub'd, insipid Thing," and the Virginia Resolves were praised in contrast with it.[7] Resistance

2. Mass. State Archives, XXVI, 202, 209. Hutchinson Correspondence, March 8, 1766. The Virginia address appeared in the *Boston Gazette*, March 25, 1765.
3. *Boston Gazette*, April 14, 1766. "B. W."
4. Mass. State Archives, XXVI, 139, June, 1765. Letter [not sent]: "They attempted last week to drop me from the council but failed there."
5. Bernard Papers, IV, 132-3. To the Lords of Trade.
6. "But soon after the resolves of the Virginia Assembly were sent hither, A new spirit appeared at once." Mass. State Archives, XXVI, 209. Hutchinson Correspondence, March 8, 1766.
7. *Boston Gazette*, July 8, 1765.

to the Stamp Act culminated in open violence against the Lieutenant-Governor and other officers of the King. Efforts to execute the Act by the agency of the General Court were futile. The General Court was allowed to sit only two days when the Governor apprehended the temper of it. But the adjournment was of no avail.[8]

After the destruction of his house, and the plunder of his personal property by a mob, Hutchinson had been warned of impending violence to his person. Consequently he resigned his office of Probate Judge near the end of the year 1765, but with characteristic prudence, for only a period of twelve months.[9]

Threats were made against the Governor because of his support of the policy of the Ministry in regard to the Stamp Act. The *Boston Gazette* carried a warning: "Great Sir, Retreat or you are ruined";[10] which the Governor understood to be a hint to him "that if I do not in the next Assembly retract what I have hitherto urged for the execution of the Stamp Act, I must expect to be ruined some way or other."[11] Bernard now was forced to admit that it was impossible for him to carry out his orders to effect distribution of the stamps.[12]

In the next General Court, the Boston members had command of the Assembly. Feeling was at such a pitch that members friendly to the administration now preferred not

---

8. ". . . there was not the least probability of my prevailing upon the Representatives to assist the execution of the Act: on the contrary a Faction in perpetual opposition to Government, which had hitherto been pretty well kept down, took the lead; & what with inflammatory Speeches within doors, & the parades of the Mob without, entirely triumphed over the little remains of Government. " Bernard Papers, IV, 170. To Conway, Nov. 25, 1765.

9. Mass. State Archives, XXVI, 187, 189, Dec., 1765: "I was in danger of violence to my person unless I immediately complied with their demands." See *Boston Evening-Post*, Jan. 6, 1766, for the appointment of Foster Hutchinson to the place.   10. Jan. 6, 1766.

11. Bernard Papers, V, 71. To Pownall, Jan. 11, 1766.

12. *Ibid.*, V, 63. To Gray Cooper, Dec. 22, 1765.

to attend the Court, and intimidation was being used. Early in 1766 a committee on grievances was appointed with a twofold purpose: to secure an Act of the General Court for opening the courts, in defiance of the Stamp Act; and to bring in an Act to exclude the judges and officers of the government from the Council. The committee reported that it was a grievance for one person to hold two offices, executive or legislative.[13] The latter measure was voted down, after argument, by a majority of 3 to 1, according to Bernard. But it followed that the same result could be brought about by another method.

A resolution that the courts of justice throughout the province should be opened and function without the use of stamps passed the House by a final vote of 66 to 4. That this vote was brought about by intimidation was explained by Bernard.[14] The resolve was non-concurred by the Council, after a reference of the question to the judges of the Superior Court, who gave an equivocal opinion.[15] This opinion of the judges, which seemingly played into executive hands, was voted to be unsatisfactory by the House. Executive domination of the Council and of the Superior Court appeared to have been demonstrated, and the time had come when the domination would no longer be tolerated. The

13. *Ibid.*, IV, 211. To Lords of Trade, March 10, 1766.
14. ". . . I am convinced it was against the Sense of a considerable Majority of the House: to so great a pitch has the power of intimidation been carried. Those Members who opposed the Question were told that if they voted against it, they would not be able to return in Safety to their Homes; some of the first 7 (an earlier vote) were insulted in the Streets as they went from the House: above 20 Members kept away to avoid voting; the small Minority of 7 were reduced to 4, by taking a second Vote by entring the Names upon the Journal so as to mark the Nays for resentment; these 4 were desired to quit the house that it might be unanimous & refused; whilst some of the most assured friends of Government were frightened into voting for the Question. Such is the popular Despotism which at present governs the Councils of this province." Bernard Papers, IV, 199. To Conway, Jan. 25, 1766.
15. *Ibid.*, IV, 209. See *Boston Gazette*, Jan. 7, 1766, for Hutchinson's action in the Council.

combination, the "Junto," was now attacked successfully by the popular party.

Prior to the elections of 1766, the most vigorous campaign yet undertaken against the executive, legislative, and judicial combination got under way. The Stamp Act had, in the meantime, been repealed, but official news of the repeal did not reach Boston until after the election. Disaffection had been bred, and the danger of parliamentary taxation still impended. The demonstration to the people that the "ring" within the government could be used to defeat their interests had been sufficient, and they now proceeded to destroy it.[16] The press now was wholly against the administration.[17]

In the *Boston Gazette*, and also in the *Boston Evening-Post*,[18] there was published a list of thirty-two representatives, with the names of their towns opposite, carrying a recommendation that their conduct should be scrutinized: ". . . and in particular, if they have in any shape discovered an approbation of the *Stamp Act*, and manifested a willingness that it should take place in this province:—Then, without doubt, they are justly to be accounted *enemies to their country*. . . ." In order to bring about "a *general purgation*, and thorough reformation, in *both houses*," which was now recognized to be of absolute necessity, the people were urged to "purge" out "*the old leaven, which has so long corrupted the whole lump*," and then to seek "good and honest and *Free* Men . . . Men that are *unshackled* with posts and preferments; Men who will not *warp*, nor be cajoled into

16. John Adams, *History of the Dispute with America*, pp. 58, 59: "The Public, accordingly, found all these springs and wheels in the Constitution set in motion to promote submission to the Stamp Act, and to discountenance resistance to it; and they thought they had a violent presumption, that they would for ever be employed to encourage a compliance with all Ministerial measures, and Parliamentary claims, of whatever character they might be."

17. Bernard Papers, IV, 229-30. To Lords of Trade, July 7, 1766: ". . . no pen was used in its defence. . . ."

18. *Boston Gazette*, March 31, 1766. *Boston Evening-Post*, April 28, 1766, Supplement.

any measures that will tend to impoverish and enslave their country." Nineteen of the representatives on the list failed of re-election.[19]

In the numerous articles written for the voters in 1766, it is apparent that public opinion was agreed on the necessity of breaking up the combination of executive, judicial, and legislative offices in the government. Such was said to be the "settled" opinion by a "Gentleman in the Country":

". . . the most judicious persons in the country, are now of a settled opinion, that it is the *real interest* of the province—*that no Judge of Probate, Judge of Admiralty, Attorney-General, Adjutant-General, Sheriff, nor any Gentleman in Close Connexion with the Chair,* should have a seat at the Board."[20] Another writer, who signed himself "One of the Sons of Liberty in Bristol County," said that few things had of late been more complained of by the patrons of true liberty, than the "unrighteous practice of blending the executive with the legislative power; or uniting them in the same person. . . ." It was pointed out that it was unreasonable "that men should make the laws that they judge of, and put in execution," and objection was made to justices and attorneys acting as representatives.[21]

A reply to this writer, by a "Son of Liberty in Boston," calls the separation of legislative and executive powers an "important essential maxim of English liberty." But the writer was against "misapplication" of the principle, by carrying it to extremes.[22] Model instructions, offered by "A Countryman" to representatives to the General Court, would require of them:

First. That you use the whole of your influence, and endeavour that no person holding any fee or military office what-

---

19. *Journal of the House, 1766*, p. 4; Francis Bowen, *Life of James Otis*, p. 135.
20. *Boston Evening-Post*, May 26, 1766.
21. *Ibid.*, April 21, 1766.   22. *Boston Evening-Post*, May 12, 1766.

soever, especially judges of the superior court, secretary, etc. be chosen into his Majesty's Council of this province; and that you attend at the election of counsellors, and give your vote accordingly. . . .

Fifth. That you endeavour that there be no monopolizing of public offices in this government; and that one man be not invested with more than one office at one time, except it be compatible with the true interest of the people in general.[23]

Several towns gave instructions along these lines to their representatives. Worcester gave very sweeping instructions, which corresponded closely to the model instructions above, as to the articles quoted.[24] The Worcester article against monopoly in public offices followed the fifth article of the model instructions quoted above exactly. Worcester also included an article attacking executive influence in the House of Representatives by advocating the dismissal of any representative receiving an appointment from the Governor, unless he should be re-elected by his constituents.[25]

Boston gave instructions based upon the common-law rule: "That you be not parsimonious in the support of executive officers of government, but at the same time use all your influence against any one officer's holding two or more places inconsistent or interfering with each other." The Boston representatives were also instructed (for their political guidance) that they should take particular care in their choice of councillors and other officers of government for the next year, to see that they should be "men of integrity, and wis-

[23]. *Boston Gazette*, March 31, 1766.
[24]. Appendix III, section 1, *infra*.
[25]. "That you Endeavour as aforesaid that there be a Law made that wherever any Representative shall Receive any office or Commission from ye Governour he shall be Dismissed ye House & not allowed to act as a member thereof without he should be Chosen a New by his Constituents and that the said Constituents be forthwith served with a New Precept to call a meeting for ye Choice of some meet & Suitable Person to Represent them in ye Great & General Court. . . ." *Worcester Town Records, 1753-83*, IV, 138-9.

dom, lovers of liberty and of our civil and ecclesiastical constitutions"; that they should not give their vote for "any whose characters are doubtful, or who are of a timid or wavering disposition."[26]

The sweeping changes in the list of representatives returned in the elections of 1766 made it obvious that the administration would be at a disadvantage in the election of councillors. Forty-two new representatives were elected to the General Court.[27] Otis boasted before the election of the Council took place that the judges and the Crown officers (the Secretary and the Lieutenant-Governor) would be turned out.[28] The Governor, apparently, was not restrained by the dignity of his office from retaliating with threats. He was reported to have threatened "diverse negatives, should the elections be not to his mind. . . ." And he declared quite publicly that "it should be his fault, if he had not a good council this year."[29]

The popular party made good their boasts in the election of councillors. When the General Court met, its character was indicated by the choice made of James Otis as Speaker of the House and of Samuel Adams as Clerk. Bernard defied the House and disapproved of Otis, not foreseeing that the Ministry would favor conciliation. The Governor by this action gave another rallying point to the opposition, and kept alive controversy.

As the formalities for the election of the Council were being completed, Judges Lynde and Leonard resigned their seats in the Council. According to Bernard, they were

26. *Boston Evening-Post*, June 2, 1766. Report of the Boston Record Commission, *Boston Town Records*, 1758-69, XVI, 183.
27. Bernard Papers, V, 118; *Boston Evening-Post*, June 2, 1766.
28. Bernard Papers, IV, 230.
29. *Boston Gazette*, Nov. 24, 1766. "John Hampden," *ibid.*, Dec. 22, 1766. "A." ". . . in case certain crown-officers were not re-chosen into the c . . . l, [he] would strike as good a stroke, at what he politely call'd their tail, as they should give at their head. . . ."

"teized" into resigning.[80] In the ensuing elections, the Chief Justice and Lieutenant-Governor Hutchinson, Judge Oliver, Secretary Oliver, and Attorney-General Trowbridge were all dropped from the Council.[81] At this overthrow, the Governor in chagrin negatived the candidates chosen in place of these Crown officers and the judges, although the Governor's veto in the election of councillors had not been used for some years.[32] The new candidates whom he negatived, the Governor said, had no pretensions to a seat in the Council, or at least very little other pretension than "a constant & uniform opposition to the Administration of Government upon all occasions." Two of the old councillors (Colonel Otis and Colonel Sparhawk), Bernard said he negatived on the ground that they were "out of all doubt promoters of the exclusion."[33]

The Governor made an unsuccessful attempt to compromise with the opposition and to restore the Council to its former make-up, but his effort was rejected disdainfully. In the end, the Governor apparently declared that the places of the Crown officers in the Council would not be filled.[34] The result of the election demonstrated, the Governor said, "what a fatal Ingredient in the Composition of this Government has been the making of the King's Council annually elective."[35] He marveled at the irony of a King's Council in which "an official relation to the King becomes a plausible pretence to exclude Men of the first-rate abilities from a Seat in it."[36]

30. Bernard Papers, IV, 291. To Shelburne, Dec. 24, 1766. *Journal of the House*, 1766, p. 7.   31. *Boston Evening-Post*, June 2, 1766.
32. Bernard Papers, IV, 233. To Lords of Trade, July 7, 1766.
33. Bernard Papers, IV, 233; V, 116. To J. Pownall, May 30, 1766.
34. *Boston Gazette*, April 27, 1767. "Freeborn American." Cushing, *Writings of S. Adams*, I, 350. Petition of the House to the King, June 27, 1769: "He has declared that certain seats at the Council board shall be kept vacant, 'till certain Gentlemen, who are his favourites, shall be re-elected."
35. Bernard Papers, IV, 236. To Lords of Trade, July 7, 1766.
36. *Ibid.*, p. 232.

The next day, in his address to the two houses of the General Court, the Governor took the opportunity to upbraid them severely for their action. This course of the Governor was later disclaimed by the conciliatory attitude adopted by the Ministry. The Governor said that he could not be indifferent "when the Government is attacked in form; when there is a profest Intention to deprive it of its best and most able Servants, whose only Crime is their Fidelity to the Crown"; and that he felt himself obliged "to exercise every legal and constitutional Power to maintain the King's Authority against this ill-judged and ill-timed Oppugnation of it."[37]

The reply of the House was probably written by Samuel Adams, but pointed with sarcasm by Otis.[38] The House declared they were wholly at a loss to conceive how "a full, free and fair Election" could be called "an attack upon the Government in Form," "a professed intention to deprive it of its best and most able Servants," "an ill-judged and ill-timed Oppugnation of the King's Authority." The Governor's accusations against the two houses were termed "high and grievous Charges," such as "no crowned Head since the Revolution has thought fit to bring against the Houses of Parliament."[39] A facetious explanation of the "Oppugnation" with which the Governor charged the two houses was then advanced by the House: they had released those Superior Court judges who had a seat in the Council from "the Cares and Perplexities of Politicks," and given them an opportunity

37. *Journal of the House, 1766*, p. 12. See Cushing, *Writings of S. Adams*, I, 101, letter to de Berdt, Nov. 15, 1766, for the comment: ". . . his Excy was displeased with the two Houses for the Elections they had made, & gave them a Speech wch displeased them as much."
38. Wells, *Samuel Adams*, I, 121. Wells states that the answer "was drafted by Samuel Adams," though Hutchinson states that Otis "was supposed to have had a principal share in the composition of this answer." Hutchinson, *History*, III, 150. See also Cushing, *Writings of S. Adams*, I, 74, 83.
39. *Journal of the House, 1766*, p. 26. Appendix III, section 2, *infra*.

to make "still further Advances in the knowledge of the Law," and to perform their duty of administering justice. Other officers also were left "more at Leasure" to perform the duties of their important offices. All this was surely not to deprive the government of its "best and ablest Servants," nor could it be called an "Oppugnation" of anything, except a "dangerous Union of Legislative, and Executive Power in the Same Persons, which was a grievance that had been long complained of by their Constituents," and the redress of which some of them had special instructions "to endeavour at this very Election to obtain."[40]

The Governor was not silenced by this impertinence, but a few days later found occasion to add to his censures, accusing the members of being actuated by the private interests of a few men of the two houses: It must be understood that the Gentlemen were turned out for their Deference to Acts of the British Legislature. It was "impossible to give any tolerable Colouring to this Proceeding."[41] The Governor indicated, however, that it might not be too late to reconsider the action which had been taken: He wished that some measures might be found "to draw a Veil over it," or at least "to palliate it and prevent its bad effects," which would surely be very hurtful to the province, if it should be persisted in.[42] If any "Expedients can be found out for this Purpose," the Governor said, he would "heartily concur in them."

The colonists were given to comparing their constitutional struggles with those of Parliament in the seventeenth century. These two addresses of Bernard were said to be "perhaps as infamous & irritating as ever came from a Stuart to

---

40. *Journal of the House, 1766*, pp. 26-7. Appendix III, section 3, *infra*.
41. *Journal of the House, 1766*, pp. 29-30, June 3, 1766.
42. *Ibid.*, p. 30.

the English parliam^t."^{43} The House, in answer to the Governor, rejected the suggestion of reconsideration of their action, and turned the Governor's statements to ridicule. First they asserted their charter right of a free election of the Council, from which they refused to be deterred by "unprovoked asperity of Expression" on the part of the Governor. The strictest examination of the proceedings at the election, the House declared, gave them not "the least Reason for Regret." So long as their Charter privileges were continued, they said, ". . . we must think ourselves inexcusable, if we should suffer ourselves to be intimidated in the free Exercise of them. . . ." The impropriety of the Governor's commenting on the result of the election was stressed. If he had informed them of his sentiments and opinion of the candidates before the election, it could not have been more a breach of their privileges. The matter was beyond remedy for the present year at least, and as for the Assembly of another year they would act for themselves, or "under such Influence and Direction as they may think fit." As for the Crown officers who were previously in the Council, and who were not chosen at the election: "This Province has subsisted and flourished, and the Administration of Government has been carried on here intirely to the Royal Approbation, when no Crown Officers had a Seat at the Board, and we trust this may be the Case again."[44]

The true reason for the exclusion of the judicial and executive officers from the Council had already been given, the House declared, in their answer to the Governor's first Speech of the Session. The House also replied to the Governor's charge that it was impossible to give "any tolerable colouring" to their proceeding, that the integrity and up-

43. Cushing, *Writings of S. Adams*, II, 165. April 19, 1771.
44. *Journal of the House, 1766*, pp. 42-3. Appendix III, section 4, *infra*.

rightness of their conduct was such that no "colouring" was requisite, and therefore they would excuse themselves from attempting any.[45] The House also asked to be excused from an attempt to palliate the bad effects of the election, since they had no apprehensions of such effects, especially when they reflected on the ability and integrity of the Council to which the Governor had given his approval.[46] The address of the House concluded with the impertinent suggestion: ". . . With Regard to the Rest of your Excellency's Speech, we are sorry we are constrained to observe, that the general Air and Style of it savours much more of an Act of free Grace and Pardon, than of a Parliamentary Address to the two Houses of Assembly; and we most sincerely wish your Excellency had been pleased to reserve it (if needful) for a Proclamation."[47]

While the dialectics ended in failure and humiliation for the Governor, it was not without retaliation from him. The empty seats in the Council went unfilled. The Governor's resentment also visited itself upon certain members of the House who held military commissions from him and who notwithstanding had failed to support the administration. Scarcely was the General Court prorogued after the elections when several colonels of the militia who were members of the House were abruptly dismissed from their appointments by Bernard.[48] No reason was assigned for the dismissals, but various critics willingly clarified the reason in newspaper articles.[49] One of the officers dismissed was Colonel Ward,

---

45. *Journal of the House,* 1766, p. 43. Appendix III, section 5, *infra.*
46. *Journal of the House,* 1766, pp. 44-5. Appendix III, section 6, *infra.*
47. *Journal of the House,* 1766, p. 46.
48. *Boston Gazette,* Nov. 24, 1766. "John Hampden," *i.e.,* Otis, according to John Adams, *Life and Works,* II, 174.
49. ". . . he hath disgracefully torn away the com—ssi—ns of several honorable gentlemen, because they were hardy enough to confront the advances of tyranny, and maintained the prerogative to think for themselves, and afterwards hung those badges of inf—y on his temporizing sycophants." *Boston Gazette,* May 11, 1767. "Philalethes."

and a captain "who had the faculty of pleasing"[50] was advanced to his place. Prior to the next elections, someone wrote: "G—r B—d is at his old Trade of rubbing up old Tools, and making new ones, against the ensuing Election. . . . Com—ssi—ns are shamefully prostituted to obtain an Ass—m—y that shall be subservient to his Designs."[51] Henceforward, however, the influence which the Governor's patronage could exercise over the House was negligible.[52]

It is worth passing notice that, although he had been dropped from the Council in the elections, Hutchinson still struggled to keep his seat in the Council on the ground that he had a seat there by virtue of his office of Lieutenant-Governor. Even before the elections of 1766 (in which Hutchinson was dropped), Otis and Hawley had started an agitation to establish that the Lieutenant-Governor had no right, ex officio, either to sit or preside in the Council without being elected as a councillor. Otis charged that Hutchinson, who had been presiding over the Council, had usurped the place: "There are elder Councellors, and he sits not as Lieu^t. but as Councellor."[53]

The Council attempted to settle the point by voting on the question, "Whether his Honor the Lieutenant-Governor hath usurped the Place of President of the Board?" The result was a resolution, not too clear, to the effect that when Hutchinson first began to preside over the "Board," he had done so after resolution by the "Board," on which he did

50. *Ibid.*, Nov. 24, 1766.
51. *Ibid.*, May 4, 1767. "Intelligence Extraordinary." Somewhat later, one of the customs officers, Timothy Folgier, was dismissed, apparently because he voted for a measure which the administration opposed. *Boston Gazette*, March 14 and April 11, 1768.
52. See, however, *Boston Gazette*, Feb. 20, 1775. "Novanglus." "The Governor had to the last hour of the house's existence, always some seekers and expectants in the house, who never failed to oppose. . . ."
53. *Boston Gazette*, Jan. 27, 1766. "Freeborn Armstrong." Bernard Papers, IV, 210. Mass. State Archives, XXV, 225.

not vote and after there had been search of "the Books for Precedents in the like Cases."[54]

This resolution Otis characterized as a "summary decision" in favor of Hutchinson's right to preside in the Council. He declared that the question was a legal one, and unless it had support in the Charter, or in the laws of the province, the right was at least doubtful. There was nothing, however, either in the Charter or laws of the province that entitled the Lieutenant-Governor to a seat in the Council, much less to the presidency. Furthermore, there was no usage that gave him a right to sit in the Council.[55]

When the General Court met in January, 1767, the House objected to Hutchinson's sitting in the Council.[56] The House declared to the Governor that his appearance was "not only in itself an impropriety, but repugnant to the constitution, and the letter of the charter"; and, they said, with resentment: "If the honourable gentleman was introduced by your Excellency, we apprehend the happiest means of supporting the authority of the government or maintaining the honour of the province, were not consulted therein: But if he came in and took a seat of his own motion we are constrained to say, that it affords a new and additional instance of ambition, and a lust of power, to what we have heretofore observed."[57]

There was no clause in the charter which could be plausibly construed to give the Lieutenant-Governor a seat in the General Court, while the Governor was present. As the House pointed out, the Charter defined the General Court to consist "of the Governor, and Council or Assistants for the time being, and such Freeholders of the Province, as shall be

---

54. *Boston Gazette*, Feb. 3, 1766. Appendix III, section 7, *infra*.
55. *Boston Gazette*, Feb. 3, 1766. Appendix III, section 8, *infra*.
56. *Journal of the House, 1766-7*, p. 393.
57. *Ibid.*, p. 233, Jan. 31, 1767.

from time to time elected or deputed by the major part of the Freeholders and other Inhabitants qualified."[58]

Secretary Oliver, at the direction of the Governor, drew up a report on the usage followed during the province period in regard to the Lieutenant-Governor's sitting in the Council from the very beginning.[59] From this report, the Governor found: ". . . that ev'ry Lieut. Governor since the opening the present Charter, has usually and frequently when not elected a Councellor sat in Council, until the time of Governor Belcher, who excluded the Lieut. Governor from a seat in the Council. . . ."[60] The House could not agree with this finding. Only two instances of the Lieutenant-Governor's appearing in the Assembly when the Governor was present could be found, their reply said, and "no precedents can prevail in support of any conduct, repugnant to the constitution[61] and letter of the charter." The House emphasized that the Lieutenant-Governor, unless elected a councillor, had been excluded from the Council under Governors Belcher, Shirley, and Pownall—for a period of nearly forty years.

The question was determined by resolution of the House that the Lieutenant-Governor "not being elected a Councellor, has not a Right to a Seat at the Council Board, with or without a Voice, while the Commander in Chief is in the Province," and by a similar resolution passed by the Council.[62] Hutchinson therefore gave up his claim to sit in the Council, while Bernard awaited instructions from the Secretary of State on the point.

The House, in the meantime, explained their position in this controversy in a long and vehement letter to the province agent, de Berdt, which they published in the House Journal:[63]

58. *Journal of the House*, 1766-7, p. 233.
59. *Ibid.*, p. 260.
60. *Ibid.*, p. 260.   61. *Ibid.*, p. 294.
62. *Journal of the House*, 1766-7, pp. 267, 368. Feb. 10, March 7, 1767.
63. *Ibid.*, p. 393. March 16, 1767. Major Hawley, James Otis, and

We cannot but think this attempt of his Honor the more unnatural [wrote the House], as he has so long enjoy'd every honor and favor in the power of his native country to confer upon him. Some of his high offices are so incompatible with others of them, that in all probability they never will hereafter be, as they never were heretofore thus accumulated by any man. This gentleman was for years together Lieutenant Governor, Councellor [sic], Chief Justice of the province, and a Judge of the probate. Three of these lucrative as well as honorary places he now enjoys, and yet is not content. It is easy to conceive how undue an influence the two first must give.

The House then gave an argument to demonstrate the incompatibility of "modern" politics with the Chief Justiceship, which had been used more than once before in the controversy over plural office-holding in Massachusetts:

The cool and impartial administration of common justice can never harmonize with the meanders and windings of a modern politician. The integrity of the judge may sometimes embarrass the politician, but there is infinitely more danger in the long run of the politicians spoiling the good and upright Judge. This has often been the case, and in the course of things may be expected again.[64]

The Earl of Shelburne gave a final determination to the controversy by writing that the question of admitting the Lieutenant-Governor to the Council rested exclusively with the Council.[65]

With Hutchinson out of the Council, his place as leader of the Council was assumed by Bowdoin, who was in close

---

Samuel Adams were all members of the committee to draw up this document (*ibid.*, p. 350), though Wells claims authorship for Samuel Adams. Wells, *Samuel Adams*, I, 135.

64. *Journal of the House, 1766-7*, p. 404. March 16, 1767.

65. *Ibid., 1767-8*, Appendix, p. 35. "But the question concerning his admission seems to lie, after all, in the breast of the Council only, as being the proper judges of their own Privileges, and as having the best right to determine whom they will admit to be present at their deliberations." To Bernard, Sept. 17, 1767. See also Wells, *Samuel Adams*, I, 175.

agreement with the leaders in the House. Hutchinson is authority that Bowdoin attained a greater influence over the Council than he himself ever had.[66] Thenceforward the Council worked in unity with the House on matters of provincial policy, and the Governor found himself, on controversial questions, opposed by a combination of the two houses.[67]

The Massachusetts custom of combining executive, legislative, and judicial offices of government in a few prominent men had lost its hold in 1766, if it was not completely abolished. The policy to be followed in the future, it proved, was that of excluding judicial and executive officers from the Council. The seat of a councillor, which under the province Charter had generally carried with it other offices of varying powers, now tended to become a distinct and separate place. With each of the immediately following years, new holders of judicial and executive offices were discovered and displaced from the Council.

The "supporters of government" now found themselves on the defensive in the General Court. According to Bernard, intimidation continued to be used by the popular party, and members who did not conform continued to be threatened. Of Otis, Bernard wrote that it was common for him to tell a member of the House who spoke on the side "of Government, that He should not sit in that House the next year."[68] Subsequent to the elections of 1766, the "Government" found itself outnumbered in the General Court, with the opposition in control. The Governor's power to negative councillors was found to be an ineffective protection, since if the houses refused to nominate other candidates, the number in the Council was reduced, and the Council was the more easily out-voted by the House.[69]

66. *History*, III, 156. 67. *Ibid.*, III, 156, 193.
68. Bernard Papers, IV, 279. To Shelburne, Dec. 22, 1766.
69. Mass. State Archives, XXVI, 306. Hutchinson Correspondence.

Prior to the elections of the next year, Bernard attempted a compromise with the leaders of the House, of which he gave a first-hand account:

For this purpose I engaged some principal Members of the House to make (as from themselves) a proposal to the opposite Party, that if they would agree to remove the Indignity done to the Kings Commissions by electing the L^t. Govr. & the Secretary into the Council, they, the Proposers, would join with them in electing the two Negatived Councillors, (of whom Otis's Father was one) & bring in the four old Councellors with a full vote: in which Case the Governor would most probably consent to all four. That this Compromise should not extend to the rest of the Election, & if it did not immediately remove all Dissatisfaction, it would lay a Foundation for a perfect Reconciliation, as it would remove the principal Causes of the Contention.

The leaders of the popular party, however, were not to be induced to compromise, and they rejected the offer.[70]

The opposition now proceeded to elect the six councillors whom the Governor had refused to accept the year before. In addition, they dropped from the Council Israel Williams, Chief Judge of the Court of Common Pleas and Judge of Probate for Hampshire County. Governor Bernard used his negative on five of the six candidates proposed anew, relenting in the case of Nathaniel Sparhawk, he "having conciliated himself by a very decent Behavior."[71] In 1758 Otis directly interfered to defeat Hutchinson: "our great incendiary was enraged and ran about the House in a fury with votes for my Competitor crying Pensioner or no Pensioner a term which among Americans conveys a very odious Idea & upon a third trial prevailed against me." Of Colonel James Otis, Hutchinson said: ". . . the father of my principal opponent . . . de-

70. Bernard Papers, VI, 211. To Shelburne, May 30, 1767: "To this the Party answered that they should make the Election by themselves, & did not want their, the proposers, Assistance; & therefore they should enter into no Compromise with them."

71. Bernard Papers, VI, 305. To Hillsborough, May 30, 1768. *Ibid.*, XII, 183. *Journal of the House, 1767-8*, p. 7. May 28, 1767.

clared before the Election he had rather not only renounce any Share in the government himself but also lose his whole Estate which is not a small one than the L G should be chose."[72] Hutchinson's friends had thought that they could restore him to his seat in the Council by a great majority. Hutchinson attributed the defeat to the news of the salary grant from the Crown, and the interference of Otis.

The House explained their action in the elections to the Earl of Hillsborough, early in 1768, to be a matter of the principle of a separation of powers, and "by no means the effect of party prejudice, private resentment, or motives still more blameable." It was the result of calm reflection upon the dangers that might result to the constitution and the liberties of the people, from *too great* a union of "the legislative, executive and judiciary powers" of government, which in the opinion of the greatest writers, ought always to be kept separate. This opinion, they said, was not a recently formed one, but it had been for many years the prevailing view of many of the most sensible and unexceptionable gentlemen of the province, and was based upon principles which Hillsborough's thorough knowledge of the constitution and the balance of powers of government would certainly justify.

As a precaution, they wished to warn against possible misrepresentation of the province, "even by persons in station here"; and if there were any such persons, they indicated that their removal would be agreeable to the province: ". . . they flatter themselves, that their removal will render this people happy in the esteem of the parent country, and much more so in the smiles of the best of Kings."[73]

Before the elections of 1768 took place, Bernard had

72. Mass. State Archives, XXVI, 308. Hutchinson Correspondence. June 4, 1768.
73. *Ibid., 1767-8*, Appendix, p. 24. Feb. 22, 1768. See Appendix III, section 9, *infra*.

sought a compromise to bring Hutchinson back into the Council. But Colonel Otis himself was unwilling that a compromise should be made on the point, even though it would result in his own return to the Council. The attitude of Colonel Otis on the matter of compromise was described as follows by Bernard: "The Old Man upon this occasion said that He would quit all his offices (which are the first in honor & profit in his County & of my gift) & bring himself to the lowest of the People rather than the Lieut. Governor should get into the Council."[74] The strength of the opposition was shown by the fact that John Chandler, Judge of Probate for Worcester County, and Andrew Belcher, Register of the Court of Vice-Admiralty,[75] were dropped from the Council in the elections. Bernard negatived six candidates proposed by the House to fill vacancies in the Council, although he admitted Samuel Dexter, whom he had negatived the two previous years, "having Reason to think he was tired of his Party."[76] The Council in 1768 consisted of only twenty-two members, instead of the usual number of twenty-eight.[77]

As the elections of 1769 approached, Governor Bernard abandoned hope of controlling the Council.[78] "It will be of

74. Bernard Papers, VI, 116. To J. Pownall, May 30, 1768. Also, p. 120.
75. Mass. Hist. Soc. *Proceedings*, 2nd Series, XVI, 66; Whitmore, *Mass. Civil List*, p. 119.
76. *Journal of the House, 1768*, p. 7, May 26, 1768. Bernard Papers, XII, 183. *Ibid.*, VI, 122, 307, 308.
77. Mass. State Archives, XXVI, 309, Hutchinson Correspondence. To R. Jackson, June 4, 1768: "The same Int. which kept us out brought in half a doz obnoxious to the G. to all of whom he has Refused his consent so that the C this year consist of 22 only instead of 28 for the House are sullen after a negative."
78. Bernard Papers, VII, 285. To J. Pownall, April 23, 1769: ". . . The Delinquency in the Council is become so general, that it is not in the power of the Governor to correct it by Negatives. If therefore I shall consent to the whole of the next Council, it must not be understood as an Approbation of all the Persons elected, but because the exceptional Part of them is too large for the Negative of a Governor. The Reformation of

no Use," he wrote, "to make any more Negatives: for now the Delinquency is become so general, that there is more exception to be taken to Persons within the Council than out of it." The popular party declared their intention of clearing the Council of "Tories." In pursuance of this aim a number of officers were dropped from the Council: Thomas Flucker, Justice of the Peace and of the Quorum for Essex County;[79] Nathaniel Ropes, Chief Judge of the Court of Common Pleas and Judge of Probate for Essex County; Timothy Paine, Register of the County of Worcester, and of the Court of Probate for that county; and John Worthington, who was Justice of the Peace for Hampshire County.[80] Bernard's opinion of these "Tories" was that they were "4 Gentlemen of the very first Reputation in the Country & the only Men remaining of Disposition & Ability to serve the King's cause."[81]

In spite of his stated conviction of the futility of the use of his negative, Bernard retaliated in the election of the Council by negativing eleven nominated to the Council, including two councillors of many years' standing, Brattle and Bowdoin, who were leaders of the opposition in the Council.[82] Joseph Gerrish, Thomas Sanders, Colonel Otis, and Jerathmeel Bowers had been the subjects of the Governor's negative annually since the year 1766. To them had been added John Hancock, Benjamin Greenleaf, Artemas Ward, Joshua Henshaw, and Walter Spooner. Joseph Hawley had declined election to the Council, preferring to remain in the

---

the Council must now be made in the Body & not in the Members; it must be done at Westminster & can't be done here." *Ibid.*, p. 292. To J. Pownall, May 15, 1769.

79. Whitmore, *Mass. Civil List*, p. 131.
80. *Ibid.*, pp. 84, 86, 119, 134. Washburn, *Judicial History*, p. 229. Bernard Papers, XII, 183.
81. *Ibid.*, VII, 295. To J. Pownall, June 1, 1769.
82. Bernard Papers, VII, 295. To J. Pownall, June 1, 1769. *Ibid.*, VII, 168. To Hillsborough, June 1, 1769.

House. The Governor had as a result, in 1769, a Council consisting of sixteen members, while the Charter provided for twenty-eight.[83]

The popular party in the elections showed itself to be in such absolute control of both houses that the Governor gave up hope of the redemption of the Council: "The Boston Faction has taken Possession of the two Houses in such a Manner that there are not 10 Men in both who dare contradict them," he wrote. "There is not now one Man in the Council who has either Spirit or Power to oppose the Faction; & the Friends of Government are so thin in the House, that they won't attempt to make any Opposition: so that Otis Adams etc. are now in full Possession of this Government."[84]

Thus the Governor found himself with a Council from which he could expect no support and in this extremity he resorted to government with a "select Council." Even before the popular party gained control of the Council, Bernard had on special occasions made use of such a group of the Council.[85] The working of this expedient, which came to be used by Hutchinson, as well as Bernard, in the later years of the province government, has been described by Samuel Adams. It was the practice of the Governor, Adams said, to summon the Council while the Assembly was in session, when the whole number of councillors were assembled. They were then adjourned in their capacity of the Governor's advisory body from week to week until the Assembly was over, when the country gentlemen members of the Council returned home. Then the Council having been kept alive by adjournments, the executive business was done by seven or eight members living in and about the town, and if the Governor could manage a majority of this small number, he

---

83. Whitmore, *Mass. Civil List*, p. 65. Mass. State Archives, XXVI, 353, May 29, 1769.
84. Bernard Papers, VII, 295-6. To J. Pownall, June 1, 1769.
85. Bernard Papers, IV, 197. To Conway, Jan. 23, 1766.

could prevail in his own plans.[86] Adams added that by far the greater number of civil officers "have been appointed at these adjournments; so that it is much the same as if they were appointed solely by our ostensible Governor. . . ."

In 1767 it was charged that an appointment to the Superior Court had been made by such a "select Council" even though this was in violation of the charter, which required that no nomination or appointment of officers should be made "without notice *first given or summons issued out seven days before such nomination or appointment, unto such of the said councellors or assistants as shall be at that time residing within our said province.*" The General Court, it was said, had been in session only a week previously, and the nomination was at that time expected.[87] This method of getting around popular opposition only served to increase resentment against the Governor. Newspaper articles denounced the practice as "unconstitutional," "a Privy Council," and a "prostitution of regular . . . government." Bernard was accused of attempting to "overthrow the constitution" of the colony, and of having "true *Stuartine* notions of government."[88]

While Bernard was thus attempting to govern in defiance of a "democratic" Council, sometimes with the advice of only the three principal Crown officers,[89] the Council undertook to meet separately and to transact business without the Governor. The minutes of their proceedings and their resolutions

86. Cushing, *Writings of S. Adams*, II, 265. To A. Lee, Oct. 31, 1775. *Boston Gazette*, Nov. 11, 1771. "Fidelis." See Appendix III, section 10, *infra*.
87. *Boston Gazette*, April 27, 1767. "Freeborn American." The appointment was apparently that of Edmund Trowbridge, March 25, 1767. See *The Mass. Civil List*, p. 70.
88. *Boston Gazette*, April 27, May 11, 1767; May 21, 1770.
89. Bernard Papers, VII, 124. To Hillsborough, Jan. 24, 1769: "To enable me to execute my present Orders & such of the like kind as I may hereafter receive, as I have at present no privy Council that will give me real Assistance, I have formed a Cabinet Council consisting of the 3 principal officers of the Crown, whose Zeal Fidelity & Ability cannot be suspected."

found their way into print without having been submitted to the Governor.[90] From the point of view of the Governor, there was a question whether the Charter was not forfeited by this action.[91]

During his difficulties, Governor Bernard was tirelessly submitting plans for the reform of the Council to Lord Hillsborough and other prominent members of the Ministry. It had been demonstrated that a Council elected primarily by votes of the House could not be depended upon to support the Governor when his policy diverged from that followed by the House. The idea that a Governor might bear responsibility to the legislature, or above all to the people, was foreign to the time. Bernard believed that royal control of the Council was indispensable to the maintenance of the King's authority in the colony. Annual election of the Council he considered the "Canker-Worm of the Constitution" and the "fatal Ingredient" in the Constitution of the colony.[92] The people had too much weight in the government and the remedy "must certainly emancipate the council." It seemed plain to Bernard that: "The People by the Constitution have really all the Power in their Hands. . . . The Chain is very Short: The People Elect the Council; the Governor can do nothing without the Council; therefore if the People fill the Council with their own Creatures & keep them in Constant Awe, they must govern the Governor as absolutely as those of Connecticut & Rhode Island do theirs."[93]

Not forgetting entirely the British tradition of a repre-

90. Bernard Papers, VIII, 215. State of the Disorders . . . Jan. 1774.
91. *Ibid.*, VII, 112, 245-7. Under Hutchinson, the Council continued to sit after the prorogation of the General Court, calling themselves a "Committee to correspond with & instruct their agent in the recess of the Court." Hutchinson found that it was, in effect, continuing one branch of the Assembly after prorogation. Mass. State Archives, XXVI, 437; XXVII, 204. July 11, 1771.
92. Bernard Papers, VI, 275, 276.
93. *Ibid.*, IV, 291-2. To Shelburne, Dec. 24, 1766.

sentative legislature, however, Bernard sought to distinguish the council in its executive capacity, which he called a privy council, from the council as a legislative body. The executive council should be appointive by the King. In respect to the selection of the legislative council, Bernard's statements are not consistent. As a rule he seemed to see the necessity of popular election for the legislative upper house, but he would not have advocated complete independence from royal control for the legislative council. In 1769 he wrote that from the "Duplicity of Functions" arose the objection to the councillors holding their places at the pleasure of the King, since the objection to appointment applied only in their legislative capacity. "There indeed if the Members of the upper House hold their Seats at the Pleasure of the King, they are not a separate Body but the Kings Delegates; & he may be said to have two Negatives in the Provincial Legislature. This may be said to be not constitutional that is not conformable to the sovereign Legislature."[94] But as privy councillors it was constitutional for them to hold their offices at the pleasure of the King; in fact it was necessary to government that they should do so.

While Bernard did not insist upon an appointive legislative council, therefore, he unmistakably favored a "privy Council" holding office at the pleasure of the King. It was to overlap in membership the upper house of the legislature: "Provincial privy Council might be composed cheifly of Members of the upper house with some few of the lower House, & upon some Occasions of Gentlemen who have Seats in Neither." Bernard's plans, therefore, did not encompass a complete separation of the personnel of the privy council from that of the upper legislative house. He had in mind the necessity of political control over the government, and complete separation of the personnel of the various branches

94. Bernard Papers, VII, 136. To Hillsborough, Feb. 4, 1769.

of the government would not be conducive to that result. His experience with the government of Massachusetts after some separation had taken place in practice had not been happy.

In the same letter to Lord Hillsborough which contained these observations, Bernard threw out a suggestion for an appointive legislative upper house: "If there was an upper House, besides a privy Council, both deriving their Appointments from the King, it would afford the King means to distinguish the Friends of Government & give greater encouragement to People to desire to be reckoned of that Number." The Governor suggested some such title as "Baron" for members of the upper house: "And this Method would multiply the Honors conferred by his Majesty at least five-fold in every Province, without making them cheap." But it was the opinion of the Governor that, if the King "cannot secure to himself the Appointment of the Council, it is not worth while to keep that of the Governor."[95]

Hutchinson, as well as Bernard, expressed his opinion to the Ministry that the government of Massachusetts gave too much power to the people: "We know by experience that the present form of government in this province gives too great a share both of legislative and executive power to the people, to consist with the interest of the parent state, or the welfare of the colony itself."[96] Like Bernard, Hutchinson complained also of the Council "as being under undue influence and casting their weight into that scale, which had much too great a proportion before. . . ."[97] Hutchinson wrote: "The great thing proposed is a council that are less under the restraint of the house." Hutchinson believed that the legislative and executive organization of the Council should be separated, but that the personnel need not be completely so.

95. Bernard Papers, VII, 265. To Barrington, March 18, 1769.
96. *Boston Gazette*, Aug. 14, 1775. To Lord Hillsborough. Dec., 1770.
97. *Ibid.* To Lord Hillsborough. Jan. 22, 1771.

Instead of an annually elected council, Hutchinson recommended a legislative council of the size of the province Council, triennially elected. A privy council annually chosen by the Governor was also proposed by Hutchinson:

> Let the governor annually select twelve out of the 28, who with the lieut. governor and secretary, shall be the privy council, or his majesty's council for the province for that year, and shall have all the powers except that of legislation, which the council or assistants have by charter. . . . The council meerly in their legislative capacity, would be like Cromwell's other house, of no great consequence; tho' they would be rather serviceable to the governor, who might often make an advantage of their negative upon the house, and yet they could not hurt him by their concurrence.[98]

Hutchinson was not insistent upon abolishing election of the legislative council, but he would have the election under some new regulation, if it were continued. Neither did he reject the idea of an appointive council, but doubted its practicability. It was also his opinion that some limits should be set to the number in the House of Representatives. If the election of councillors were continued under a new regulation, Hutchinson felt that limitation of the number of representatives would be more peculiarly necessary to prevent the Council from being dominated by the House: "If every town would use it's privilege the number would exceed 300, and in a few years as the law stands for settling the number, it may amount to five hundred. At present it does not exceed 130."[99]

Former Governor Pownall also formulated plans for the revision of the Council which were based upon his experience as Governor in Massachusetts, plans more liberal than those either of Bernard or Hutchinson. Pownall advocated sep-

---
98. *Ibid.*, Aug. 14, 1775. To Lord Hillsborough. Oct., 1770.
99. *Boston Gazette*, Aug. 14, 1775. To Lord Hillsborough. Dec., 1770.

arating the consultative and legislative organization of the Council. He found "the governor's council of state . . . a distinct . . . almost . . . an incompatible board,—with the council, one branch of the legislature . . . in their persons, as well as their office. . . ." Pownall would have had two councils, an appointive council of state, and an elective legislative council. The council of state should be constituted as under the Charter. It should be "composed of men of the best experience, fortune, and interest in the colony, taken in common from the legislative council, the house of representatives, or the courts, while the members of the legislative council, independent of the governor for their existence, had all and only those powers which are necessary to a branch of the legislature."[100] This separation of consultative and legislative organization, though it did not require an absolute separation of personnel, Pownall believed would assure support to the Governor without the sacrifice of independence in legislative action on the part of the Council.

The last three civil governors of the province therefore recommended that the legislative and consultative organization of the Council should be separated. They held that the Council should be responsible to the Governor in its capacity of a consultative body; and with the possible exception of Bernard they believed that the Council should be responsible to the electors, or the representative body elected by them, in its capacity of a legislative body. Consequently, two bodies instead of one would be needed for the dispatch of the functions of the Council. The Governor should have advice regarding his executive policy from an appointive Council; but for the purposes of legislation, an upper house of greater independence and more popular responsibility was recommended. The recommendations of the governors were the outgrowth of their experience in Massachusetts. While they

100. Thomas Pownall, *The Administration of the Colonies*, p. 86.

called for a separation of the functions of the Council, they did not require or even contemplate a complete separation of legislative and consultative personnel. Not one of them mentioned Montesquieu, or any other writer on the separation of powers. Unlike the popular party, the governors were seeking, it should be remarked, a separation of organization, not a complete separation of offices, nor of the personnel of Council and legislative house.

Opposition to political control, while it was the most important, was not the only cause which operated to bring about a separation of offices in Massachusetts. There was also the very obvious practical inexpediency of the union of the judicial and the councillor offices. It had become, before Bernard's administration, a practical impossibility for one man to discharge the duties of a judge of the Superior Court and those of a councillor. The Superior Court, in which several of the councillors were judges, was a circuit court which sat in turn in different counties of the province. In addition, there must have been some inexpediency in having judges of the inferior courts in the Council, as well as in the House.

Adjustment was made in two ways to enable the judges to perform their twofold duties: by shifting the sessions of the judicial courts so as not to conflict with sessions of the General Court; or by altering the time of the sittings of the General Court so as to avoid conflict with the judicial courts. Either way, the shifting caused great inconvenience. When the change was made in the schedule of the judicial courts, the passage of an Order or Act of the General Court was necessary. On the other hand, if the change were made in the sessions of the General Court it might delay and impede important political decisions, as was the case when the passage of the Stamp Act threatened.

The inferior courts, because of recurrent conflict with sessions of the General Court, were more frequently subject to alteration as to the time of their sessions than was the Superior Court. Yet their sessions were numerous, and the number of judges of the inferior courts who sat in the General Court, particularly in the House, outnumbered the justices of the Superior Court who had seats in the Council.

The Resolves of the province for several years previous to 1766, show that a number of changes in a single year were common in the schedule of the inferior courts. The reasons commonly given for changes in the time of the sittings of the inferior courts explained the situation, as, for instance:

"Whereas diverse of the Justices of the Inferior Court of Common Pleas . . . are members of this [the General] Court and the important Affairs of the Province require their attendance thereon . . ."[101]

or: ". . . divers of the Justices of the General Sessions are members of this [the General] Court and the Affairs of the Province now depending may require their Attendance thereupon at said time . . ."[102]

or: ". . . several of the Justices of said Court are now attending this Court and probably will be detained upon the business of the Government."[103]

When a conflict between the Superior Court and a session of the General Court arose, it was not uncommon for the Governor to meet the situation either by adjourning the General Court or by delaying to summon it, since such power was within his discretion. Governor Bernard acknowledged that he had taken such action in 1764, in order to give the administration an advantage at the time when it was proposed to make representations against the impending Stamp Act.[104] Since the "Town Members" wished to make

101. *Acts and Resolves*, XVII, 8-9.
102. *Ibid.*, XVII, 100.   103. *Ibid.*, XVII, 138.
104. Bernard Papers, III, 261, Nov. 17, 1764. To R. Jackson. "I was very much pressed by the Town Members . . . to call the Assembly

representation against proposed taxation by Parliament, it is obvious that the situation, from their point of view, would urgently require reform.

In the following year, the Governor adjourned the General Court, after a three days' session, because of a similar conflict which put him at a disadvantage politically, as he reported to the Lords of Trade:

> By previous questions put at the Committee, it appeared that there was a Majority of one Voice against submitting to the Act [the Stamp Act]; & it was certainly intended in their answer to Assert in positive terms the right of the Colonies to be exempted from Parliamentary Taxes. This would entirely have defeated my purpose: therefore on the third day I adjourned the general court for 26 days, giving for a reason that I saw it would be in vain to expect a full house untill the times for holding the usual Courts of Justice were over . . . the Government will be much stronger in a fuller House than it was in this.[105]

The significance of the adjournment of the General Court in such a case was not lost upon the opposition, and the episode helped to accelerate the movement for separating office-holding in different departments of the government.[106]

In 1765 the whole schedule of the Superior Court was changed and more or less arranged to fit in with the schedule of the General Court, doubtless not without influence from preceding events. The winter months, during which travel upon the circuit was difficult, were left free for the General Court. Sessions of the Superior Court, previously scheduled for the months of January and February, were moved for-

---

sooner than I did, at a time when the Superior Court was sitting in the Country, & thereby the Judges & Attorney Gen¹ & some other Members of Consequence could not attend. Which I refusing to do was abused in the public Papers for sevral Weeks together."

105. Bernard Papers, IV, 164. To Conway, to Lords of Trade, Sept. 28, 1765.

106. See *Boston Gazette*, Sept. 30, 1765. Comment;Governor's Message.

ward to summer months.[107] It was in fact during the winter session of the General Court that the greatest volume of business was usually disposed of. There still remained, however, possibility of conflict during the spring and fall sessions of the General Court, and the schedule of the Superior Court was again altered within five years.

The inconvenience to the province of such a conflict of courts had been obvious for some years. In 1762, in his "Considerations on the Election of Counsellors," Oxenbridge Thacher had clearly pointed out the difficulties of uniting the office of councillor with that of judge.[108] The union in fact violated the common-law rule against holding incompatible offices. With the growth of the province and with the consequent increase of judicial and political business, it is evident, apart from the problem of political domination, that some separation in office-holding would have become inevitable.

---

107. *Acts and Resolves*, III, 64; IV, 733-4.

108. "It is obvious that the attendance upon the Circuit. and that upon the Council are incompatible. Even when the Superior Court sits in *Boston*, and the general court at the same time in the same place; it is not possible for those gentlemen to give the needful attendance at both courts. But when they are on the more distant parts of their circuit, they must be totally absent from one or other. Thus the public is deprived either of a counsellor or a judge, in whose attendance they are interested."

CHAPTER IV

PLURAL OFFICE-HOLDING BY PATRIOTS, 1775-1778

As THE GOVERNOR's control broke down and the province moved toward revolution, the British government tried to make the Governor and judges independent of popular support by providing for payment of their salaries by the Crown. Because repeated representations from the Massachusetts governors had affirmed that the key to the difficulties of government lay in the constitution of the Council, the mother country, by making the Council appointive, attempted to give the Governor the control which he lacked. When the report of the plan for an appointive Council reached Massachusetts, there was unavailing protest against it. The House of Representatives instructed their agent to oppose it.

In this crisis, the patriots seemed to prefer action to discussion. There was, however, some citation of Blackstone, whose *Commentaries* had come out in 1765, to prove that the three branches of the legislature should be independent, with no one of them subservient to the other two. Further, the extremity of citing Locke's theory on revolution which James Otis had justified as early as 1764, in the introduction to his *Rights of the British Colonies Asserted and Proved* was reached: such a destruction of the balance of the powers of government as was proposed in a dependent council would work an entire dissolution of the bonds of government, and set the people at liberty to establish a new legislative organ.[1]

[1]. *Boston Gazette*, Dec. 9, 1771. *Mass. Spy*, Dec. 5, 1771. "Massachusettensis."

One provision of the "Act for the better regulation of the Government of the Province of the Massachusetts-Bay" was that after August 1, 1774, the powers of the province Council should be abrogated and similar powers vested in a body of thirty-six councillors appointed by the Crown. In the province this appointive Council was commonly called the "mandamus" Council. The futility of protest seemed to be generally recognized; there was no hesitation in resorting to direct action to suppress the "mandamus" Council.

Although the province Council had come to an end "de jure," the "mandamus" Council was not allowed to function. Those who accepted appointments to the King's Council were required by the Provincial Congress of 1774 to publish in all the Boston newspapers a renunciation of their commissions from the Crown under penalty of being considered "infamous Betrayers" of their country and of having their names published as rebels to the state.[2] It is well known that more direct and forceful methods were used by the "Sons of Liberty" upon those appointive councillors who were reluctant to renounce their commissions.[3] Only twenty-four of the "mandamus" councillors ever took the oath of office; nine of these afterward resigned, leaving a Council of only fifteen.[4]

With such intimidation of the "mandamus" Council, all hope of a manageable General Court vanished, and the writs issued for the Court to meet on October 5, 1774, were cancelled by the Governor.[5] The appointment of "mandamus" councillors was one more grievance. The Congressional Declaration of 1774 complained that: ". . . the exercise of legislative power in several Colonies, by a Council appointed

2. *Boston Gazette*, Oct. 24, 1774.
3. A. Matthews, "Documents relating to the last meetings of Mass. Royal Council," *Pub. of the Col. Soc. Mass.*, XXXII, 460-504.
4. *New-England Historical and Genealogical Register*, XXVIII, 62.
5. *Mass. Spy*, Oct. 6, 1774.

during pleasure by the Crown, is unconstitutional, dangerous, and destructive to the freedom of American legislation."[6] The grievance of an appointive council was thought important enough to be referred to by the Continental Congress in 1775 thus: "Counsellors, holding their commissions during pleasure, exercise legislative authority."[7]

In spite of the cancellation of the writs for the General Court, it assembled as a revolutionary body on October 7, 1774, and functioned on behalf of the revolution.[8] On July 21, 1775, the members of the revolutionary Assembly elected councillors, since, it was said, the Governor was considered to have deserted his office. The powers of the province Governor, as well as those of the Council, were taken over by the Council, and government was carried on under the province Charter, as amended by the revolutionary Assembly.[9] Thus the province government, constructed on the unworkable principle of dual responsibility to the British Crown and to the people of Massachusetts, came to an end. This revolutionary alteration followed the advice of the Continental Congress to Massachusetts ". . . to conform as near as may be to the spirit and substance of the charter . . ." and the suggestion that no obedience was due "to a Governor or Lieutenant-Governor who will not observe the directions of, but endeavor to subvert, that charter, the Governor and Lieutenant-Governor of that Colony are to be considered as absent, and their offices vacant. . . ."[10] Government under the revolutionized Charter was continued until October 25, 1780.

From the later years of Bernard's administration until the revolutionary government began to function, the problem

6. John Adams, *Life and Works*, II, 540.
7. *Boston Gazette*, Jan. 30, 1775.
8. *Mass. Spy*, Oct. 13, 1774; Dec. 16, 1774.
9. *Journal of the House*, 1775, p. 6.
10. John Adams, *Life and Works*, III, 17.

of plural office-holding was not in active agitation. Questions of order and of peace or war were more immediately in the forefront of discussion. From 1766 until 1774, the popular party in Massachusetts had the Council largely under control,[11] and the question of changes in its constitution was no longer of great importance to the popular party. The General Court exercised executive as well as legislative powers.

Under the decapitated Assembly which governed Massachusetts from October 7, 1774, to the adoption of the Constitution of 1780, the necessity of a separation in office-holding was once more demonstrated to the province and to the state. The separation of departments and the question of plural office-holding was once more discussed in the newspapers, and once more the question became an important political issue.

It was indeed disillusioning that the Provincial Congress, with the distribution of offices in its power, now discredited the government of the people by resorting to plural office-holding, for the most part by its own members. Thus it reverted to the example of the Crown officers under the province government, but on an even more extensive scale. It was discovered almost as soon as the revolutionary government was set up that the danger from "place men & pensioners" was still present. As early as July, 1775, the town of Worcester thought it necessary to give instructions on the subject to its representative in the General Court. These instructions opened with a sympathetic warning of the temptations which might beset a representative: "The Accumulated difficulties that we labor under at this time aded to

11. Mass. State Archives, XVII, 491. (Not addressed. Not sent.): "I have my Lord, been in one continued scene of trouble vexation & the most violent opposition for between three & four years past, with little or no support from any other Parts of the Administration having never had a majority of the Council in Sentiment with me upon the measures I thought my duty to the King required me to pursue, at Present I have only two or three left among the whole number who are not in sentiment with their Electors...."

those passions that too often lead men into error, makes the task of a virtuous Representative truly arduous. An inordinate desire of Riches and Power have induced some men to barter the rights and liberties of their Constituents for a lucrative office or some post of Command. . . ."

The mother country furnished no example in this respect: ". . . by the accounts we often receive, the Members of the British Parliament are very Generous in Granting pensions & places to each other." The instructions sought a separation of offices:

You are therefore to Endeavor that none be Elected Councellors, but persons of Established charracters [*sic*] for Probity & virtue. And as it is expected that they will appoint Executive officers, and may perhaps appoint each other into the most lucrative offices & Continue the fees as heretofore Established, or refuse to give their Concurence to a more Equitable law for the Regulation of that Matter, you are to use your influence that the legislative and Executive authority be kept in seperate hand [*sic*] as much as may be, for we look upon it as incompatible with the principles of equity for men to appoint themselves into Executive offices & establish their own fees. . . .

A disqualifying act to debar any member of the legislature who accepted an executive office from taking his seat unless he were re-elected, and the directing of an election for the purpose was advocated.[12] This proposal would have followed the English practice, which by the Act of 1705, had dealt with the problem by such a compromise.

A committee of the Provincial Congress was appointed, which brought in a bill to define "what Offices are compatible to be held by one Person at the same Time . . ." but after one reading, the bill was dropped.[13] The English statutes for excluding "placemen & pensioners" were precedents for

12. Worcester Papers, MSS. I, 38, July 14, 1775. Appendix IV, section 1, *infra*.
13. *Journal of the House*, 1775-6, pp. 111, 154, 188, 195, 197, 229.

such a bill, but it did not accord with the interests of the members of the Provincial Congress.

Of the first Council elected under the revolutionary government, that of 1775, it must be recorded that every member received for himself some additional appointment. For the most part, each of the twenty-eight councillors was given a judicial appointment of some kind, frequently more than one.[14] The most common judicial appointment assumed by the councillors was for a local or county office, such as Justice of the Peace and of the Quorum. In addition, some councillors became chief justices in their counties, and sometimes judges of probate.

Thus Thomas Cushing, a prominent patriot, who was a delegate from Massachusetts to the Continental Congress, was, for the County of Suffolk, Chief Justice of the County Court, Justice of Probate, Justice of the Peace and of the Quorum, Special Justice of the Pleas, and Justice throughout the "colony."[15] Robert Treat Paine, another delegate to the Continental Congress, was Justice of the Peace and of the Quorum for Bristol County, and Justice throughout the "colony." He was also appointed to the Superior Court, but declined the office.[16] Colonel James Otis was made Judge of Probate for Barnstable County, Justice of the Pleas for Barnstable County, Justice of the Peace and of the Quorum for Barnstable County, and Justice of the Peace throughout the "colony."[17]

Samuel Adams was delegate from Massachusetts to the Continental Congress, Justice of the Peace and of the Quo-

14. *Ibid.*, July 19, 1775, to Feb. 20, 1776; MSS. I, Incomplete; *Journal of the House*, July 19, 1775, to May 10, 1776, pp. 6, 13, 14, etc. for the Council; *Boston Gazette*, Oct. 2, 9, 1775, for a list of civil officers; Mass. State Archives, Council Records, XVII, XVIII, XIX, also for appointments.
15. Council Records, XVII, 251, 43, 90, 153, 161. *Journal of the House*, 1775-6, p. 269, Nov. 11, 1775.
16. Mass. State Archives, Records of Civil Commissions, 1775-1787—A.
17. Council Records, XVII, 66, 65, 90, 128. Appendix IV, section 2, *infra*.

rum for Suffolk County, Justice throughout the "colony," and Secretary of the revolutionary government of Massachusetts.[18] It is obvious that his appointment as delegate to the Continental Congress, which necessitated attendance for a large part of the year, added to the difficulties of occupying other important "colony" or "State" offices. When Secretary Adams was absent in Philadelphia, his duties as Secretary were carried out by a deputy.[19] As no one except Otis and Thacher had been more active than Adams in the struggle to separate the councillor and judicial offices in the province government, it is of some interest to note his point of view on the same practice under the patriot government, especially at a time when he himself was a holder of plural offices. He told how his scruples were allayed:

> We have also complaind, that a Plurality of Places incompatible with each other have sometimes been vested in one person. . . . Tell me how a Judge of Probate can consistently sit at the Council Board and joyn in a Decision there upon an appeal from *his own* Judgment? Perhaps, being personally interested in *another* Appointment, I may view it with a partial Eye.

Adams had not accepted the office without hesitation:

> But you may well remember that the Secretary of the Colony declind taking a Seat at the Council Board, to which he had been elected *prior* to his Appointment, until, in the House of Representatives he had publickly requested their opinion of the Propriety of it, and there heard it explicitly declared by an eminent and truly patriotick Member as his Opinion, that as the Place was not then as it formerly had been, the Gift of the Crown, but of the People, there was no Impropriety in his holding it. The rest of the Members were silent. Major H(awley) has as much of the stern Virtue and Spirit of a Roman Censor as any Gentleman I ever conversed with.

18. Council Records, XVII, 90, 161, 26 *Boston Gazette*, Oct. 2, 9, 1775.
19. Council Records, XVII, 26. At first, Perez Morton. Wells, *Samuel Adams*, II, 322, 448.

The appointment had been made without solicitation on his part:

> The appointment of the Secretary and his Election to a Seat at the Board were both made in the Time of his Absence from the Colony and without the Solicitation of any of his Friends that he knew of—most assuredly without his own. As he is resolv'd never wittingly to disgrace himself or his Country, he still employs his Mind on the Subject, and wishes for your candid and impartial Sentiments.[20]

While Samuel Adams declared that he was not entirely clear in his mind as to the propriety of multiple office-holding on the part of the patriots, he continued as Secretary until the inauguration of the state government, when the appointment went to his deputy, John Avery, who had been performing the functions of the office during his absence.[21]

Evidently the people did not agree with Major Hawley as to the propriety of holding multiple offices, provided they were of the gift of the people, for in the spring of 1776, Samuel Adams failed of election to the Council.

Another illustrious member of the Council in 1775, John Adams, in addition to representing Massachusetts in the Continental Congress, was made Justice of the Peace and of the Quorum for the County of Suffolk, Justice throughout the "colony," and finally, Chief Justice of the Superior Court of Judicature, on October 11, 1775.[22] John Adams also held

---

20. *Mass. Hist. Soc. Coll.*, LXXII, 173. Samuel Adams to James Warren, Nov. 4, 1775.

21. Wells, *Samuel Adams*, II, 448; III, 116, Nov., 1780. See also letter of S. Adams to Elbridge Gerry, Oct. 29, 1775, quoted in Wells, *Samuel Adams*, II, 332: "It is in your power, also, to prevent a plurality of places incompatible with each other being vested in the same person. This our patriots have loudly and very justly complained of in time past, and it will be an everlasting disgrace to them if they suffer the practice to continue. Care, I am informed, is taking to prevent the evil with as little inconvenience as possible; but it is my opinion that the remedy ought to be deep and thorough."

22. Council Records, XVII, 128, 154, 90, 161, 173; John Adams, *Life and Works*, III, 23.

from the Continental Congress a commission as President of the Board of War.[23] Adams was, in the Continental Congress, a member of at least ninety different committees, and chairman of at least twenty-five.[24] Some embarrassment was encountered in reconciling the services of Adams as a member of the Continental Congress in Philadelphia with those of the Chief Justice of the Superior Court of Judicature, sitting in Massachusetts. The difficulty was tentatively arranged as follows: "It was agreed that the court should go on, for a time, without his presence. If no difficulties should occur in the establishment of its authority, then he was to continue his labors in Congress so long as he might deem them important to the establishment of the great objects Massachusetts had at heart. To these conditions he seems to have assented."[25] With this understanding, the Chief Justiceship of the Superior Court of Massachusetts was held for John Adams from October 11, 1775, until February 10, 1777, when he resigned the office.[26]

In the meantime, the plural office-holding of John Adams must have become the subject of widespread criticism, for the Maryland delegates to the Continental Congress were given an instruction to move a "self-denying" ordinance, which was directed against John Adams. His enemies represented him as interested in the establishment of independence because of his judicial appointment under the new government in Massachusetts. "I soon found there was a whispering among the partisans in opposition to independence, that I was interested," wrote Adams; "that I held an office under the new government of Massachusetts; that I was afraid of losing it, if we did not declare independence."[27] The whispers circulated "not only in the city of Philadelphia

23. *Ibid.*, IX, 633. To Josiah Quincy, Feb. 18, 1811.
24. J. Q. and C. F. Adams, *Life of John Adams*, I, 311, 314, 332.
25. *Ibid.*, I, 268.
26. John Adams, *Life and Works*, III, 25.
27. *Ibid.*, III, 25, Feb., 1776.

and State of Pennsylvania, but in the neighboring States, particularly Maryland, and very probably in private letters throughout the Union."[28] The Continental Congress was composed largely of office-holders, either under the old, or the new governments.[29] Adams commented on the Maryland attack as follows, to one of the delegates from Maryland: "I have one bone to pick with your colony," he wrote, "I suspect they levelled one of their instructions at my head. . . . One of your colleagues moved a resolution that no member of Congress should hold office under any of the new governments. . . ."[30] The move in the Continental Congress was cleverly deflected by a counter-proposal on the part of Adams to extend the resolution to all office-holding, whether under the new or the old governments.[31]

However, as agitation was under way in Massachusetts against appointment of members of the Provincial Congress to offices under the new government, John Adams resigned his seat in the Council before the elections in May, 1776.[32] "I cannot think it becoming in me to deprive the colony of the advice of a counsellor, for the sake of keeping open a seat for me," he wrote. Nevertheless, he continued to hold the appointment of Chief Justice for another year, though still in the Continental Congress. Five other office-holders resigned from the Council likewise; it may have been because re-election was dubious.[33] Samuel Adams, John Hancock, and Robert Treat Paine, also delegates from Massachusetts to the Continental Congress, did not resign from the Council, but they were not re-elected to the Council in 1776.[34]

28. *Ibid.*, III, 27.
29. *Ibid.*, IX, 397. To Samuel Chase.
30. *Ibid.*, IX, 397. To Samuel Chase, June 14, 1776.
31. *Ibid.*, IX, 397.
32. *Ibid.*, IX, 374. To James Otis, April 29, 1776.
33. *Journal of the House*, May 29, 1776; Nov. 9, 1776, p. 9. *Boston Gazette*, June 3, 1776.
34. *Ibid.*

The inexpediency of holding the Chief Justiceship *in absentia* was becoming apparent to John Adams, as he resigned from the Council: ". . . this is not a Time if ever there was or can be one for Sinecures," he wrote, "fill up every Place—they ought to be full. I believe I must resign the office, which the Board have assigned me for the same Reason, but I shall think a little more about that and take Advice."[35] As noted above Adams relinquished the Chief Justiceship only on February 10, 1777.[36]

The number of "disinterested patriots"[37] who were multiple office-holders in the House of Representatives also would form a long catalogue. The Speaker of the House, James Warren, was also Sheriff of Plymouth County. The clerk of the House of Representatives, Samuel Freeman, was at the same time register of probate, clerk of the Inferior Court and the Court of Sessions, and justice of the peace for the County of Cumberland.[38] A very large proportion of the multiple office-holders in the House (the Journal in 1776 shows about one-third) also held military commissions.

The volume of protest which was raised against this retrogression in principles of government is indicated in newspaper articles of the time. The surprising difference was observed "between the assembly which left all the executive officers out of the council, and that which has devoted all their ingenuity and great part of their time in distributing their respective offices among them." The province was said to suffer from "blending the executive and legislative powers," and the electors were urged to end the inconvenience at the next election.[39] The question, directed at many members of the General Court, was asked: "Does not our conduct re-

35. *Mass. Historical Society Coll.*, LXXII; Warren-Adams Letters, I, 243-4, May 12, 1776.
36. John Adams, *Life and Works*, III, 25.
37. T. Parsons, *Memoir of Theophilus Parsons*, p. 40.
38. *Manual of the Constitutional Convention of 1917*, p. 13.
39. *Mass. Spy*, May 18, 1776. "O. P. Q."

proach us with doing the same things we have abhorred in others?"[40]

The detriment of the practice of plural office-holding to the province in a critical time was emphasized by a writer in the *Massachusetts Spy*. Since the General Assembly was formed the previous May, the members of the Assembly, he wrote, had divided among themselves and their particular friends all the civil and military offices in the colony. The distraction resulting from the holding of executive office made attendance in the Assembly erratic, seldom leaving a quorum, to the great detriment of the public business at a time when the constant attendance of the best members (such were those among whom the executive offices were distributed) was of the highest importance to the colony.[41]

A self-denying enactment by the General Assembly to secure separation in office-holding was again suggested by some towns. Boston, in 1776, instructed its representatives that it was essential to liberty that the legislative, judicial, and executive powers of government be "as nearly as possible" independent of and separate from each other; for, the instructions said, where they were united in the same persons, or number of persons, that mutual check which was the principal security against the making of arbitrary laws and wanton exercise of power in the execution of them would be wanting. The representatives were therefore instructed to procure the enactment of a law or laws which should make it incompatible for the same person to hold a seat in the legislative and executive departments of government at one and the same time: "And to prevent the Multiplicity of Offices in the same Person, that such Salaries be settled upon them, as will place them above the Necessity of stooping to any indirect or collateral Means for Subsistance."[42]

40. *Boston Gazette*, Dec. 30, 1776.   41. May 18, 1776.
42. *New-England Chronicle*, May 30, 1776; *Boston Gazette*, June 10, 1776; Appendix IV, section 3, *infra*.

A combination of offices in the hands of leading men continued to be resented, the important circumstance that those men were responsible to the electorate seemingly not altering the feeling against the practice. When the Continental Congress by a resolution of May 15, 1776, declared it necessary that "every kind of authority under the Crown should be totally suppressed," and that it be recommended to the assemblies of the colonies, in the absence of adequate government, "to adopt such government as shall, in the opinion of the representatives of the people, best conduce to the happiness and safety of their constituents in particular, and America in general,"[43] discussion of the essentials of a constitution began in Massachusetts.

In the fall of 1776, the Provincial Congress took steps toward the formation of a constitution by proposing to make a constitution themselves. By a Resolve of the House of Representatives of September 17, 1776,[44] the towns were asked to consider and determine "whether they will give their Consent that the present House of Representatives of this State of the *Massachusetts-Bay* in *New-England*, together with the Council, if they consent in one Body with the House, and by equal Voice, should consult, agree on, and enact such a Constitution and Form of Government for this State. . . ." This suggested addition to the powers of the Assembly provoked a determination to resist in many towns. The town of Boston, which had formerly led the Assembly, particularly opposed the attempt. Only the proviso that "they would direct that the same be made Public for the Inspection and Perusal of the Inhabitants, before the Ratification thereof by the Assembly," secured its acceptance by a majority of the towns.[45]

The town of Norton declared its inability to assent since

43. John Adams, *Life and Works*, III, 46; IV, 214.
44. Mass. State Archives, CLVI, 180, Sept. 17, 1776.
45. See Mass. State Archives, CLVI, 152, 169.

the House and Council were not separately elected for the purpose by the people. And the town stated very frankly, "The Requision of the Hono^r. House being so pregnant with power we cannot think it will be conducive to the future good of this people to comply with their proposal."[46]

The town of Lexington (on October 21, 1776) rebuked the General Assembly for the proposal, feeling obliged to withhold "a chearful Compliance" with the Resolve, as a matter of keeping faith with themselves and posterity. They were outspoken in the reasons for their refusal to comply: the present House of Representatives had not been elected to draw up a constitution, and their constituents had no intimation of anything of the kind in the precept for their election: ". . . therefore the proposing themselves to the People, and asking their Consent as Candidates for this Service, appears to us to be a Clog to that Freedom of Election, which ought always to be exercised, by a free People, in Matters of Importance. . . ." It was feared, if the Resolve of the House were complied with, that it would be "an established Precedent, in all future Time, for the Decency & Propriety of Persons offering themselves Candidates for the Election of the People, to offices of Trust & Importance;—a Practice which hath always been held, by the judicious & virtuous, dangerous to the Liberties of the People, and a Practice by which corrupt & designing Men, in every age, have too often availed themselves of Places of Power & Authority, to the great Disadvantage of those that *elected them*, if not to the Gross Violation of their most sacred Rights."[47]

A number of other towns recommended that a convention be called to frame the new constitution. Concord, for example, stated its Resolution: that the "Supreme Legislative," sitting either in its proper capacity, or in joint session, was

---

46. *Ibid.*, p. 146. Oct. 7, 1776.   47. *Ibid.*, pp. 178-9.

not a body proper to form and establish a constitution, since a constitution was a set of principles established to secure the subject in the possession of rights and privileges, against the encroachment of the government; as the same body that made a constitution must have the power to alter it, a constitution that could be changed by the legislature would be no security at all for the subject against governmental encroachment.[48] Hence they argued that a convention should be chosen to draw up the proposed constitution.

The town of Stoughton characterized the Resolve as "unadviseable and irrational, and a measure that ought not by any means to be complied with, for these reasons, viz. That we are totally unacquainted with the capacities, patriotism and characters of the Members that compose the said House and Council (excepting our own Members). Also because they were never elected by the People for that purpose, and also because the present embarrassed state of our public affairs calls for the steady attention of every Member of said Court."[49]

The pulpit helped to form public opinion on the subject. The Reverend Peter Whitney, in a "Lecture Appointed for Publishing the Declaration of Independence," asked for cool examination of the constitutions already adopted by other states and improvement upon them. He explained the need for a separation of the personnel of the departments: "Power is too intoxicating, to be committed for *any* great length of time, to the hands of *any* man, or *any* body of men." Each branch of government should be entirely independent of every other, "that it may not in the least be influenced by the other."[50]

As the time for the General Court to meet drew near in the spring of 1777, committees of the towns of Berkshire

48. *Ibid.*, p. 182.
49. *Independent Chronicle*, Oct. 10, 1776. Mass. State Archives, CLVI, 125, Oct. 2, 1776.
50. Pp. 48-49.

County met, and resolved unanimously in favor of the method of constitution-making proposed by Worcester County, that is, by state convention.[51] Through the newspapers, vent was given to a barrage of criticism directed against the Resolve of the General Court. In the *Independent Chronicle*, "Cato Censorinus" sounded a warning against impending tyranny. Every government known to history had shown a disposition to invade the liberty of the subject. What had been the case with every other government would be the case with the Massachusetts government, unless care were taken to give no color for such proceedings. Massachusetts should then take care not to lay the foundations of tyranny in the midst of the struggle for liberty. The present Assembly would be less apt to distribute the powers of government in such a way as to preserve the liberty of the people, certainly, than would a body of men who had no concern in the government.[52]

Another writer in the same paper, who signed his article "The Observer," expressed his opinion in a rugged style: "One thing strikest me disagreeably then, and that is, That they who are immediately to set upon the constitution, should previously frame it; it seems to me liable to this exception, that a bias will take for self, and so preclude or prevent some very salutary strokes in the constitution. For instance, will one, I might say any one, be so likely to oppose a monopoly of offices in one person, if himself or connections are thereby deprived of some place of honor or profit."[53]

In the *Independent Chronicle* of July 10, 1777, "Clitus" observed that the constitution should be formed by a disinterested body. To the objection that the General Court might be of little importance, and that men would not care to sit in the House unless it afforded an opportunity to arrive

---

51. *Continental Journal*, March 20, 1777.
52. *Independent Chronicle*, June 19, 1777.
53. *Ibid.*, May 22, 1777. *The Observer*, No. II.

at places of honor or profit for themselves or their friends, he answered that the result would be a House of disinterested members, who, having no interest of their own to seek, would devote their whole time to the public good; that there would then be but one interest, the good of the people at large. Those who expected to be chosen to represent the people under the new form of government were certainly not the proper persons to draw up that form of government.

Characteristic of popular interest in political thought at this time was the model constitution of a writer under the pseudonym of "Phileleutherus" which was published in the *Independent Chronicle* of March 6, 1777. Article 14 of this constitution showed clearly that a separation of departments meant a separation of offices:

That the Legislative, Executive and Judiciary Departments, shall be as separate and distinct as possible; so that neither shall, without necessity, exercise the powers belonging to the other; nor shall any person exercise the powers of more than one of them at the same time; except that the Justices of the County-Courts shall be eligible to either the General Court, or Council of Safety; and excepting also, That the Council of Safety, shall sit as Justices in Cases of Impeachment, and in cases of Appeal from the Probate Court.

Article 42 of this model constitution would disqualify any officeholder under the United States from holding a state office for reasons which were given:

. . . in order to preserve Liberty,—to distribute the burdens and favors attending the several offices, in the several parts of this Government—and to prevent, as far as possible, any one man —family—or their connections, from engrossing many places of honor and profit.

The general principle of a separation of offices was set forth:

Nor shall any one man hold more than one office or place in the service of this State, at one and the same time, whether by commission or otherwise, excepting only through necessity, or as is herein before in this act excepted.

To gain approval for their undertaking, and no doubt also because of the insistence by the towns on their own powers in respect to constitution-making in their returns on the Resolve, a further Resolve was passed by the Provincial Assembly on May 5, 1777. It was here recommended to the towns in choosing their members to the General Assembly that "in addition to the common and ordinary powers of Representation," they "instruct them in one Body with the Council, to form such a Constitution of Government, as they shall judge best calculated to promote the happiness of this State; and when compleated, to cause the same to be printed —in order to its being by each Town and Plantation, duly considered."[54]

Far from instructing their representatives to form a constitution "in one Body with the Council," the town of Boston gave an unmistakable refusal, citing the need of the commonly accepted principle of a separation of offices:

With respect to the General Courts forming a new Constitution, you are directed by a unanimous vote of a full meeting. on no terms to consent to it, but to use your influence, and oppose it heartily, if such an attempt should be made; for we apprehend this matter *(at a suitable time)* will properly come before the people at large, to delegate *a select number for that purpose, and that alone;* when some things which we esteem *absolutely necessary* to a good form, may be viewed by a General Court, in the light of *self-denying ordinances,* which it is natural to conclude, are *always* disagreeable to human nature; among other things we have *particularly in view, making the Council intirely independent of the House, and to prevent the lately too prevalent custom of accumulating offices in one person;* we could wish to establish it, as a certain rule, that no person whatever be entrusted with more than *one* office at a time, *(and for the discharge of it,*

54. Mass. State Archives, CLVI, 199. May 5, 1777.

let there be honorable allowance;) and to keep the *members of the General Court from accepting any:* This we apprehend will have a happy effect upon the State at large, and is agreeable to the custom of all States, until corruption and bribery, destroy the principals of virtue.⁵⁵

In spite of the fact that some of its members were charged with such contrary instructions, the Provincial Congress proceeded with the work of drawing up a constitution, the members who were given no powers to frame a constitution seeming to take part in the proceedings, as did the others. But the members from Boston were not given a leading part.⁵⁶

During the year 1776, the people of Massachusetts were given an opportunity to peruse the constitutions drawn up by South Carolina, Virginia, New Jersey, and Pennsylvania.⁵⁷ These constitutions all provided for a separation of departments, which took the form of a separation in office-holding. Virginia was the first of the states to incorporate such a separation of departments in its constitution. The Virginia provision, perhaps, went farther than the others in the general statement that no person might hold an office in more than one department, with a single exception. The Virginia provision read: "The legislative, executive, and judiciary department, shall be separate and distinct, so that neither exercise the powers properly belonging to the other: nor shall any person exercise the powers of more than one of them, at the same time; except that the Justices of the County Courts shall be eligible to either House of Assembly." The fifth Article of the Declaration of Rights provided "that the Legislative and Executive powers of the State should be distinct from the Judicative. . . ."⁵⁸

55. *Boston Gazette*, June 2, 1777.
56. See the committee membership, *Continental Journal*, June 19, 1777.
57. *Continental Journal*, June 6, 13; Aug. 2, Aug. 8; *New-England Chronicle*, Nov. 21, 1776.
58. B. P. Poore, *Federal and State Constitutions*, II, 1910.

One of the political writers of the time, the Reverend William Gordon of Roxbury, began an analysis of the articles of the Virginia Constitution in the *New-England Chronicle*, on September 6, 1776. He discussed the provisions in the constitutions of South Carolina, New Jersey, and Virginia; he urged the necessity of following Virginia's example in the matter of a separation of departments, which he evidently understood to mean a separation of offices. He referred to the clamor which had been raised under the royal governors against having certain officers in the Council, and to the fact that they were left out. If the combination of offices were allowed under the new government, the clamor would appear to have been needless and merely partisan in purpose. To avoid the error of plural office-holding, Gordon advocated paying judicial and executive officers generously.

"Pay well," he advised, "and suitable men will be found that will be content with single places, and apply themselves to the proper discharge of the duties thereof. ... But," he added, "it clashes so with contrary cases among ourselves, that I am fearful whether it will be adopted."[59]

Also of influence in Massachusetts while the Constitution of 1778 was in process of formation were the Articles of Confederation, of which Article V prohibited the delegates to the Congress from holding any other lucrative office under the United States. The prohibition read: "nor shall any person, being a delegate, be capable of holding any office under the United States, for which he or another for his benefit, receives any salary, fee, or emolument of any kind."[60]

The acceptance of the Articles of Confederation was considered in the Provincial Congress of January, 1778,[61] and the Provincial Congress drew up an address to be published in the newspapers with the Articles. On January 8 a letter to the Convention was published which quoted the above

---

59. *New-England Chronicle*, Sept. 12, 1776.
60. Article V, paragraph 2.   61. *Journal*, Jan. 1, 1778.

provision of Article V of the Articles of Confederation as an example for Massachusetts. Should not a similar exclusion of placemen from the Massachusetts General Court be adopted, the writer asked, instead of confining the exclusion to some few only? If the people were not wise and cautious enough to exclude placemen from the beginning, when the constitution was being framed, they would never be powerful enough to exclude them by acts of the General Court.[62]

Another writer who commented on Article V of the Articles of Confederation, in proposing a Senate, suggested a rule against dual places for the senators, with a single exception: ". . . no senator to wear two characters in the legislative capacity, unless he be a justice of the peace; provided he be a judge of any Court, or lawyer at the bar, that shall disqualify him to be a senator. . . ."[63]

Without formulating a theory of separation of departments, the Constitution of 1778 followed the experience of the province, for it provided very concretely for a separation of offices. Article IV provided that:

The Judges of the Superior Court, Secretary, Treasurer General, Commissary General, and settled Ministers of the Gospel, while in office; also all Military Officers, while in the pay of this or of the United States, shall be considered as disqualified for holding a seat in the General Court; and the Judges and Registers of Probate for holding a Seat in the Senate.[64]

Membership in the Continental Congress and certain state offices were mutually exclusive by Article XXVIII:

If any person holding the office of Governor, Lieutenant Governor, Senator, Judge of the Superior Court, Secretary,

62. *Ibid.*, Jan. 8, 1778; Jan. 22, 1778.   63. *Ibid.*, April 2, 1778.
64. *Journal of the Constitutional Convention of 1779-80*, Appendix, No. 5, 255; *Boston Gazette*, March 23, 1778; Sparks MSS. XLIX, 5, Misc. Papers—Report of a Committee of Convention of a Form of Government—Pub. Dec. 11, 1777; Journal of the Committee appointed by the Convention (of 1777) to form a Constitution, Pickering MSS., John Pickering's Journal.

Attorney-General, Treasurer-General, or Commissary-General, shall be chosen a member of Congress, and accept the trust, the place, which he so held as aforesaid, shall be considered as vacated thereby, and some other person chosen to succeed him therein. And if any person, serving for this State at said Congress, shall be appointed to either of the aforesaid offices, and accept thereof, he shall be considered as resigning his seat in Congress, and some other person shall be chosen in his stead.

Article XIX of the Constitution of 1778 was objected to in the returns of some of the towns, as affording an opportunity to members of the General Court to assume additional offices themselves. It provided for the election by the General Court of those civil officers who were on an annual basis; all other civil officers, and all military officers were to be appointed "by the Governor and Senate."

No provision was made for approval or rejection of separate articles of the Constitution of 1778. It was to be accepted or rejected as a whole by the people. Nevertheless, so extensively had the spirit of self-government permeated the revolutionary state that a number of towns returned their objections against the Constitution of 1778, article by article. Some towns explained their action. The prevalent attitude was thus expressed by the town of Beverly: "We ... expect a candid reception of these general hints as originating from a sincere desire to secure the invaluable liberties of the people."[65]

Some towns rejected the proposed Constitution, as did the town of Bristol, because they found no provision made for them "to approve of the artickels we Like & Disaprove and vote against the artickels we Disliked, it is for these Reasons this Town voted against the Whol Form of Government."[66] One hundred and twenty towns neglected to express any opinion at all upon the Constitution of 1778. It was re-

---

65. Mass. State Archives, CLVI, 432. 66. Ibid., CLVI, 420.

jected, it is said, by five-sixths of the 12,000 persons who voted on it.[67] Most of the towns rejected it without stating specific reasons for their action.

Of those towns which stated their objections to the Constitution, a number expressly declared that it did not go far enough in providing for a separation of the departments of government. There was no expression of opinion on the part of any town against a separation of departments, which points to the conclusion that there was agreement of opinion among the voters as to the necessity of a separation of departments, to be effected by a separation of offices.

While there was no difference of opinion as to the necessity of such separation, the opinions expressed on the exact offices to be separated were various. The town of Upton, in unanimously rejecting the Constitution of 1778, among other reasons stated:

We are of opinion, that all Salary men in the State, and all whose fees of office are worth annually eighty pounds should be uneligible into either House of Assembly. . . . Sheriffs, Register or Registers of deeds and Coroners . . . that each of these be uneligible for either House of Assembly.

Also it appears to us that Legislative, Judiciary and Executive departments ought to be preserved more distinct than is provided for in the proposed Constitution of Government.[68]

Lexington directed its objections to a Constitution made by the Legislature, but also found the separation of departments inadequate:

We have complained of it, in Times past, under the Charter, and still look upon it of dangerous Tendency, to have the Legislative and Executive Powers blended in the same Persons. And the Wise & judicious in all Ages have spoken of it as a very great Greivance to have, in the Supreme Council, or Legislative Body

67. John Adams, *Life and Works*, IV, 214; Mass. State Archives, CLX, 123.
68. Mass. State Archives, CLVI, 389.

of a State, Placemen and Pensioners; or which amounts almost to the same Thing, Persons who hold Lucretive Posts, in the Gift of that Court, or are dependent thereupon for their Offices, and the Salaries or Perquisites annexed thereunto. And we cannot persuade ourselves, that the Provision made, in this Constitution, would be an adequate Remedy.[69]

Rochester apparently agreed with Sir Edward Coke as to what the public welfare required in office-holding: "that no person whatsoever hold no more than one office under the State at one & the same Time."[70]

Westminster, in its return, was mindful of recent experience with the Assembly in the matter of appointments:

... if the General Court must be authorized to Elect all officers Will they not Monopalise all places of Honour and prophit to themselves to the Exclusion of many others perhaps as capeable as themselves. ... and further When they have made a band of officers perhapps Verry Disagreeable to the people, no power is Left in the people to Disband them. . . .[71]

Lenox was mindful of the common-law rule against holding incompatible offices, finding the appointing power of the Senate

... more power than can be safe in the hands of one Branch of the Legislature, it give [sic] them too great an opportunity to provide for their Connections to the injury of the Public, ... Members of Congress as well as all other Officers of the State ought not to hold a plurality of Offices, the execution of which requires them to be at different Places at the same time and different requisite Talants. . . .[72]

Plymouth also feared the appointing power of the Governor and Senate:

... which power of Appointing, may Enable a Sett of enterprizing Intrigueing Men, to Establish an intrist, & Influance, thro' the State, that may be Daingerous, to the liberties, of the people.[73]

69. *Ibid.*, CLX, 26.   70. *Ibid.*, CLVI, 336.   71. *Ibid.*, CLX, 18.
72. *Ibid.*, CLVI, 379-80. Also *Continental Journal*, June 4, 1778. Return of the Town of Dartmouth.
73. Mass. State Archives, CLVI, 426; *ibid.*, CLVI, 419.

Boston found the provisions just as inadequate as they expected in a constitution framed by the legislative assembly method of constitution-making to which they were opposed:

> ... it is hard for the General Court, upon a matter of this kind to divest themselves of the idea of their being *members;* and the probability that they may continue *such,* may induce them to form the government, with peculiar reference to themselves; to this, we suppose it is owing, that the legislative and executive branches, are so blended, and that nothing appears, but that the members of the Court may monopolize to themselves a variety of offices; while we are fully persuaded the best Form of Government, will ever keep those branches intirely distinct, and the members confined to their particular duties, without incumbrance. . . .[74]

The *Essex Result,* which had a great influence in discrediting the Constitution of 1778,[75] pictured at some length the evils which would arise if the three "powers" of government were united in the same hands, making the government an absolutism. From a union of the legislative and judicial powers would arise an uncertainty in respect to law, since the maker of the law would also interpret it. "And what people," it queried, "are so unhappy as those, whose laws are uncertain?" And from a union of executive and legislative powers, "mischiefs the most terrible" were said to follow. The executive power would make itself absolute, and the government would prove a tyranny. If the executive and judicial powers were united, security of person and property would be annihilated.[76]

So the conclusion was drawn "that the legislative, judicial,

---

74. *Continental Journal,* June 4, 1776. Instructions to Representatives.
75. *Mass. Hist. Soc. Coll.,* LXXIII, 20. Warren-Adams Letters—Jas. Warren to John Adams, Boston, June 7, 1778: "The Town of Boston (whose wise Observations you will see in the Papers) and the County of Essex have had a great Share, and Influence in this Determination. . . ."
76. *Memoir of Theophilus Parsons,* pp. 373-4.

and executive powers, are to be lodged in different hands, that each branch is to be independent, and further, to be so ballanced, and be able to exert such checks upon the others, as will preserve it from a dependence on, or an union with them."[77] The *Essex Result* also advocated a division of the Council in its two capacities, a small privy Council advisory to the executive, and chosen from the Senate, and a legislative upper house or Senate.

Commenting on the Constitution of 1778, the Reverend William Gordon wrote in the *Independent Chronicle* that the provisions for a separation of offices were sadly inadequate from the point of view of the public good: ". . . all members of the Board of War ought to have been excluded from seats in the General Court,—the Attorney-General also. . . . The nature of his office requiring that he should attend every Superior Court through the State, clashes with an attendance in General Court." Mr. Gordon then went back to the necessity of excluding "placemen" from the General Court: "Indeed care should have been taken to have excluded placemen of every kind from being chosen into the Senate or House of Assembly: By the fifth Article of Confederation every delegate is declared incapable 'of holding any office under the United States, for which he or another for his benefit, receives any salary, fee, or emolument of any kind.' Why was not a similar paragraph wrought into the articles of the Constitution? O dear! that would have counteracted the influence and interests of individuals, *to which the public good ought to give place.*"[78]

In criticizing the irregularity of allowing all members of the General Court to take part in framing a constitution whether instructed to or not, the Reverend Mr. Gordon wrote that the body was assembled by "a certain State leger-

77. *Ibid.*, pp. 395-6.
78. *Independent Chronicle*, April 30, 1778; *Continental Journal*, April 23, 1778.

demain, a kin to British legislative omnipotence." He asked, "And ought not the representatives who had not been instructed to join in forming a Constitution, much more those who had been instructed to the contrary, to have absented themselves, instead of taking an active part?"[79] For this criticism, the General Court summarily dismissed Mr. Gordon from serving as its chaplain, giving as the reason that he had, in this article, "grossly reflected upon the General Court as having acted a legerdemain part in assembling the late Convention."[80]

Another discussion of the detriment to the public good of plural office-holding appeared in the *Boston Gazette* of May 25, 1778. The writer frankly recommended that in the election of the Council no man should receive a vote who had an important office in the executive department. He referred to the experience of the province with executive officers in the Council, and observed that candidates for office who had opposed the practice some years back now seemed to discredit that opposition by holding plural offices themselves:

The opposition made a few years since by some gentlemen to persons under this predicament, having a seat in council, must have been founded in reason and sound policy, had not those very gentlemen (of whose understanding and political improvements none can entertain a doubt) ever since held their seats under the same, etc. did they not still continue to be put up by their friends, who have ever avowed the same sentiments, as candidates.

The writer would not call the integrity of these gentlemen in question, but he would deny the argument which they advanced to justify themselves, that there could not be found ten men of equal abilities to put in their places, although he could not but applaud the modesty of their defense. Nor could he allow a further argument which was made for the

79. *Independent Chronicle*, April 2, 1778; *Continental Journal*, April 2, 1778.
80. *Acts and Resolves*, XX, 345, April 6, 1778.

practice, that these men by their long continuance in office had acquired a peculiar facility in conducting the public business which would more than balance the mischiefs arising from their holding of incompatible offices. His conclusion was:

> ... that if the gentlemen above refer'd to and their friends will not wave the privilege of monopolizing places in government when the principle is so inadmissible, and the effect so dangerous, we can entertain no very sanguine hopes from a constitution to be form'd under their direction, by which they are to have both the arrangement and disposal of offices.[81]

It seems obvious that the motive in this widespread demand for a separation of offices was concern for the public good. The town of Stoughton pointed this out directly to its representative in 1778:

> ... you are on no terms to accept of any office of honor or post of profit while you are the Representative of the town, without the approbation of your constituents, in order that you may be influenced by no motive, only by that of serving public; and that you may be always thus influenced, is agreeable to the earnest wishes and prayers of your Constituents.[82]

"Mentor," in the *Independent Chronicle*, gave reasons for the separation of offices which expressed clearly the general objection to plural office-holding:

> And take this with you, my countrymen, that the multiplying offices in one man, has a tendency to produce an aristocracy, which of all governments is the worst calculated for the people's freedom or happiness. For Consider, when all the principal offices of the State, are got into few hands, how great must be the influence of these few.[83]

It was obvious, therefore, that there was a volume of opinion in the state calling for a greater separation of offices

---

81. *Boston Gazette*, May 25, 1778. "Alociapt."
82. *Continental Journal*, June 18, 1778.
83. *Independent Chronicle*, Nov. 27, 1778.

for the good of the state than that provided for by the Constitution of 1778. One of the principal reasons[84] underlying the rejection of the Constitution of 1778, in short, was opposition to a constitution made by a General Court, the members of which had shown themselves to be anything but disinterested in the organization of the government. The widespread expression of opinion showed what would be acceptable in a subsequent constitution, with regard to a separation in office-holding.

84. See the reasons given for rejection of the Constitution of 1778: lack of a bill of rights, property qualifications for the suffrage, inefficacy of the executive. *Memoir of Theophilus Parsons*, p. 46. The provisions for a religious establishment also alienated many people.

CHAPTER V

ACHIEVEMENT OF A "SEPARATION" OF DEPARTMENTS

IT IS NOT SURPRISING that the Assembly appeared somewhat chastened after their unpopular attempt at constitution-making. Before trying again, they admitted some hesitation, saying: ". . . it is doubtful, from the Representations made to this Court, what are the Sentiments of the major Part of the good People of this State as to the Expediency of now Proceeding to form a new Constitution of Government. . . ." The questions were put to the towns as to whether they chose to have a new constitution made at the time and as to whether they would empower their representatives to vote for calling a state convention to form a new constitution.[1]

As it appeared from the returns on these questions that more than two-thirds of the towns were in favor of a new constitution, and that it should be made by a convention specially authorized for the purpose,[2] a call was issued for a convention for the sole purpose of forming a constitution. It was to meet in Cambridge on September 1, 1779. Although the Resolve of the Provincial Congress did not call for instructions to the delegates to the proposed convention, they were nevertheless given by some towns. From the instructions available, it appears that it was well understood that a separation of departments was one of the fundamental principles required in a constitution.

Among the towns which gave such instructions was Sandisfield. Sandisfield declared in phrases by this time threadbare

1. Mass. State Archives, CLX, 116, Feb. 20, 1779.
2. *Ibid.*, p. 134, June 21, 1779.

that certain judicial and executive officers should be disqualified from sitting in the General Court, and that a judge of probate should not hear an appeal from his own judgment.³ The town of Dudley, in one of five brief articles of instruction, stipulated against salaried or executive officers sitting in the Assembly.⁴ Stoughton's instruction on the subject is also available. It called for a separation of departments, which was to be achieved by a separation of personnel, stating "That yᵉ. Supreme power is divisible into Several Departments, viz. yᵉ. legislative Judicial & executive; & that yᵉ. powers particular to each may & ought to be delegated to certain Distinct and Seperate Bodies of men in Such Manner that yᵉ. powers beloging [*sic*] to all or either two of yᵉ. branches may not be exercised by any one of them. . . ."⁵

The proceedings of the Constitutional Convention itself show that the Report of the Committee of Thirty to the Convention provided for a separation of departments in at least four different clauses of the draft. A brief article (XXXI) in the Declaration of Rights on the separation of departments read: "The judicial department of the State ought to be separate from, and independent of, the legislative and executive powers."⁶ This article uses "department" synonymously with "power" and aims at establishing primarily the independence of the judicial department. The second paragraph of the preamble to the Frame of Government went further in providing for a separation of the three departments

3. *Ibid.*, p. 259: ". . . the Judges of the Superiour Court, Secretary, Treasurer Genˡ. Commissary Genˡ. Setled Ministers while in Office, Military Officrs [*sic*] while in pay of this or the United States & Judges & Registers of Probate ought to be considered as Disqualified from having a seat in the Genˡ. Court, & the Judge of Probate ought not to hear & Determine an Appeal from his own Judgment."
4. *Ibid.*, p. 283: ". . . that no Sallery men or none of the Executive Authority shall have a Seat in the Assembly."
5. *Ibid.*, 160: 271.
6. *Journal of the Constitutional Convention of 1780*, App. II, 197; John Adams, *Life and Works*, IV, 230.

of government as follows: "In the Government of the Commonwealth of Massachusetts, the legislative, executive, and judicial power, shall be placed in separate departments, to the end that it might be a government of laws and not of men."[7]

Another article relevant to the subject was Article I, Section I, Chapter II. It aimed at the independence of the executive and judicial departments: "And the first magistrate shall have a negative upon all the laws—that he may have power to preserve the independence of the executive and judicial departments."[8] Also, the second article of the Chapter on the Judiciary (Chapter IV), provided for a very limited separation in office-holding: "No Justice of the Superior Court of Judicature, Court of Assize, and General Gaol Delivery, shall have a seat in the Senate, or House of Representatives."[9]

These provisions on the separation of departments in the Report of the Committee of Thirty were probably the work of John Adams. Of this Report, Adams boasted: "I had the honor to be principal engineer."[10] According to the account given in his *Life and Works*, John Adams was a member of a sub-committee of three, to whom the Committee of Thirty delegated the task of preparing a draft of a constitution. And of this sub-committee, John Adams, the account goes, was the most important member (the other members were James Bowdoin and Samuel Adams), because to him the sub-committee in turn delegated its work. The draft prepared by John Adams has not been preserved; but of the Report of the Committee of Thirty, his biographers say: "In its leading features, and in most of its language, the plan of Mr. Adams is preserved in the report."[11]

7. Chapter II. *Journal of the Constitutional Convention*, p. 197.
8. *Ibid.*
9. *Journal of the Constitutional Convention*, p. 211.
10. *Life and Works*, IV, 216.
11. John Adams, *Life and Works*, IV, 215-16.

At any rate, the various scattered statements on the separation of departments in the Report might have been expected from John Adams, as the principle was of primary importance in his philosophy of the state. Also the statement of the purpose of the separation of departments, "that it might be a government of laws and not of men," was no doubt the contribution of Adams. This statement is very important, as it was carried over into the Constitution of 1780 in the same words. This principle was found by Adams in the writings of more than one political theorist, and it fitted aptly the experience and problem of Massachusetts.

Adams considered that the only good government was republican;[12] and a republic he found defined by the theorists "to be a government of laws, and not of men."[13] On the necessity of a government of laws, Adams wrote earnestly if not brilliantly. A government of laws had been suggested as a remedy in the same connection in England by Harrington: ". . . where the public interest governs, it is a government of laws, and not of men . . . and where private interest governs, it is a government of men, and not of laws"; and, more explicitly, on government directed to a private end: ". . . because the laws in such cases are made according to the interest of a man, or a few families, it may be said to be an empire of men, and not of laws."[14]

Government by a faction which was a group animated by private interest, and for some other end than the interest of the public, therefore, Adams would have aimed to prevent by such a provision. It would have been designed to prevent a recurrence of government by a few, of which Massachusetts had had considerable experience in the province period. Even in the state government, during the revolutionary period, it

12. Thoughts on Government, *Continental Journal*, Sept. 23, 1779.
13. *Life and Works*, IV, 106, 448.
14. *Life and Works*, IV, 404. Plato had described his perfect commonwealth as a state where "in one word . . . the *laws* govern." *Ibid.*, IV, 448.

was Adams' observation that human nature was above all things self-seeking or "self-engrossing," as he put it. Hence the need for a separation of departments to be effected by a separation in office-holding, and for checks and balances among the different departments.

Adams' philosophy on the subject of the need of a separation of departments was contained in the following passage: "We have all along contended, that the predominant passion of all men in power, whether kings, nobles, or plebeians, is the same; that tyranny will be the effect, whoever are the governors, whether the one, the few, or the many, if uncontrolled by equal laws, made by common consent, and supported, protected, and enforced by three different orders of men *in equilibrio*."[15]

Other writers of the time had a similar interpretation of the phrase, "a government of laws." The English writer Richard Price, in his "Observations on the Nature of Civil Liberty," extracts from which were printed in the *New-England Chronicle* of July 4, 1776, said that it was not enough to define liberty as a government of laws and not of men: "Liberty, therefore, is too imperfectly defined when it is said to be 'a government by *laws*, and not by *men*.' If the laws are made by one man, or a junto of men in a state, and not by *common consent*, a government by them does not differ from slavery. In this case, it would be a contradiction in terms to say that the state 'governs itself.'"[16] Hence the several branches of government should be organized on the basis of separate and distinct departments, or in departments as nearly independent of each other as possible.

Such was the understanding of the meaning of a "government of laws" at the time; the object was to secure government in the public interest. Only distinct departments

---

15. Adams, *Life and Works*, V, 9-10.
16. Commented upon in Adams, *Life and Works*, IV, 401-2. See Appendix V, section 1, *infra*.

Achievement of a "Separation" of Departments 141

could adequately check each other, and only adequate checks could maintain a measure of popular control. The theoretical statement of the purpose of a separation of departments which was placed in the Report of the Committee of Thirty to the Convention, was carried over into the final draft of the Declaration of Rights of the Constitution of 1780. It underwent restatement, however, and its practical application in the provisions of the Frame of Government proper was considerably altered in the Convention. Although he no doubt had a large or the sole part in drawing the original articles, John Adams had no part in this alteration.

The determination of these articles of the Report did not come before the Convention until January, 1780, although there was brief debate on them on November 8 and 9, 1779. Because of the severity of the winter and the difficulties of travel,[17] the attendance at the winter session was very scanty. The Convention adjourned from time to time until the end of January. On January 29, 1780, the Convention published an advertisement to the towns in the newspapers, urging a better attendance of delegates, with the information that "The most important articles, such as Representation;—the several Departments of Government, with their respective powers and checks;—the mode of appointing militia and other officers;—and other matters of great weight, have not, as yet, been taken up, from the expectation of a more general attendance."[18]

John Adams had left for France the previous November,[19] and so was not present when the consideration of the separation of departments got under way in the Convention. There are only a few summary passages in the Journal of the Convention relating to the adoption of Article XXX of the Bill of Rights. The long history which has been given

17. *Journal of the Constitutional Convention*, p. 53.
18. *Journal of the Constitutional Convention*, p. 63.
19. *Life and Works*, IV, 215.

of a separation of departments in Massachusetts forms the background of the relationship, scarcely evident from the Journal, between Article II of Chapter VI, on the "Exclusion and Incompatibility of Offices," and Article XXX of the Declaration of Rights, which provided the theory of a distribution of powers among separate departments.

In the Report of the Committee of Thirty to the Convention, Article XXXI had emphasized the independence of the judicial department: "The judicial department of the State ought to be separate from, and independent of, the legislative and executive powers."[20]

On February 10, Article XXXI came under consideration and a motion was made that the words "separate from and" should be omitted from the Article, which however was superseded by a motion that Article XXXI of the Declaration of Rights of the Report should be expunged and a substitute article passed, "by which the article aforesaid, and the 2d paragraph in the preamble of the 2d chapter, formerly voted to be considered together, may be consolidated, and the sense of both expressed...."[21]

The "2d paragraph in the preamble of the 2d chapter" in the Report of the Committee read: "In the Government of the Commonwealth of Massachusetts, the legislative, executive, and judicial power, shall be placed in separate departments, to the end that it might be a government of laws and not of men."[22]

Another provision of the Report in regard to the independence of departments, constituting Section I of Article I of Chapter II, was dropped by vote of the Convention on February 21:[23] "And the first magistrate shall have a negative

---

20. *Journal of the Constitutional Convention*, p. 197, Appendix II.
21. *Ibid.*, pp. 44, 95.
22. *Journal of the Constitutional Convention*, p. 197.
23. *Ibid.*, pp. 126, 197.

upon all the laws—that he may have power to preserve the independence of the executive and judicial departments. . . ."

The substitute article which was passed on February 10 constitutes the well-known Article XXX of the Declaration of Rights of the Massachusetts Constitution. This article which, it is generally said, provides for a rigid separation of departments, as passed by the Convention actually contained neither the word "separation" nor "department!" That the framers of the Constitution did not intend a "rigid" separation of departments may be inferred from the fact that the words "separate from" contained in the original provision on the subject in the draft [Article XXXI] were omitted in the final provision. Article XXX as it passed the Convention read: "In the Government of this Commonwealth, the Legislative shall never exercise the Executive and Judicial powers, or either of them. The Executive shall never exercise the Legislative and Judicial powers or either of them. The Judicial shall never exercise the Legislative and Executive powers or either of them, to the end that it may be a government of laws and not of men."[24]

To this article the word "department" was added after the word "Legislative" in the first sentence, evidently by the Committee on "clerkship and arrangements."[25] Otherwise it would be hard to account for its addition. As the history of a separation of departments has been followed in Massachusetts, it should be clear that it was to be attained chiefly by a separation in office-holding, and not by a separation of powers according to abstract type. Evidently the terms

24. While Article XXX passed the Convention in this form, after the word "Legislative" in the first sentence, the word "Department" was *added* in the final draft of the Constitution, a change which can scarcely be attributed to any source but the Committee on Clerkship and Arrangement. *Journal of the Constitutional Convention*, p. 95. For the appointment of this committee, see *ibid.*, p. 158.

25. *Ibid.*, p. 158.

"Executive," "Legislative," and "Judicial" powers in Article XXX refer to the powers of those various departments. The separation of departments has been shown to have had for its purpose the same end which English theory and law on the subject, as well as Montesquieu, had aimed at; that is, "a government of laws," or a government to protect the rights of all groups in the state. In the Constitution of 1780, Article XXX of the Declaration of Rights and Article II of Chapter VI must have had a correlation in the understanding of the people of the time; the first being a theoretical statement, the second a practical provision for the attainment of the same end, which was "a government of laws, and not of men."

On January 29, the article providing for a limited separation in office-holding (Article II of Chapter VI of the Report) came up,[26] and it was obviously considered inadequate by the Convention, for it was recommitted, "after very extensive debates," to a committee of seven.[27] The committee was instructed to report an article of three headings "which shall ascertain what offices, to be held under the Commonwealth, shall be declared incompatible with each other; what offices shall disqualify the possessor from holding a seat in either House of Assembly; and also what number and kind of offices, it may be inconsistent with the public good should be held by any one person. . . ."

Several days later, the committee reported an article excluding a long list of executive and judicial officers from sitting in the General Court. The Governor and Lieutenant-Governor were not named in the Report, it is to be noted,

---

26. "No Justice of the Superior Court of Judicature, Court of Assize, and General Gaol Delivery, shall have a seat in the Senate, or House of Representatives." See page 138, above. *Journal of the Constitutional Convention*, pp. 65, 211.

27. James Bowdoin, John Lowell, Rev. Jonas Clark, John Pickering, Jonathan Jackson, Israel Washburn, and Amos Bradley. *Journal of the Constitutional Convention*, p. 65. George Cabot and Rev. Henry Cummings were added to this committee on Feb. 8; Robert Treat Paine and Timothy Danielson were added March 1. *Journal*, pp. 91, 158.

but otherwise every state officer of any significance was excluded from the General Court, and even the president, professors, tutors and instructors of Harvard College, and ordained or settled ministers of the gospel, were barred from sitting in the legislature.[28]

The exclusion from the General Court of each officer on the reported list was considered separately by the Convention. The exclusion of these officers, except judges of the Inferior Court and judges of the Maritime Court, militia officers, and ministers of the gospel, was eventually accepted; and clerks of the Inferior Courts of Common Pleas and clerks of the Supreme Court were added to the list by the Convention.[29]

Strangely inconsistent with the modern interpretation of Article XXX of the Declaration of Rights was a motion adopted, obviously as a result of English practice, which gave to a committee consideration of re-election to palliate holding of an office incompatible with a legislative seat. A committee of one was appointed on February 24 "to bring in an article making provision for the issuing precept for a new choice of a member or members, when any person or persons, returned to serve in either House of the Legislature shall be appointed to and accept of places under the government, the holding of which is, or shall be declared to be incompatible with the retaining a seat in the same."[30] In practice in England, such a provision in the Place Act of 1705 worked out to be a mere formality, not obstructing the development of the Cabinet system. Article XXX of the Declaration of Rights, which provides for a separation of departments, had already been adopted when the above instruction was voted by the Convention. A provision was also considered whereby

28. *Journal of the Constitutional Convention*, p. 81. Appendix V, section 2, *infra*.
29. *Journal of the Constitutional Convention*, p. 138, Feb. 24. Also, pp. 92, 94, 137-8, 158.
30. *Ibid.*, p. 139. Judge Sullivan was appointed as the committee.

the seat of any member of the Senate or House of Representatives chosen as delegate to Congress should be vacated and re-election required, following the English precedent.[31]

A separate chapter for the list of persons excluded from a seat in either house (with other matters) was voted on February 25.[32] The report on "Incompatibility of Offices" dealing with the chief offices of state, and their incompatibility, was accepted on March 1. It contained two paragraphs which were placed at the beginning of Article II of Chapter VI of the Constitution.[33] It was not until the last day of the Convention that the article on exclusion of certain officers from the House, the Senate, and the Council was agreed upon. Even on that last day, there was some difference of opinion as to separation in the holding of certain offices. The above two reports, combined, form Article II of Chapter VI of the Massachusetts Constitution.[34] This article on "Exclusion and Incompatibility" was the last one to be accepted by the Convention. It was accepted and voted to be placed in the "Miscellaneous Chapter" of the Constitution on March 2, 1780.

The first paragraph of this article (Article II, Chapter VI) affords a general rule against a combination of offices and places in the chief officers of state, executive and judicial, they being excluded from any other office or "place" in the Commonwealth, with minor exceptions. Far more systematic than the general terms of the common-law rule, the provision does not yet attempt a complete separation. It went farther, however, than any of the English place bills (except that provision of the Act of Settlement which never went into effect) in that it required a separation in the holding of the principal offices of state. It was obviously designed to prevent a plurality of offices but not a complete separation: "No Governor, Lieutenant Governor, or Judge of the

31. *Ibid.*, pp. 163, 167. 32. *Ibid.*, p. 140.
33. *Ibid.*, pp. 158, 160. 34. *Ibid.*, pp. 163, 165-6.

Supreme Judicial Court, shall hold any other office or place under the authority of this Commonwealth, except such as by this Constitution they are admitted to hold, saving that the Judges of the said Court may hold the office of Justices of the Peace through the State." The office of justice of the peace was a local one, and the possible union of it with a place on the Supreme Court was allowed by the Convention only after repeated consideration.[35] The phrase "except such as by this Constitution they are admitted to hold" would seem to refer to incident offices given by the Constitution, such as that, for example, of President of the Council to the Governor and Lieutenant-Governor. The prohibition of plural office-holding by the chief officers, in view of a later, more specific clause, does not apply to seats in the General Court. These were not considered "offices," although they were considered "places."[36]

The article goes on to deal with less important offices and their incompatibility. In regard to them, it secures a more limited separation, since the incumbents of these offices are not forbidden to hold any other office whatsoever, only any other one of these designated offices. While the offices named are made incompatible and exclusive of each other, they are not necessarily exclusive of other offices not named: "No person shall be capable of holding or exercising at the same time, within this State, more than one of the following offices, viz: Judge of Probate, Sheriff, Register of Probate, or Register of Deeds. . . ."

As to certain other offices (not the chief offices of state, yet obviously important by reason of the methods of selection to these offices), the prohibition extended only to the holding of more than two by any one person: ". . . and never more than any two offices which are to be held by appointment

35. *Ibid.*, pp. 158, 163. Chapter VI, Article II, of the Constitution of Massachusetts.
36. It was extended even farther by Amendment VIII to the Constitution. See Worthy v. Barrett, 63 N. C. 199, drawing the distinction that a legislative seat is not an "office," but is a "place."

of the Governor, or the Governor and Council, or the Senate, or the House of Representatives, or by the election of the People of the State at large, or of the People of any county, military Offices and the offices of Justices of the Peace excepted, shall be held by any one person." The object of this second paragraph of Article II of Chapter VI as a whole was evidently to define how far plural office-holding was permitted, and in what cases two offices might be combined without danger to the Commonwealth. Evidently, the danger of tyranny would depend upon the importance of the offices combined, and in the case of the offices named above in paragraph two, the danger appeared not as great as in the case of the chief offices of state.

The third paragraph of the Article on Exclusion and Incompatibility of Offices defines what officers were to be excluded from a seat in the General Court. Both judicial and executive officers are included under this head but, surprising to note, the Governor and Lieutenant-Governor are not included. In fact, the Governor and Lieutenant-Governor seem to have been intentionally omitted from the list. Acceptance of any of the named offices operated as a resignation of the legislative seat. The expedient of re-election was not permitted:

No person holding the office of Judge of the Supreme Judicial Court—Secretary—Attorney General—Soliciter General—Treasurer or Receiver General—Judge of Probate—Commissary General—President, Professor, or Instructor of Harvard College—Sheriff—Clerk of the House of Representatives—Register of Probate—Register of Deeds—Clerk of the Supreme Judicial Court—Clerk of the Inferior Court of Common Pleas—or Officer of the Customs, including in this description Naval Officers—shall at the same time have a seat in the Senate or House of Representatives; but their being chosen or appointed to, and accepting the same, shall operate as a resignation of their seat in the Senate or House of Representatives; and the place so vacated shall be filled up.

The paragraph thus follows the English place bills in excluding an enumerated list but not *all* officers from a seat in the legislature. As to vacating the seat on accepting an incompatible office, it follows the common-law rule rather than the English Act of 1705:

And the same rule shall take place in case any judge of the said Supreme Judicial Court, or Judge of Probate, shall accept a seat in Council; or any Counsellor shall accept of either of those offices or places.[37]

The last paragraph in the Article deals with bribery and corruption as a disqualification for public office. The English experience of associating these safeguards (since bribery, like plural office-holding, destroyed the independence of action of office-holders) must have accounted for this inclusion. Outright bribery did not appear in the records at least as one of Massachusetts' political vices. The provision reads:

And no person shall ever be admitted to hold a seat in the Legislature, or any office of trust or importance under the Government of this Commonwealth, who shall, in the due course of law, have been convicted of bribery or corruption in obtaining an election or appointment.

An interesting provision which showed the influence of the English Bill of Rights, in providing for the independence of the legislative branch of the government, was that against suspension of the laws, except by the legislature:

The power of suspending the laws, or the execution of the laws, ought never to be exercised but by the legislature, or by authority derived from it, to be exercised in such particular cases only as the legislature shall expressly provide for.[38]

Another provision which seemed to be the result of English experience and which dealt with a separation of powers was Article XXV of the Declaration of Rights:

37. F. R. Mechem, *A Treatise on the Law of Public Office and Officers*, p. 420; *Journal of the Constitutional Convention*, pp. 247, 160; *Acts and Laws of Massachusetts, 1780-81; Constitution*, p. 28.

38. *Journal of the Constitutional Convention*, p. 225. Article X of the Declaration of Rights.

No subject ought, in any case, or in any time, to be declared guilty of treason or felony by the legislature.[39]

Of considerable significance are certain articles which the Convention voted down in connection with the Exclusion and Incompatibility of offices. That a committee of one was set up to report a provision "on vacating seats in the Assembly on accepting appointments to civil offices" has already been noted. The committee (Judge James Sullivan) reported a provision on February 26, which would have allowed a union of certain civil offices with a legislative seat, providing re-election took place, as in the English Act of 1705:

When any member of the House of Representatives shall be appointed to, and accept of, any civil office, his seat in the House of Representatives shall thereupon become vacant, and a precept shall be issued to his town for a new election.

Provided nevertheless, that if the office so accepted shall be such, as is not incompatible with a seat in the House, and his town shall upon (a) new election, he be entitled to his seat.[40]

Although this report was voted down, it only indicates that the Convention preferred the common-law rule rather than the expedient of re-election. It is noteworthy that a jurist should recommend such a provision, after Article XXX of the Bill of Rights had already been adopted, and that it should have been considered by the Convention.

Also of significance was the rejection of an article which would have provided for vacating the seat of any member of the Senate or House of Representatives chosen as a delegate to Congress and which would have required re-election.[41]

Otherwise, beyond a change in the constitution of the

---

[38] Journal of the Constitutional Convention, p. 225; Article X of the Declaration of Rights.

[39] Laws of Massachusetts, 1780-81; Constitution, p. 28.

[40] Journal of the Constitutional Convention, pp. 144-45. For the detailed instruction given to the Committee, ibid., 139, quoted above, page 145.

[41] Journal of the Constitutional Convention, pp. 163, 167. Later adopted as Amendment VIII to the Constitution, but re-election was not permitted. 4 Journal of the Constitutional Convention, pp. 247; 1601.

Council, the powers of government were left practically where they had been under the province Charter, which was far from being separated into three different types on the basis of departments. Such change as was made in the constitution of the Council was required by Massachusetts experience under the province Charter. The councillors obviously sat in two—if not indeed three—different departments of the government, and a change was essential to secure some separation of the personnel of the departments. Not only was there the notorious failure of the Council as an advisory body in the last years of Bernard's and Hutchinson's administrations, but there were the repeated complaints of the Governors, the experiment with the "mandamus" Council, and lastly, the example of several other states to guide Massachusetts in separating the legislative and executive functions of the Council in the new Constitution.[42] Virginia, which had been the first of the states to provide for a separation in the personnel of the departments, to be attained by a separation in office-holding, had created a small advisory council to exercise the executive functions of the Charter Council, while its legislative functions were to continue to be exercised by the upper house of the legislature. This method of separating the legislative upper house from the executive Council was followed by Massachusetts.[43]

The executive or advisory Council in Massachusetts was to consist of a small number of councillors to be chosen from the members of the upper house annually by a joint vote of both houses,[44] a change which would seem to have

42. A member of the Convention, Rev. Jonas Clark, said of the Council: "Not only to preserve, as distinct as possible, the several departments of government, that so they might be a mutual check upon each other; but also to give dignity to government and energy to the laws, as well as ease to administration, were evidently in view, by adopting this branch in the Constitution." Election Sermon, May 30, 1781, p. 57.

43. See Wm. Gordon, *New-England Chronicle*, Sept. 12, 1776.

44. Nine, besides the Lieutenant-Governor. *Journal of the Constitutional Convention*, p. 240, Article I, Section III, Chapter II.

been designed to give the legislature some control over the executive. To this Council, the judicial powers of the province Council were given "until the Legislature shall, by law, make other provision." (Chapter III, Article V.) A Senate elective by the voters was created to act as the upper house of the legislature in the place of the province Council.[45]

Beyond these changes, the framers of the Constitution of 1780 apparently considered that conformity to a separation of departments required no substantial alterations in the previous organization of the departments of government, and apparently attempted no such alterations. Only a few changes were made otherwise in the organization of the various departments, and these were made in practically every case as a result of experience under the province Charter and hence cannot be ascribed merely to an effort to secure a separation of different specific powers of government.

The veto given the Governor undoubtedly received discussion in the Convention. Actually, the qualified veto (which might be overridden by a two-thirds vote of both houses of the legislature), was not a great deviation from the province practice, and was no greater a change than the alteration of status from colony to state would have required. In granting a veto over legislation to the Governor, other considerations than a separation of specific powers of government, notably the English and the Massachusetts experience, were paramount. In the Report of the Committee of Thirty, the provision on the veto had read: "And the first magistrate shall have a negative upon all the laws—that he may have power to preserve the independence of the executive and judicial departments."[46] This provision was in accord with the theories of John Adams,[47] who not only thought a veto

---

45. *The Constitution of 1780*, Chapt. I, Sect. II; Chapt. I, Sect. 1, Art. I.
46. *Journal of the Constitutional Convention*, pp. 126, 197.
47. *Life and Works*, IV, 358: "The Americans have not indeed imitated it (i.e., the English practice) in giving a negative upon their legislature

of the Governor upon legislation necessary, but that it should have been unqualified: ". . . the executive power," he said, "being an object of jealousy and envy to the people, and the legislative an object of their confidence and affection, the latter will always be able to render the former unpopular, and undermine its influence."[48] But the Convention threw out the provision thus made in the Report of the Committee of Thirty for an absolute veto on the part of the Governor, "that he may have power to preserve the independence of the executive and judicial departments," and instead gave the Governor a qualified veto. They did not thereby obviously show a lack of concern for the independence of the departments, because they at the same time revised the provision for a separation of departments, incorporated in Article XXX of the Declaration of Rights.[49]

On the contrary, it is very probable that the independence of the departments was the primary concern of the framers of the Constitution, as it had been of English legislators, and of the theorist Montesquieu, who was so often quoted. Montesquieu, however, had advocated an absolute veto: "The executive power . . . ought to have a share in the legislature by the power of rejecting, otherwise it would soon be stripped of its prerogative. . . . If the prince were to have a part in the legislature by the power of resolving, liberty would be lost. But as it is necessary he should have a share in the legislature for the support of his own prerogative, this share must consist in the power of rejecting."[50] In giving the Governor a qualified veto, therefore, the framers of the Constitution were preferring their own experience to theory, although like Montesquieu, they advocated checks among the departments for the purpose of securing liberty. It

---
to the executive power; in this respect their balances are incomplete, very much I confess to my mortification."
48. *Life and Works*, IV, 587.   49. See p. 142, *supra*.
50. *Spirit of the Laws*, I, Book XI, Ch. VI.

should be noted that the separation of the departments and checks in the interest of the public were not to be attained through a separation of abstract powers. Following previous practice, the chief executive was not denied a part in the making of the laws. Although he was not given the power of a legislator he was not forbidden election to the General Court.[51]

Thus noting the changes in the separation of departments in the Constitution of 1780 from the governmental organization under the province Charter, it is obvious that there was little attempt to separate specific powers of three different types in the new Constitution. The question as to whether there was any analysis or definition in the Convention of three different kinds of power allotted to different departments, so far as the records show, must be answered in the negative. If an allocation of three different types of power to three different departments was intended by Article XXX of the Declaration of Rights, some serious analysis of the nature of the different powers of government must have been undertaken in the Convention, and some decided alterations from the province practice must have been determined upon in the distribution of powers to the different departments of government. No such study was made; indeed, not even a definition of the three different powers of government was attempted or laid down by the Convention. What is found rather is the extended consideration of a separation in the holding of various offices, which it has seemed necessary to narrate here at some length, and the incorporation in the Constitution of a long list of incompatibilities among offices of government and exclusions from the legislature.

Further exposition of the meaning of the separation of departments may also be found in the "Address of the Con-

---

51. The article on the veto was drawn up by a committee consisting of Ellis Gray, Rev. Mr. Clark, General Danielson, Theophilus Parsons, and Mr. Spooner.

Achievement of a "Separation" of Departments

vention to their Constituents," in which the "Grounds and Reasons" for the various provisions of the Constitution are given. From the discussion of the "superstructure" of the government in the "Address," it seems clear that the word "power" is used in more than one sense. Sometimes it is used synonymously with "department," as indeed it seems to have been used fairly frequently in the eighteenth century:

> Unless a due Proportion of Weight is given to each of the Powers of Government, there will soon be a Confusion of the whole. An overbearing of any one of its Parts on the rest, would destroy the Balance and accelerate its Dissolution and Ruin: And, a Power without *any* Restraint is Tyranny. The Powers of Government must then be balanced: To do this accurately requires the highest Skill in political Architecture.

In the foregoing discussion, the "Powers" of government are the departments, which are to be maintained in a state of balance, that no one "Power" may dominate another.

However, the "Address" goes on:

> Those who are to be invested with the Administration, should have such Powers given to them, as are requisite to render them useful in their respective places; and such *checks* should be added to every Branch of Power as may be sufficient to prevent its becoming formidable and injurious to the Commonwealth. . . . in this point of the greatest importance . . . *You* are the judges how far we have succeeded; and whether we have raised our Superstructure, agreeably to our professed Design, upon the Principles of a *Free Commonwealth*.[52]

In the first part of this paragraph "powers" is used in the distinct sense of legal capacity. The "powers" requisite to the officers of government are here defined as those which will "render them useful," rather than powers of any distinct type. Later "Branch of Power" is equivalent to "department."

---

52. *Journal of the Constitutional Convention*, p. 217.

In the exposition regarding the Governor's veto over legislation, the "Address" makes it clear that the primary consideration was to prevent members of any one department from attaining undue influence. The purpose of the veto was stated to be:

> ... that a due balance may be preserved in the three capital powers of Government. The Legislative, the Judicial and Executive Powers naturally exist in every Government: And the History of the rise and fall of the Empires of the World affords us ample proof, that when the same Man or Body of Men enact, interpret and execute the Laws, property becomes too precarious to be valuable, and a People are finally borne down with the force of corruption resulting from the Union of those Powers.[53]

Substantiating the conclusions of this study is the fact that the connection between the separation of departments and a separation in office-holding, as provided for by Article XXX of the Bill of Rights and by Article II of Chapter VI (on Exclusion and Incompatibility), was quite explicitly stated in the "Address" with an implication of the common-law rule against holding incompatible offices:

> Your Delegates have further provided that the Supreme Judicial Department, by fixed and ample Salaries, may be enabled to devote themselves wholly to the Duties of their important Office. And for this reason, as well as to keep this Department separate from the others in Government, have excluded them from a Seat in the Legislature; and when our Constituents consider that the final Decision of their Lives and Property must be had in this Court, we conceive they will universally approve the measure. The Judges of Probate, and those other officers whose presence is always necessary in their respective Counties, are also excluded.[54]

---

53. *Ibid.*, p. 219. Here, no doubt, as in other writings of the time, a union of powers was understood to take place when one man held several offices, in different departments. In other words, it was the result of a union of offices.

54. *Journal of the Constitutional Convention*, p. 220.

Also of importance in explaining the understanding of the separation of departments are the returns of the towns on the Constitution. A truly formidable volume of objection to the Constitution appeared. No doubt the town delegates to the Convention led the debates in the town-meetings in many cases. It seems probable, however, that Article XXX of the Declaration of Rights, and also the Article on Exclusion and Incompatibility of Offices were acceptable to the required two-thirds of the inhabitants voting on the Constitution, whatever they thought about some other parts of the Constitution. No authorization, however, was given to the voters to accept the Constitution by articles. There was comparatively little criticism of these articles, the great majority of the towns which accepted these articles making no comment. The only opinion on the part of the towns may therefore be said to come from those towns which had some objection, and this should be noted that quotation of it may not give an erroneous impression. Generally, the objection was to the effect that the separation provided did not go far enough, or that there was a discrepancy with the theory stated in Article XXX.

In the return of Petersham, for example, the connection between Article XXX and the Article on Exclusion and Incompatibility of Offices is clearly expressed:

The Thirtieth Article we think might be amended by an Addition in the Following Manner Namely, and such Separate Departments of Goverment [sic] shall ever be Exercised in Seperate and Distinct hands and if it should at any time So Happen that any one person who may sustain any office or offices in any one of such Departments should be Elected or Appointed to office in any of such Different Departments or that any person shall be Elected or appointed to office in such Different Departments in such Case such person or persons shall hold and Sustain office in But one of the aforesaid Departments and may chuse in which he Will Hold.[55]

55. Mass. State Archives, CCLXXII, 104.

In other words, the separation of departments of Article XXX was to be attained by a separation in office-holding. However, Petersham also stated an objection which might seem further to anticipate a separation of powers of a theoretical kind, but which might equally well disclose that independence of action in the departments is the end sought:

The Constituting the Gen¹. Coart a Judiciary For the Tryal of all officers we think Inconsistant with the thirtyeth Article which Expressly makes Provition that such Departments shall not Interfere in the Duties of the others we rather Chuse that all officers Shall be Inditable and Tryable at the Superior Coart and that all officers thus tryed shall have the priviledge of Being tryed By a Jury this will in Some Measure keep up, and Support the Supremacy of the People.

This article can only refer to the power of the House of Representatives to impeach and the power of the Senate to try impeachments. The objection was no doubt based on jealousy of the power of the General Court, certainly not on English constitutional theory. The purpose was to attain "Supremacy of the People." The return is one of several to be found in which complaint is made by the towns that the independence of the departments was not made as absolute as theory would require. This statement of objection indicates the view that a separation of departments should achieve independence of the departments. The provision, however, as stated does not necessarily require a separation of powers, but rather it might be said to require freedom from interference by one department with another.

Wrentham called attention to a discrepancy: Article XXX was "much too strongly expressed," the Frame of Government did not secure the complete separation of departments which Article XXX seemed to call for; hence it suggested amendment of Article XXX to agree with the Frame of Government: "The 30th Article in the Declaration of rights we think it much too Strongly expressed and Absolutely Militates with Article 2d page 15th. & Article 5th. page 40th. of the frame of Government. . . ." The articles here referred to are those giving the Governor a veto power over legislation, and the Governor and Council judicial powers in cases of marriage, divorce and alimony, and appeals from the judges of probate. The Wrentham return recommended not that complete separation should be attempted but that Article XXX should be amended to agree with the separation actually achieved. Wrentham would not go so far as to require such complete separation: "We apprehend said 30th. Article ought to be amended by inserting towards the latter end of it thes words exceping [*sic*] so far as is expressed in this Constitution."[56]

Two of the towns, Wells and Groton, recommended that an absolute veto be given the Governor. The town of Groton explained that the absolute veto would prevent domination by the legislature of the executive and judicial departments: ". . . being in the hands of the Governor will have a manifest Tendency to prevent the other Branches from making dangerous encroachments upon the executive and Judicial Departments, preserve a proper Balance in the three Capital powers of Government. . . ."[57]

There were several towns, however, Lincoln, Middleborough, Sandisfield, and Wilbraham, which objected to giving the Governor a veto upon legislation, on the ground that a separation of departments required a separation of powers. They understood the veto to give the Governor the power of a legislator. Wilbraham stated:

That the Governor shall have no power in Legislation— which we conceive he has in his Objecting to Bills and the Consequence thereof according to the Art (Part 2: Chap & Sect 1st): —Reasons; Because we think it is Important for the Safety of

56. *Ibid.*, pp. CCLXXV, CCLXXVII.
57. *Ibid.*, p. 14. "Powers" here is used synonymously with "departments," it is obvious.

the Rights of the People that the three Branches of Government Should be kept Distinct and that a Union of them would be Dangerous—to this purpose you very well Express the Matter in your Address in these words—that when the same man or Body of men Enact Interpret and execute the Laws Property Becomes too precarious to be Valuable. and the People are finally born down with the force of Corruption Resulting from the Union of those Powers . . . we also conceive it to be repugnant to the 30: Art: of the Declaration of Rights where it is Declared that the Executive Shall never Exercise the Legislative and Judicial Powers or either of them . . . But the Governor in Consequence of his Election as Chief Executive Officer—has a Considerable Influence in Legislation by the Art: But we are of Opinion that the Chief Executive Officer ought to be excluded a Voice in Legislation as much as the Supream Judicial Judges."[58]

In the above statement, the separation of departments would seem to be understood to extend to a separation of powers. The Constitution did not go far enough in separating the departments of government, in the opinion of these towns.

Lincoln disapproved of the Governor's veto: "1st because we think the Legislative Executive and Judicial powers Ought to be in seperate Departments and not exercised by the same Body or Bodies of men either in part Or in whole. . . ."[59]

Sandisfield objected to the Governor's veto (Chapter I, Article II): "Art 2d is Contrary to the bill of rights as Expresd in Art: 30th. . ." and regarding justices of the peace declared: "they being of a Judicial Department are by the bill of rights Art. 30th forbid a Seat in Legislature."[60]

Middleborough suggested an amendment, which would have gone farther than the Constitution, which was understood not to provide a complete separation of departments

58. *Ibid.*, CCLXXVI, 72.
59. *Ibid.*, CCLXXVII, 17.   60. *Ibid.*, CCLXXVI, 20.

as Article XXX required: "That the governor Shall have nothing to do in the Legislative Department as he must be the Supreme Executive Magistrate ... for Reasons against it we appeal to the 30th article in the Bill of Rights, where no one Shall act in Two Branches of Power."[61]

Most of the objections of the towns in this connection, however, referred to the article on the actual separation of offices. None of them suggested that the separation was too far-reaching as provided in the Constitution. For the most part, they suggested additional offices to be added to the list of incompatibility or exclusion in offices. Some towns objected to any accumulation of offices, as did Bellingham. As a substitute for Article II, Chapter VI, Bellingham suggested: "... no officer whose office is in the Gift of this State shall hold more than one such office at the same time ... and ad that every Person that shall have accepted any office aforesaid shall not be elegeable to any other office that Year."[62] Shrewsbury suggested as an "alteration" of the same article, that "all feemen to be excluded a Seate in the house ... and a further Alteration that No Man shall hold more than one Commission Civil or Military at the same time...."[63]

Braintree, the home seat of John Adams, who had been at the same time a member of the General Court and a delegate to Congress, suggested prohibiting such a combination of offices: "And in case any Member of the House, Senate, or Council, shall be elected a Delegate to Congress, & accept thereof, his former Seat shall be vacated. And no Member of Congress, shall be eligible to a Seat in the House, Senate or Council."[64] Barre objected to the same combination of

---

61. *Ibid.*, CCLXXVII, 40.   62. *Ibid.*, p. 60.
63. *Ibid.*, p. 108. See p. 1 for return of Acton.
64. *Ibid.*, p. 63. This separation was effected later by Amendment VIII of the Constitution.

offices, giving as a reason: "We think such a practice Would open a way for some persons to have an undue influence in government and Derogetory to the liberties of the people."[65]

A number of towns among these offering objections in regard to the separation of departments considered the exclusion of judges from the legislature inadequate. Northborough proposed, on Chapter VI: ". . . that in order to keep the legislative and judicial departments distinct, that the several Counties may not suffer through a delay of Justice, the Justices of the inferior Court of Common pleas Should be excluded from a Seat in the house of representatives and Senate; at least in the Senate."[66] Barnstable apparently had the same idea: ". . . that the Justices of the inferior Courts ought not to sit as Legislatures. . . ."[67] Grafton objected likewise "that all Justices out [sic] to be excluded having any hand in Legislation."[68]

Rehoboth, in rejecting the Constitution, stated among its objections: ". . . no Legelative officer to be an Judicial officer & no Judicial officer to be an Executive Officer etc. all which Objections & amendments we think Absolutely Necessary for Enjoying a free well Regulated Gover^t."[69] West Springfield voted for additional exclusions from a legislative seat "that no Minister of the Gospel, Judge of the Inferior Court or Justices of the Peace shall be a Member of the Senate Council or House of Representatives." The exclusion was necessary because of the separation of departments, as provided for in Article XXX of the Bill of Rights: "The Reason why we should have Judges of the Inferior Court & Justices of the Peace excluded is set forth in the 30th. Art. of the Bill of Rights."[70] The town of Norton voted on Article II, Chapter VI "that no Judge of the Admiralty or

---

65. *Ibid.*, pp. 79, 84. See p. 120 for return of Wrentham. Worcester favored the same exclusion.   66. *Ibid.*, p. 100.
67. *Ibid.*, p. 48.   68. *Ibid.*, p. 91.
69. *Ibid.*, CCLXXVI, 35. See also CCLXXVII, pp. 15, 117.
70. *Ibid.*, CCLXXVI, 71.

Judge of the Inferior Court should have a seat in the General Court. for reasons to us as obvious and as Just, as the Exclusion of many others in s^d Section."[71]

The members of the Board of War were suggested for exclusion from the legislature by Weymouth.[72] Many of the towns offering objections to the stated separation in office-holding suggested that ministers of the gospel should be excluded from the General Court. Their exemption from taxes was considered as disqualifying them as legislators, especially, it was stated, in matters of taxation. The political and religious offices were regarded as incompatible, and their union as presenting a possible inconvenience.[73]

Just because the provisions of the Constitution on the separation of departments were satisfactory to the great majority of the towns, there is very little contemporary comment in support of the provisions to be found in the newspapers or writings of the time. Among the few specific estimates to be found is the following statement of rationale in "Memoirs of the Revolution of Massachusetts-Bay," by Thomas Pemberton:

And to avoid the inconveniences of the old Constitution. of one man holding two offices at one. & the same time incompatible with each other, the bill of rights in a very explicit manner settles this matter in the 30th or last article "In the government of the commonwealth, The *legislative* department shall never exercise the executive and Judicial powers. or either of them. The *Executive* shall never exercise the legislative & judicial powers. or either

---

71. *Ibid.*, p. 34. 72. *Ibid.*, CCLXXVII, 80.
73. *Ibid.*, CCLXXVI, 49, 70; CCLXXVII, 5, 24, 70, 72, 78, 95. Ministers had been excluded from the General Court in the Constitution of 1778 (Article IV). An interesting comment on the opinion to exclude ministers was made by the Rev. Wm. Gordon: "But if the Convention meant to exclude them under the notion that, like the judges, secretary, etc. they are officers of the State, I must declare as to myself, in matters of religion, I call no authority on earth Lord and Master . . . I am not, nor ever will submit to be a *state minister.*" *Independent Chronicle,* April 9, 1778.

of them. The Judicial shall never exercise the legislative and executive powers or either of them, to the end it may be a government of laws, and not of men.[74]

In the "Commonplace Book" of John Metcalfe, also, is found a rough-hewn analysis of the separation of departments in the Constitution to the same import:

... the Constitution has Devided this Government officers into three Parts viz (1) the law makers that is the representatives & the Senators

(2) the Executors of those laws viz. The Governour the Sheriffs and all the Mellesha officers

(3) the Judges of the Superiour & Inferiour Courts & the Justices of Peace who are the Judges of the laws between man & man

And these three are Never to Interfeir withe one another that is they are not to act in any other Part, only in their own Part of the Buisness set to them to act.

therefore the Generall Court are never to execute the laws they make nor to Judge upon the Laws they make.

And the Governour the sheriffs nor the millisha officers are Never to be law makers nor Judges on the laws

Nither are any of the Judges of the Superiour or Inferior Courts nor the Justices of Peace Ever to be law makers or to Executors [sic] of the laws.

And if any towns ever chuse any of the Sheriffs or Judges of any of the Courts or any of the Justices of the Peace to be either Senators or Representatives, to Sett in Generall Court; the Senate & house of Representatives ought, When they are first forming them Selves, to reject all those so chosen as being uncostitunaly [sic] chosen.

And the Senate & house of Representatives ought in like maner & at the same time to reject every mellisha officer so chosen as being unconstitutionaly chosen.

And the General Court to send to such towns to chuse constitutionaly others in their Room.

74. Mass. Hist. Soc. MSS., II, 393.

... That the House of Representatives ought to reject out of their house & not allow a seat with them, every man that has a Commission as a Juditial officer or millitary officer unless he will utterly relinquish & totaly resign up his Commission.

... And the Senit ought as well as the Representatives to reject all such officers.[75]

The narrative leaves no doubt as to Metcalfe's attitude on a separation of departments, and of his understanding that the separation to be achieved by the Constitution was a separation in office-holding.

In the election sermons of the time, there is also some reflection on the principle of a separation of departments. Of relevance is the Election Sermon preached on May 30, 1781, to the Governor and General Court under the new Constitution, since it was preached by Jonas Clark, who had been the delegate from Lexington to the Convention, and who sat as a member of the committee on "Incompatibility and Exclusion" from offices. Discussing "disadjustment" of the parts of government, the Reverend Mr. Clark delivered the following warning against a "government of men":

It is of the highest importance to the well being of society, that every man, that all the members should know their place, and the duties of their station, in the Commonwealth, whether in authority, or subordination: And everything that tends to an alteration, or abridgment, of the powers of government, on the one hand, or of the rights of the people, on the other, should awaken the attention of both rulers and people, and put all upon their guard.

For instance: The compromise of *individuals*, the plans of a *junto*, the schemes of a *faction*, or the intrigues of a *court* for the disposal of offices or the obtaining elections, have a threatening aspect on the liberties of the people, the powers of government and the constitution itself.

75. Mass. Hist. Soc. MSS. (1787), pp. 48-50.

Such compromise and compact on the part of the first triumvirate was responsible for the fall of the Roman Republic and the usurpation of the government by Julius Caesar, Mr. Clark pointed out:

> In all such cases, therefore, *"Obsta Principiis,"* is a good maxim, and worthy the attention of all: And the first appearances of such baneful machinations should be beheld with abhorrence and check'd with severity, by all orders of men in a *free Commonwealth*, as they are friends to their country and wish to preserve the liberties of the people, the powers of government, or the rights of the constitution, inviolate to the State.[76]

Other ministers prayed over the separation of departments, sometimes becoming surprisingly eloquent. The Reverend Jonathan French, in delivering an election sermon at a later date, prayed as follows:

> May the various branches of the State and Federal governments, under the influence of the religion of Jesus, each in its proper sphere, like the various orbs above, keep their proper places and balances, the one never encroaching upon, or interfering with the other, move on in harmonious round till time shall be no more.[77]

The Reverend John Shipping Lathrop also called upon the Deity to supply a harmony to the departments of government which might be found wanting in practice, for in his book of prayers is to be found the following passage, in a "Fourth of July" prayer:

> To thee we commend the Governmt of this Common-Wealth, and pray, that while the several important Branches are kept destinct and independent of each other, they may support a good understanding, & always act in the most perfect harmony.[78]

---

76. Pp. 30-31.
77. Jonathan French, *A sermon preached before His Excellency, Samuel Adams . . . May 25, 1796*, p. 22.
78. Mass. Hist. Soc. MSS.

Achievement of a "Separation" of Departments

With those articles in the new Constitution providing for a separation of departments, then, there seems to have been general satisfaction. They were not slipped into the Constitution as an excursion into the field of political theory, though Article XXX of the Bill of Rights, taken alone, might give that impression. The practical provisions should be of greater significance than Article XXX, since they were a concrete application of its theory, the result of experience with a "government of men." The need of checks and a separation of departments had appeared not only in the mother country but in Massachusetts in the province period, as a protection against an administration the springs of which were largely beyond popular control, and also against the revolutionary statesmen who should have been subject to popular control. Not all of the members of the Constitutional Convention were impractical theorists. There were some who realized that governments are not made on paper.[79]

It is possible, too, that some people of the time even understood that a separation of departments might impede the processes of government: "This may indeed, in some instances, retard the operations of government, but will add dignity to its deliberate counsels, and weight to its dictates."[80] But they believed that a separation of departments was necessary as a protection of government for the benefit of all

---

[79] "The business of Government making however easy it may be esteem'd, or however plausible it may appear, I have long been of opinion is rarely if ever accomplish'd by consultation.—Governments make themselves or grow up out of the ground, that is, out of the Habits, the wants, the wishes of the People, & if all the Wise Men of the East, & of the South were to meet in the Center & form a system that other people would admire & lavishly extol, I suspect it would turn out like Shakespears. "baseless fabrick of a Vision." What then is to be done? blunder on—mend where we can, bear where we cannot—lose on this side—gain on that & leave to time, accident, or artifice the formation of a better plan." Judge Lowell to Benjamin Lincoln, Mass. Hist. Soc. MSS., p. 159, Nov. 20, 1782.

[80] Samuel Cooke, *A Sermon Preached at Cambridge, May 30, 1770*, pp. 9-10.

groups in the state, and to prevent government in the interests of any one group, or of a few. The aim they sought was stated to be "a government of laws, and not of men."

Indicative also of the interpretation of the separation of departments of government which the Constitution of 1780 set out to achieve should be the practice followed in government under the new Constitution. An examination of the records of the General Court for the years immediately succeeding the adoption of the new Constitution discloses a body exercising powers which the modern observer might classify as legislative, judicial, and executive as well, but which at that time there was little or no attempt to differentiate. The powers exercised by the General Court were undoubtedly those considered proper to such a body at the time. The General Court indeed occupied a position of such dominance in the government that it could accurately be described, as was the General Court of the seventeenth century in Massachusetts, in reflection of the English theory of parliamentary supremacy as "the chiefe civill power of the commonwealth."

Far from exercising powers merely legislative in the modern point of view, the General Court directly on the adoption of the new Constitution may be found acting as a high court of appeal from all other courts of the state, setting aside their decisions, awarding new trials, issuing directions to the Supreme Judicial Court respecting the disposition of cases and, on the other hand, ordering the appearance of individuals before it for examination, issuing writs for the apprehension of certain persons, and committing of them to jail with minute instructions for their custody.

The power of the General Court extended to granting a continuance in all actions scheduled for a certain session of an inferior court to a later session of the court "as if the same had been continued in due form of law."[81] The rec-

81. *Acts and Laws of the Commonwealth of Massachusetts* . . . *1780-81*, p. 457.

Achievement of a "Separation" of Departments 169

ords show the General Court authorizing the judges of the Supreme Judicial Court to grant a new trial to a felon convicted of theft some months before, if they should find "sufficient reason therefor," on the ground that since the trial he had found new evidence in his favor.[82] In a contract action pending in the Inferior Court of Common Pleas of Lincoln County for the purchase price of a sloop, which had been lost in government service before it was paid for, whence it was feared the owner would "be involved in ruinous circumstances, unless prevented by the equitable intervention of the Legislature," the General Court "directed" the justices by resolve to continue the action from term to term.[83] The privilege of the writ of habeas corpus was suspended when "expedient and necessary" by the General Court.[84] The General Court could also remove an action from one district of the Maritime Court to another.[85] Leave to appeal from an inferior court to a higher court might be granted by the General Court, in the meantime all process against the petitioner being "staid."[86]

The General Court could on petition grant a "rehearing" of an action which had already proceeded to judgment in a lower court, and the parties could be "admitted to the same pleadings and privilege, as by law they were entitled to previous to any judgment or process had thereon."[87]

The General Court could even permit a case which had been decided more than three years before by the highest court of the state to be reopened by "impowering" the petitioner to purchase a "writ of review" from the clerk of the Supreme Judicial Court, and to serve the adverse party with the writ and with a copy of the resolve of the General Court.[88]

Execution by the sheriff of its judgment might be directed

82. *Ibid.*, p. 339.
83. *Ibid.*, pp. 402-3.
84. *Ibid.*, 1782-3, pp. 6, 105.
85. *Ibid.*, 1780-1, pp. 813-14.
86. *Ibid.*, pp. 471-2.
87. *Ibid.*, p. 871.
88. *Ibid.*, p. 422.

by the General Court, as to apprehend a certain suspected Loyalist, who had been given leave to depart for New York some months before, but had not yet sailed, and to commit him to the county jail until he should depart from the state. And the keeper of the jail was directed to deprive the prisoner of the use of paper, pen and ink, and not to allow any writing to reach him except by express order of the selectmen of Cambridge.[89]

Too numerous for comment were the orders issued by the General Court for the administration of estates, appointing administrators and trustees and providing for sale of the property, with the most minute disposition of the proceeds such as giving the power to collect back rents and to lease.[90] Not only did the General Court review judicial action therefore, but it exercised original jurisdiction at its discretion. In a controversy between the House of Representatives and the Senate as to the meaning of the term "money-bills" in the Constitution, the judges of the Supreme Judicial Court were "directed" to deliver their opinions on the subject in writing to both houses of the General Court within two days' time.[91] The powers of the General Court were analogous to those of a high court of appeal, therefore, and they included supervision of the administration of justice in the state by and large.

But the judges of the Supreme Judicial Court were also "directed" to perform certain non-judicial functions, an important one being the determination of the value of the bills of public credit at least every three months (oftener if they thought necessary), but when the fluctuation rendered an adjustment "unfit," the General Court directed the judges to postpone their settlement of the value of the bills.[92] The judges were also appointed to adjust and liquidate the principal and interest due upon the depreciation notes given to

89. *Ibid.*, p. 264.
91. *Ibid.*, p. 289.
90. *Ibid.*, pp. 170, 173, 336.
92. *Ibid.*, p. 471.

Achievement of a "Separation" of Departments 171

the army, on the basis of the average price of certain commodities: "sheeps-wool, sole-leather, Indian-corn and beef," in different parts of the state.[93] The justices of the Court of General Sessions of the Peace of the counties of the Commonwealth drew up the estimates for the county budget, and apportioned payment on the towns after the passage of the budget by the General Court.[94]

In the direction and control which the General Court maintained over executive action the Court rivalled the Governor in occupying the position of chief executive, issuing directions to the Governor and Council, and to the other executive officers, implying that responsibility for their action lay to the General Court.

Thus the General Court by resolve empowered the Governor and Council to take up and pass upon all matters pending before the Council at the time when the new Constitution was adopted.[95] The General Court also set up a committee of both houses to consider the necessity of augmenting the powers of the Governor and Council in the recess of the Court, and on the basis of the report of the committee resolved that it was not necessary to augment those powers, beyond the powers delegated by the Constitution.[96]

However, a few months later the General Court "empowered" the Governor with the advice of Council to adopt such measures in the recess of the Court as he should find necessary for the defence of the eastern part of the Commonwealth. The Court granted a fund not to exceed six thousand dollars for the purpose, but requested the Governor "to give order that the account of the expenditure of the money . . . be laid before the General Court for examination."[97]

93. *Ibid.*, p. 324.
94. *Ibid.*, pp. 537-8.
95. *Ibid.*, p. 169.
96. *Ibid.*, p. 201.
97. *Ibid.*, p. 372.

In military matters the General Court kept control largely in its own hands, determined upon the action to be taken, then requesting the Governor to inform the officers in charge of the plans adopted. Thus the Governor was requested to inform the colonel in charge of the eastern part of the Commonwealth, that "measures are now adopting for the immediate defence of the Eastern parts of this Commonwealth," and that in the meantime, he "be directed to take the most effectual measures for the security of the provisions and stores at *Thomaston.*"[98]

Delegates to the United States Congress were elected by the two houses of the legislature jointly and were from time to time given instructions by the General Court.[99] The General Court directly elected a commissioner from Massachusetts to attend a conference with delegates from other states on the subject of supplies for the French army and navy, and gave him his instructions.[100] The Court was opposed to entering into a contract for the purpose, but if after conference and "the most mature deliberation" the commissioner was of the opinion that a contract would be for the interest of the Commonwealth, the commissioner was directed not to "engage in behalf of this Commonwealth in any contract for supplying them until you have laid the same before the General Court of said Commonwealth, for their approbation." The commissioner was empowered to deliberate on any other matter which the delegates considered would be for the public good, and to "lay an account of your proceedings before the General Court as soon as may be after your return."[101] The Governor was at times "requested" to inform other states of certain policies adopted by the General Court.[102]

Executive officers of the Commonwealth might be "directed" to take certain action.[103] Thus the Treasurer might

98. *Ibid.*, p. 349.
100. *Ibid.*, pp. 223, 475, 795-6.
102. *Ibid.*, p. 801.
99. *Ibid.*, p. 772.
101. *Ibid.*, pp. 223-224.
103. *Ibid.*, p. 426.

Achievement of a "Separation" of Departments

be directed to recall execution against a town for delinquency in military enlistments.[104] At times executive officers might be required not only to lay reports and accounts of their action before the General Court, but might be "directed to give their immediate attendance at the General Court" to give information regarding the conduct of their offices as the General Court thought necessary.[105]

The selectmen of various towns were notified to appear before the General Court at times, as when their towns were delinquent in paying their taxes, "to give their reasons, if any they have," for their neglect. The Treasurer might be "directed" at the same time to issue execution against the collectors.[106]

The General Court not only might "request" the Governor to take certain action, but might request that he act "with Advice of Council" and apparently this direction was carried out.[107] For example the General Court in one instance summoned citizens to appear before it "to Answer Certain Questions" and then requested the Governor "with Advice of Council" to lay these persons under "restrictions."[108]

The General Court also at times descended into the minutiae of administration. When the physician in charge of the State Hospital petitioned in respect to the patients in the Hospital, it was resolved that two of the patients, wounded in battle and out-patients of the Hospital, were no longer under his direction, and he was forbidden to allow them rations.[109] In response to a petition from two minor employees of the government, the General Court awarded each a "suit of cloathes."[110] As a result of another petition, the Treasurer was directed to exchange twenty dollars which had become defaced and unfit for circulation for the petitioner.[111]

The General Court therefore directed and controlled the

---

104. *Ibid.*, p. 872.
106. *Ibid.*, p. 451.
108. *Ibid.*, pp. 270, 363.
110. *Ibid.*, p. 355.
105. *Ibid.*, pp. 252, 255.
107. *Ibid.*, p. 334.
109. *Ibid.*, p. 234.
111. *Ibid.*, p. 135.

executive department of the government as thoroughly as it did the courts. That its powers were quite other than those of a merely legislative body is obvious.[112] The General Court maintained a status of supremacy over the other departments of government and the ultimate responsibility of the General Court for the conduct of government was implicit in the acts of the Court. This was the concept of the General Court which was followed in practice immediately after the adoption of the Constitution of 1780, rather than that of a department of government separated as to powers from the judicial and executive departments.

The form which the separation of departments assumed in the Massachusetts Constitution of 1780 was far from being a complete separation. It was principally a separation in the holding of offices in the various departments. Nor was the separation in office-holding made absolute by the Constitution of 1780, although it did curtail plural office-holding by all more important officers of government. There was only attempt to carry separation so far as to prevent the possibility of any man, or any group in the state, gaining so much power as to threaten the commonwealth with a tyranny. Independence of the departments from control or influence by each other secured by provisions which followed the English statutes and common law was the aim of the Constitution makers. Nothing so theoretical as an analysis and separation of three different types of power was attempted by the Convention of 1780, and the actual powers of government were left very largely where they had been under the province Charter. Far from being a failure or "impossible of execution," therefore, the separation in office-holding which the framers of the Massachusetts Constitution established was so completely successful that plural office-holding called for very little regulation thereafter in the state.

112. E. S. Corwin, Marbury v. Madison and the Doctrine of Judicial Review, XII, *Michigan Law Review*, 256.

Achievement of a "Separation" of Departments 175

The provisions against plural office-holding, particularly those which excluded important executive officers, the Secretary, the Attorney-General, the Solicitor-General, the Treasurer, from holding a seat in the General Court, might be the subject of criticism by advocates of a "Cabinet" system. To such critics it should be pointed out, however, that the Governor and Lieutenant-Governor of the Commonwealth were not among the officers excluded from the General Court; in fact they were carefully omitted from the exclusion. The provision which restricted plural office-holding by the Governor and Lieutenant-Governor was a general one: "any other office or place under the authority of this Commonwealth" and in the usage of the time, a "seat" in the legislature was not an "office," though it was a "place." Generally both terms were reserved for executive and judicial offices or appointments only. In view of the very specific provision listing every officer who was to be excluded from the General Court, it would seem that the general statement on the separation of departments in Article XXX and that of Article II of Chapter VI would not prevail to exclude the Governor and Lieutenant-Governor, by the principle of legal interpretation that specific provision prevails over the general.

Rather it was perhaps the innovation of popular election by the voters of the Governor (although not of the Lieutenant-Governor), together with the provincial tradition of an independent Governor, which thwarted the development of a "Cabinet" system in Massachusetts, and not the provisions for a separation of departments. In practice the Governor and Lieutenant-Governor did not run for seats in the legislature, although constitutionally, there was nothing to prevent their doing so nor to prevent a legislative leader from being a candidate for the Governorship. But a Governor who proved to be independent of the General Court for office could scarcely be held responsible for policy by the

General Court. The Lieutenant-Governor, however, was dependent on the General Court for election.

In this connection, it may be pointed out that the Governor's Council which was designed to act as part of the executive branch of the government, was to be chosen by the two houses of the legislature from the members of the Senate, the councillors thereupon vacating their seats in the Senate. This method of constitution of the Council should have furnished an indirect control over the executive by the General Court. In practice, however, the above method of selection of the Council fell into disuse because Senators declined to give up their seats for Council membership, and councillors came to be elected at large, and thus possible connection between legislature and executive disintegrated.[113]

The exclusion of judges from the General Court was a reform much needed in Massachusetts on the basis of experience. The principle of independence of the judiciary is now so universally accepted that this provision needs no defense. It might be pointed out, however, that even in respect to the justices the exclusion was not complete, only the judges of the Supreme Judicial Court and judges of probate being excluded from seats in the General Court. That a further exclusion of judges from the Legislature would have been desirable would no doubt be the point of view of a modern critic, and was indeed the opinion of many at the time.

As to the abolition of plural office-holding in general, it must be regarded as a very necessary reform. Apart from the fact that the custom lent itself to the destruction of integrity in political life and as well to neglect of the public service, it was a formidable obstacle to popular control of the government, either in a legislative, judicial, or executive capacity. Of little avail was selection of the Governor's

---

113. *Journal of the Debates and Proceedings in the Convention of Delegates, chosen to revise the Constitution of Massachusetts, 1820*, pp. 76-77.

Achievement of a "Separation" of Departments 177

Council by the two houses of the General Court, if councillors could be reduced to compliance with a policy objectionable to the people of Massachusetts by having further offices or appointments conferred upon them. Nor could the impartial administration of justice be expected of judges who sat to advise and be advised by the Governor in his Council, who assisted in the making of laws in the General Court which they were later to apply in the courts. The principle that the holding of incompatible offices was contrary to the public welfare had been stated by Sir Edward Coke, but derived from a much earlier period.

Of vital importance, moreover, from the point of view of the people of Massachusetts was the safeguarding of the independence of the House of Representatives against corruption and executive influence through the use of patronage, because it was only through this body that the people had been able to maintain indispensable checks over the province government. Subject to a Governor appointed by the British government, they could not hope to control executive policy, but through a series of governmental checks staunchly premised and maintained by the House, they struggled to prevent the government from pursuing a policy detrimental to their interests. The value of checks and balances in the province organization rested upon this division of interests, one part of the government being representative of the people, another part, the Governor, representing an interest alien and at times directly opposed to their purposes, which could not be controlled, but only checked, in the public interest.

The very limited experience which the Provincial Congresses furnished to Massachusetts of a government responsible to the people in its various departments did not reassure them as to absence of necessity of provisions for checks in government and for a separation of departments. The prevalence of plural office-holding among members of the Provincial

Congresses only confirmed the need for solid reform in this direction. The separation of departments set up by the Constitution of 1780 was not an end in itself, but merely the means to make the checks and balances effective, by which the constitutional statesmen hoped to attain government under the control of the people and in the public interest: a "government of laws" as they expressed the purpose themselves. Their much-criticized "checks and balances" were thus one step in the direction of democracy.

The separation of departments which the Massachusetts statesmen established to achieve this end must be characterized as exceedingly moderate and, from the persistence of the debates, they can scarcely have regarded the provisions as final. The problem of a separation of departments in the Massachusetts of 1780 was a question of how much and what separation, not whether there should be a separation. Regarding the necessity of a separation, there could be no difference of opinion, either in the eighteenth century or now. And the measure of separation which the framers used in the Massachusetts Constitution—as much separation of departments as experience showed to be necessary to secure government in the public interest—" a government of laws"—is as valid today as it was in 1780.

APPENDICES

Appendix I

1. Hutchinson's Report to a Committee of the House of Representatives, the date of which it seems was December 27, 1765, gave some interesting details regarding the circuit:
"The last year they were pleased to make me a grant of Forty pounds a motion for which in each of the three preceding years had been rejected. Our attendance upon the courts takes about six months in the year, our travel is about eight hundred miles our fees communibus annis for three years from 1761 were short of forty pounds a year, each justice, according to the best computation I can make. My expenses in travelling, including my horses servant & equipment of every sort I estimate one hundred pounds a year so that the nett profits from my place of chief justice the three first years was about ninety to one hundred pounds each year. The last year as I have observed was forty pounds more. The fees of that year were more than the preceding perhaps eight or ten pounds."[1]

2. John Adams' comment on plural office-holding by the Lieutenant-Governor and his connections is worthy of quotation:
"Has not his Honor the Lieutenant-Governor discovered to the people, in innumerable instances, a very ambitious and avaricious disposition? Has he not grasped four of the most important offices in the Province into his own hands? Has not his brother-in-law, Oliver, another of the greatest places in government? Is not a brother of the Secretary, a judge of the superior court? Has not that brother a son in the House? Has not the Secretary a son in the House, who is also a judge in one of the counties? Did not that son marry the daughter of another of the Judges of the Superior Court? Has not the Lieutenant-

[1] Mass. State Archives, XXV, 23, Dec. 27, 1765 [?]; *ibid.*, XXVI, 277; see *ibid.*, CXXI, 427, stating that a Superior Court judge travelled 1,134 miles in one year.

Governor a brother, a Judge of the pleas in Boston, and a namesake and near relation who is another Judge? Has not the Lieutenant-Governor a near relation who is register of his own court of probate, and deputy secretary? Has he not another near relation who is Clerk of the House of Representatives? Is not this amazing ascendency of one family foundation sufficient on which to erect a tyranny? Is it not enough to excite jealousies among the people?"[2]

Regarding the family ties after Hutchinson became Governor, Samuel Adams wrote as follows:

"You will not then be surprisd if I tell you that among the five Judges of our Superior Court of Justice, there are the following near Connections with the first & second in Station in the province. Mr Lynde is Chiefe Justice; his Daughter is married to the Son of Mr Oliver, the Lt Govr; Mr Oliver another of the Judges is his Brother; his Son married Gov Hutchinsons Daughter; & Judge Hutchinson lately appointed, who is also Judge of the probate of Wills for the first County, an important department, is the Gov^{rs} brother. Besides which the young Mr Oliver is a Justice of the Common pleas for the County of Essex. Mr Cotton a Brother in Law of the Govr is deputy Secretary of the province & Register in the probate office under Mr Hutchinson; a cousin german of the Govr was sent for out of another province to fill up the place of Clerk to the Common please in this County;—I should have first mentioned that the Govr and Lt Govr are Brothers by Marriage."[3]

APPENDIX II

1. Thacher considered first the incompatibility of the office of judge and the seat of a councillor:

"It is obvious that the attendance on the circuit, and that upon the council are incompatible. Even when the superior court sits in Boston, and the general court at the same time in the same place; it is not possible for those gentlemen to give the needful attendance at both courts. But when they are on the more dis-

---

2. John Adams, *Life and Works*, II, 150. Diary, Aug. 15, 1765.
3. Cushing, *Writings of Samuel Adams*, II, 265-6. Oct. 31, 1771.

tant parts of their circuit, they must be totally absent from one or other. Thus the public is deprived either of a counsellor or a judge, in whose attendance they are interested.[1]

2. "Another reason against the choice of those Gentlemen, is, that they are paid a salary by the province in order that they may leave all other business and engagements, and devote themselves wholly to the study of the laws. Every individual hath an interest that the law should be equally administred; and that those to whom the administration thereof is trusted, should be in the best manner qualified. Now to take off their attention for so great a part of the year as the General Assembly sits, from so important a study, to engage it in political disputes, and to oblige them to shorten the work of their judicial courts, that they may attend the Council, Is it not destroying with one hand the good done by the other? The gaining a skill in the laws sufficient to qualify a man for the important station of Judge, where the properties, the liberties, and often the lives of the King's subjects are nearly concerned. And the rightly discharging so important a function, when a man is vested with the office, is as much as can be expected from any one man, unless his powers and capacities greatly exceed those of all other mortals. The rightly understanding the political interest of a people, and pursuing it in the various matters which come under the consideration of a General Court, this is another branch of skill quite distinct from the former, and no meer man since the fall, ever excelled in both.[2]

3. "Let the government for instance be democratical, and let all the offices which are usually and by the constitution delegated to many different persons, meet and center in a few, and the same persons they become tyrants. The ancient forms of liberty may be preserved, but the substance is gone.

"Every body must see, that where the whole legislative, and whole executive powers are vested in the same individuals, their power is uncontrolable. This it is confessed is not the case in the instance before us, for-as-much as the judges have many their equals in the legislative, while the whole executive may be said

[1]. *Considerations on the Election of Councellors Humbly Offered to the Electors*, pp. 4-5. Reprinted in the *Boston Gazette*, April 26, 1762.
[2]. *Ibid.*

to be lodged in them. Yet let it be considered, whether it verges toward that fatal point."

4. Thacher's explanation of the incompatibility of the judicial and legislative offices:

"Add to the above considerations, that there are many instances wherein the offices and trusts aforesaid interfere with each other. One only shall be here mentioned. Every body knows it is the part of a judge to receive no information but in court. Should he hear one party out of court on the merits of his cause, none would imagine he acted as became an upright judge. . . .

"Now it frequently happens, that prosecutions are ordered by the general court in cases of public frauds, that affect the provincial revenue, previous to the ordering which prosecutions, the subject matter of the frauds ought to be, and always is, discussed by the court who orders the prosecution. Suppose now the judges members of this court, what are they to do? are they to hear this matter, and give their opinion whether an action lays or not? if they do, and enter largely into the debates in the first instance, how shall they afterwards judge in their judicial capacity? Suppose them, on the other hand, most mindful of their sacred trust, retiring wholly from the general court whenever these debates are started, then the province is deprived of its five ablest counsellors in a matter where it needeth the best assistance. . . ."

5. Otis set forth that the British Constitution, by the best opinion, established:

"a *mixed monarchy*, or a composite of the three famous kinds, viz. of *monarchy*, supplied by the King, *aristocracy*, supplied by the lords, and of *democracy*, supplied by the commons."

Otis gave his opinion that:

"This when the checks and ballances are preserved, is perhaps the most perfect form of government, that in its present depraved state, human nature is capable of. It is a fundamental maxim in such a government, to keep the legislative, and executive powers, separate. When these powers are in the same hands, such a government is hastening fast to its ruin, and the mischiefs and miseries that must happen before that fatal period, will be as bad as those felt in the most absolute monarchy."

Appendices

6. "By the demise of the king, all civil as well as military commissions must be renewed. . . . When he came to settle the county of Barnstable, where the speaker (Col. Otis) lived, he made him an offer of taking to himself the principal offices in the county, and of naming many of his relations and friends to other offices; and the whole county was settled to his mind. He took for himself the place of first justice of the county court of common pleas, and also that of judge of probate, which gives much weight and influence in the county."

Hutchinson goes on to say:

"Mr. Otis, the son, soon after appeared in favour of a grant, made by the assembly to the governor, of the island of Mount Desert; and there was the appearance of reconciliation. It lasted but a short time. Places granted by a Massachusetts governor could not be taken away again at pleasure, except places in the militia, which were not much valued, after the title and rank derived from them, were once acquired."[3]

7. Otis' comment referring to the English practice of multiple office-holding was as follows:

"I am so unfashionable as to be of Opinion, that any Gentleman who accepts of a Place while he is a Representative, deserves to be branded with a Degree of Infamy, and disqualified from ever serving afterwards; at least, he should be sent home again, as such are from the House of Commons in Great Britain, in order to see if a Town will re-elect a Man who in all Probability has carried his Constituents to Market. If this were the Fate of all who lift their Hands at the Beck of Power, we should not see so many selling their Votes and their Country for a Feather, . . ."[4]

8. "I never heard any man contend that he should be deprived of his office of Chief Justice, or of his place of Lt. Governor, which I think are enough for any gentleman to hold. The office of judge of probate is incompatible with that of chief justice; and the commission for the latter, is in law a *supersedeas* of the former. So is the commission to be judge of the Superior Court, to that for the admiralty. And all acts & decrees made below after

3. Hutchinson, *History*, III, 95-96.
4. *Boston Gazette*, April 4, 1763.

such superior commission, are illegal and void. There is no point of law clearer than this. If the salaries and perquisites of the chief justice will not maintain him with dignity, I am for his having more pay, not more offices and power. I have always contended for this in the House, and ever shall while I have the honour of a seat there. I have long tho't it, and am far from being singular in my opinion, a great grievance, that the chief justice should have a seat in the council; and consequently so great a share of influence in making those very laws he is appointed to execute upon the lives and property of the people. But this opinion affects all the judges of the superior court, and can't therefore be founded on any particular prejudice to his Honor."[5]

9. "T. Q." [Thacher] maintained that the necessity of separation would depend upon the importance of the offices concerned:

". . . But it cannot be thought that so much is to be apprehended, from justices of the peace, who are confin'd within their own county, and to matters of *little* importance; whose influence therefore must be *inconsiderable:* as from judges of the land whose authority runs from county to county, whose influence spreads over the whole province, and upon whose decisions depend fortune, liberty and life."

Appendix III

1. "That you use ye whole of your Influence and Endeavour that no Person Holding any fee or millitary office whatsoever Especially Judges of ye Superior Court Judges of ye Probate Register of Probate Secretary Cler of Either of ye Courts Sheriffs or Province Treasurer be Chosen into his majestys Council of this Province and that you attend at ye Election of Councellors and give your vote accordingly."[1]

2. The House declared:

"We are wholly at a Loss to conceive how a full, free and fair Election can be called 'an Attack upon the Government in Form,' 'a professed Intention to deprive it of its best and most

5. *Boston Gazette*, April 11, 1763.
1. *Worcester Town Records*, IV, 138-9 (1753-83).

able Servants,' 'an ill-judged and ill-timed Oppugnation of the King's Authority.' These, May it please your Excellency, are high and grievous Charges against the two Houses, and such as we humbly conceive, no crowned Head since the Revolution has thought fit to bring against two Houses of Parliament."[2]

3. "We have releas'd those of the Judges of the Superiour Court who had the Honor of a Seat at the Board, from the Cares and Perplexities of Politicks, and given them Opportunity to make still farther Advances in the Knowledge of the Law, and to administer Right and Justice within this Jurisdiction: We have also left other Gentlemen more at Leasure to discharge the Duties and Functions of their important Offices. This surely is not to deprive the Government of its best and ablest Servants, nor can it be called an Oppugnation of any Thing, but a dangerous Union of Legislative, and Executive Power in the same Persons; a Grievance long complained of by our Constituents, and the Redress of which some of us had special Instruction, to endeavour at this very Election to obtain."[3]

4. ". . . no unprovoked asperity of Expression on the part of your Excellency can deter us from asserting our undoubted Charter Rights and Privileges. One of the principal of those is that of annually chusing his Majesty's Council for this Province, . . . nor can we on the strictest Examination of the Transactions of the Day of our General Election, so far as the House was concerned, discover the least Reason for Regret. . . . So long as we shall have our Charter Privileges continued, we must think ourselves inexcusable, if we should suffer ourselves to be intimidated in the free Exercise of them. . . .

". . . Least we should be at a Loss for the *Proceedings* and Transactions which have given your Excellency so much uneasiness, you have been pleased to inform us in express Terms, that you *mean the excluding from the King's Council the principal Crown Officers* . . . Had Your Excellency thought fit to have favour'd us with your Sentiments and Opinion of the Candidates previously to the Election, it could not have more arrested our

2. *Journal of the House*, 1766, p. 26.
3. *Ibid.*, pp. 26-27.

Attention as a Breach of our Privileges; and it would surely be as proper to give Intimations of this Kind before as now the Business is past a Remedy, for this Year at least. The Assembly of another Year will act for themselves, or under such Influence and Direction as they may think fit. The two Crown Officers who were of the Honourable Board the last Year, and not chosen this, are the Lieutenant Governor and Secretary. The other Gentlemen of the Board last Year who are not chosen this, hold only Provincial Commissions. This Province has subsisted and flourished, and the Administration of Government has been carried on here intirely to the Royal Approbation, when no Crown Officers had a Seat at the Board, and we trust this may be the Case again."[4]

5. "We cannot persuade ourselves that *it must and will be understood that those Gentlemen were turned out*, as your Excellency is pleased to express it, *for their Deference to Acts of the British Legislature*. We have given the true Reason of this Proceeding in our Answer to your Excellency's first Speech of this Session. . . .

"Your Excellency says, *it is impossible to give any tolerable colouring to this Proceeding*. The Integrity and uprightness of our Intentions and Conduct is such that no colouring is requisite, and therefore we shall excuse ourselves from attempting any."[5]

6. "Had your Excellency been pleased in Season to have favoured us with a List and positive Orders whom to chuse, we should on your Principles have been without Excuse. But even the most abject Slaves are not to be blamed for Disobeying their Masters will and Pleasure when it is wholly unknown to them. . . .

"As dear to us as our Charter is, we should think it of very little Value, if it should be adjudged that the Sense and Spirit of it require the Electors should be under the absolute Direction and Controul of the Chair even in giving their Suffrages. For whatever may be our Ideas of the Wisdom, Prudence, Mildness, and Moderation of your Administration, of your forgiving Spirit, yet we are not sure your Successor will possess those shining Virtues.

". . . Your Excellency has intimated your Readiness to concur

4. *Ibid.*, pp. 42-43.　　　　5. *Ibid.*, p. 43.

with us in any Palliative or Expedient *to prevent the bad Effects of our Elections, which you think must surely be very hurtful to the Province, if it should be maintained and vindicated.* But as we are under no Apprehensions of any such Effects, especially when we reflect on the Ability and Integrity of the Council your Excellency has approved of, we beg Leave to excuse ourselves from any unnecessary Search after Palliatives or Expedients."[6]

7. The resolution read: "That when his Honor first took the Place of President of the Board, it was determined by the Resolution of the Board at that Time, after searching the Books for Precedents in the like Cases: And it was declared by some Gentlemen who were then present, that the Motion was made, and the Question determined by the Board, the Lieutenant-Governor himself being altogether silent on the Occasion."[7]

8. "This being a Matter of Law,—unless the Title can be supported by Charter, or the Laws of the Province, it is at least dubious. Now there is nothing in either that entitles a Lieutenant Governor to a Seat at the Board, much less to the Presidency. There is nothing in the Usage of our Ancestors that gives him a Right as Lieut. Governor, to any Place at the Board. . . ."[8]

9. The House explained their action in the elections to the Earl of Hillsborough, early in 1768:

"That the non-election of several gentlemen of distinguished character and station, was by no means the effect of party prejudice, private resentment, or motives still more blameable: but the result of calm reflection upon the danger that might accrue to our excellent constitution, and the Liberties of the people, from too great a union of the legislative, executive and judiciary powers of government, which in the opinion of the greatest writers, ought always to be kept separate: Nor was this a new opinion, formed at a certain period; but it has been the prevailing sentiment of many of the most sensible and unexceptionable gentlemen in the province, for many years past; upon principles, which your Lordship's thorough knowledge of the constitution, and the just balance of the several powers of government, this House is assured, will justify."[9]

6. *Ibid.*, pp. 44-45.   7. *Boston Gazette*, Feb. 3, 1766.   8. *Ibid.*
9. *Journal of the House*, 1767-8, Appendix, p. 24.   Feb. 22, 1768.

10. The use of a "select" Council in Massachusetts was described by Samuel Adams:

". . . it has been the practice of the Governor to summon a general Council at the Time when the Assembly is sitting & of Course the whole Number of Councillors is present—but in their Capacity of Advisers to the Governor they are adjournd from week to week during the Session of the Assembly & till it is over when the Country Gentlemen Members of Council return home. Thus the general Council being kept alive by Adjournments, the principal & most important part of the Business of their executive department is done by seven or eight who live in & about the Town, & if the Governor can manage a Majority of so small a Number, Matters will be conducted according to his mind. I believe I may safely affirm that by far the greater Number of civil officers have been appointed at these adjournments; so that it is much the same as if they were appointed solely by our ostensible Governor or rather by his Master, the Minister for the time being."[10]

Appendix IV

1. "You are therefore to Endeavor that an act be passed that when ever any member of the legislative be apponted to & accepts of an executive office he shall be debared a seat in the legislative until he shall be rechosen, and that his Constituents shall be forthwith served with a precept to choose some suitable person to represent them."[1]

2. Enoch Freeman had the same several judicial appointments in Cumberland County; Jedediah Foster[2] received them in Worcester County; William Sever had the same appointments in Plymouth County. Benjamin Greenleaf was given these offices in Essex County. Moses Gill was made Justice of the Peace and of the Quorum, and Justice of the Pleas for Worcester

10. Cushing, *Writings of S. Adams*, II, 265. To A. Lee, Oct. 31, 1775. *Boston Gazette*, Nov. 11, 1771. "Fidelis."
1. Worcester Papers, MS. I, 38. July 14, 1775.
2. Foster was appointed to the Superior Court, on March 20, 1776. He then resigned as Judge of Probate for Worcester County. Mass. State Archives, Council Records, March 16-May 13, 1776, p. 10.

County, and Justice throughout the "Colony." Benjamin Chadbourne had the same offices for York County; Caleb Cushing had them for Essex County; Walter Spooner for Bristol County. John Winthrop was Justice of the Peace and of the Quorum for Middlesex County, Justice of Probate for Middlesex, and Justice throughout the "Colony." Benjamin Lincoln was Justice of the Peace and of the Quorum, and Special Justice of the Pleas for Suffolk County, and Justice throughout the "Colony"; Joseph Palmer had the same appointments in Suffolk County; Samuel Holton had them in Essex County. James Prescott held an unusual combination of commissions: Sheriff, and Justice of the Peace for Middlesex County. Michael Farley was rewarded with the commission of Sheriff in Essex County.

3. The instructions of the town of Boston to its representatives in 1776, asking for a self-denying ordinance:

" 'Tis essential to Liberty, that the legislative, judicial and executive Powers of Government, be, as nearly as possible, independant of, and separate from each other; for where they are united in the same Persons, or Number of Persons, there would be wanting that mutual Check which is the principal Security against the making of arbitrary Laws, and a wanton Exercise of Power in the Execution of them."

The representatives were therefore instructed:

"to procure the enacting such Law or Laws, as shall make it incompatible for the same Person to hold a Seat in the legislative and executive Departments of Government at one and the same Time: . . . And to prevent the Multiplicity of Offices in the same Person, that such Salaries be settled upon them, as will place them above the Necessity of stooping to any indirect or collateral Means for Subsistance."[3]

APPENDIX V

1. "Liberty, therefore, is too imperfectly defined when it is said to be 'a government by *laws*, and not by *men*.' If the laws are made by one man, or a junto of men in a state, and not by *common consent*, a government by them does not differ from

3. *New-England Chronicle*, May 30, 1776; *Boston Gazette*, June 10, 1776.

slavery. In this case it would be a contradiction in terms to say that the state governs itself.

"And such constitution ought to be . . . a foundation built on a rock, which as either the efforts of tyranny or tyrants, with all their blasts and storms of power, may never be able to throw down; . . . to this end the several branches of delegated power ought to be kept in seperate and distinct departments, and as near as possible, independent of each other. For if those branches of delegated power are suffered to unite, human nature is such, that they will soon be able to rob the body politic of its supremacy."[1]

2. ". . . the following officers and persons be excluded from a seat in either House of Assembly, besides the Judges of the Superior Court, viz.
The Judges of the Inferior Court.
Judges of the Maritime Court.
Judges of Probate.
Sheriffs, commonly called High Sheriffs.
Attorney General.
Solicitor General.
Register of Deeds.
Register of Probate.
Clerk of the House of Representatives.
Secretary.
Treasurer or Receiver General.
Commissary General.
Officers of the Customs or Excise, including in this description, Naval Officers.
Militia Officers, while in the pay of this Commonwealth, the United States, or any other State or Government.
President, Professors, Tutors and Instructors, of Harvard College.
Ordained or settled Ministers of the Gospel."[2]

1. R. Price, *Observations on the Nature of Civil Liberty.* Commented upon in John Adams, *Life and Works*, IV, 401-2.
2. *Journal of the Constitutional Convention*, p. 81.

BIBLIOGRAPHY

I. Manuscripts

Adams, John. Letters to William Tudor, 1774-1801. Tudor Papers, Massachusetts Historical Society.
Bangs, Benjamin. Diary, 1742-65. Mass. Hist. Soc.
Bernard, Sir Francis. Papers. 13 vols. Sparks Collection, Houghton Library, Harvard College.
Bollan, William. MS. copy of Memorandum in the British Museum, Additional MSS. 32, 974, fo. 368. Mass. Hist. Soc. Misc. MSS.
Hollis, Thomas. Hollis Papers, 1759-71. Mass. Hist. Soc.
Hutchinson, Thomas. Hutchinson Correspondence, 1761-70. Mass. State Archives, XXV-XXVII.
Instructions to Royal Governors. Frederick L. Gay Transcripts. State Papers, 1662-1776, 13 vols. Mass. Hist. Soc.
Lathrop, Rev. John S. A Fourth of July Prayer. 100 Sermons, etc. n.d. Mass. Hist. Soc.
Lowell, John. Letter to Benjamin Lincoln, Nov. 20, 1782. Mass. Hist. Soc.
Massachusetts State Archives. 326 vols.
Mather, Rev. Samuel. Letters from Rev. Samuel Mather to his Son, 1759-84.
Metcalf, John. Commonplace Book, 1730-90. Mass. Hist. Soc.
Oliver, Andrew. Letter Book, Oct. 20, 1767-Nov. 20, 1774. 2 vols. Frederick L. Gay Transcripts. Mass. Hist. Soc.
———. Letters, 1745-70. Mass. Hist. Soc.
Paxton, Charles. Letter to Lord Townsend, Nov. 6, 1769. Misc. Papers, Mass. Hist. Soc.
Pemberton, Thomas. Memoirs of the Revolution of Massachusetts Bay. 2 vols. Mass. Hist. Soc.
Pickering, John. Journal. Essex Institute, Salem, Mass.
Report of a Committee of Convention, of a Form of Government for the State of the Massachusetts-Bay. Published for the In-

Bibliography

spection and Perusal of the Members, Dec. 11, 1777. Sparks MSS., XLIX, Houghton Library, Harvard College.

Thacher, Oxenbridge. Papers, 1762-65. Mass. Hist. Soc.

———. Memoranda.

———. Letter to the Provincial Agent at London, 1764.

———. Address to the King and Parliament, 1764. (Rough draft, not accepted.) Mass. Hist. Soc.

Williams, Israel. Letters, 1748-80. Mass. Hist. Soc.

Worcester Papers. American Antiquarian Society MSS., Worcester, Mass.

II. PUBLISHED WORKS

A. Newspapers

Boston Evening-Post, Boston, 1736-84.
Boston Gazette, Boston, 1719-90.
Boston News-Letter, Boston, 1704-76.
Boston Weekly Post-Boy, Boston, 1735-75.
Continental Journal, 1776-87.
The Essex Gazette, Salem, 1768-75.
Essex Journal, Newburyport, 1773-77.
The Independent Advertiser, Boston, 1748-49.
The Independent Ledger, Boston, 1778-86.
Massachusetts Gazette, Boston, 1768-87.
Massachusetts Spy, Boston, 1770-75; Worcester, 1775-83.
New-England Chronicle (Independent Chronicle), Cambridge and Boston, 1775-80.

B. Books, Pamphlets, and Articles

Acherly, Roger. *The Britannic Constitution, or The Fundamental Form of Government in Britain.* London, 1741.

Adams, John. *A Defence of the Constitutions of Government of the United States of America.* 3 vols. Philadelphia, 1797.

———. *History of the Dispute with America.* London, 1784.

———. *The Works of John Adams, with a Life of the Author by his Grandson, Charles Francis Adams.* 10 vols. Boston, 1850-56.

Bibliography

Adams, R. G. *Political Ideas of the American Revolution.* Durham, N. C., 1922.
Addison, Joseph. *The Free-holder or Political essays* (periodical). London, 1716.
American Historical Association. *Report.* Governors' Commissions, 1911.
Anonymous. *The Constitutional Advocate.* London, 1776.
Anson, Sir Wm. R. *The Law and Custom of the Constitution.* 3 vols. Oxford, 1922.
Ayer, M. F. *Check-List of Boston Newspapers, 1704-1780.* Publications of the Colonial Soc. of Mass., *Collections*, IX. Boston, 1907.
Bacon, Matthew. *A New Abridgment of the Law.* 3 vols. London, 1768.
Bates, Henry M. "Trends in American Government." *Proceedings*, California State Bar, 1932.
Beard, C. A. and William. *The American Leviathan.* New York, 1930.
Becker, Carl. "Samuel Adams," in *Dictionary of American Biography.* New York, 1928.
Belcher Papers. *Collections* of the Massachusetts Historical Society, 6th Series, Vols. VI and VII. Boston, 1893, 1894.
Bernard, Sir Francis. *Select Letters on the Trade and Government of America.* London, 1774.
———. *Letters to the Ministry.* Boston, 1769.
Blackstone, Sir William. *Commentaries on the Laws of England.* 2 vols. London, 1765-69.
Bland, Richard. *An Enquiry into the Rights of the British Colonies.* London, 1769.
Blauvelt, Mary T. *The Development of Cabinet Government in England.* New York, 1902.
Bolingbroke, Henry St. John, first Viscount. *Works.* 5 vols. London, 1754.
Bondy, Wm. *The Separation of Governmental Powers in History, in Theory, and in the Constitutions.* New York, 1896.
Bowdoin, James. *Bowdoin and Temple Papers. Mass. Hist. Soc. Coll.*, 6th Series, Vol. IX, 7th Series, Vol. VI, Boston, 1897, 1907.

Bowen, Francis. *Life of James Otis.* (In the *Library of American Biography*, conducted by Jared Sparks, 2nd Series, Vol. II.) Boston, 1844.

Brennan, Ellen E. "The Massachusetts Council of the Magistrates." *New England Quarterly*, IV, Jan., 1931.

Brigham, Clarence S. *Bibliography of American Newspapers*, Part IV. *Proceedings*, American Antiquarian Society, 2nd Series, Vol. XXV. Worcester, Mass., 1915.

Burke, Edmund. *An Appeal from the New to the Old Whigs.* London, 1791.

———. *Thoughts on the Cause of the Present Discontents.* 2nd edition. London, 1770.

Burns, John F. *Controversies Between Royal Governors and Their Assemblies.* Boston, 1923.

Cam, Helen M. and Turberville, A. S. *Bibliography of English Constitutional History.* London, 1929.

Carpenter, W. S. *The Development of American Political Thought.* Princeton, 1930.

Cattelain, Fernand. *Étude sur l'influence de Montesquieu dans les constitutions Américaines.* Besançon, 1927.

Chalmers, George. *Opinions of Eminent Lawyers, on Various Points of English Jurisprudence, Chiefly Concerning the Colonies.* 2 vols. London, 1814.

———. *An Introduction to the History of the Revolt of the American Colonies.* 2 vols. Boston, 1845.

Chamberlain, Mellen. *John Adams, the Statesman of the American Revolution.* Boston, 1884.

Clark, Jonas. *A Sermon Preached Before His Excellency ... May 30, 1781.* Boston, 1781.

Cobbett, Wm. *Parliamentary History of England.* 36 vols. London, 1806-20.

Coke, Sir Edward. *The Fourth Part of the Institutes of the Laws of England.* London, 1644, 1781.

Constitutions of the States and the United States, Vol. III. New York State Constitutional Convention Committee, Albany, 1938.

Cooke, Samuel. *A Sermon Preached at Cambridge, May 30, 1770.* Boston, 1770.

Coolidge, A. C. *Theoretical and Foreign Elements in the Formation of the American Constitution.* Freiburg, 1892.

Cooper, Samuel. "Letters to Thomas Pownall, 1770." *American Historical Review*, VIII, 301-330.

Coxe, Wm. *Memoirs of the Life and Administration of Sir Robert Walpole.* 3 vols. London, 1800.

Curwen, Samuel. *Journal and Letters, 1775-1783.* Boston, 1864.

Cushing, Harry A. *History of the Transition from Provincial to Commonwealth Government in Massachusetts.* New York, 1896.

———. *Political Activity of Massachusetts Towns During the Revolution.* Am. Hist. Ass'n. *Report*, 1895, 1903, I.

———. *The Writings of Samuel Adams.* 4 vols. New York and London, 1904.

The Danger of Mercenary Parliaments. A Collection of State Tracts, Published during the Reign of King William III. Vol. II (first printed in 1693). London, 1706.

Dane, Nathan. *A General Abridgment and Digest of American Law.* 9 vols. Boston, 1823-29.

Davenant, Charles. Essays upon: The Ballance of Power. London, 1701.

Davis, Wm. T. *Constitutional History of Massachusetts.* Boston, 1937.

———. *History of the Judiciary of Massachusetts.* Boston, 1900.

Dedieu, Joseph. *Montesquieu et la tradition politique anglaise en France.* Paris, 1909.

Defoe, Daniel. *The Original Power of the . . . People of England.* London, 1702.

———. *The Free-Holders Plea Against Stock-Jobbing Elections of Parliament-Men.* London, 1701.

De Lolme, Jean Louis de. *The Constitution of England.* Dublin, 1775.

Eliot, Andrew. *Letters to Thomas Hollis, 1766-1771*. *Mass. Hist. Soc. Coll.*, 4th Series, Vol. IV. Boston, 1858.

The Federalist. New York, 1788.

Feiling, Keith. *A History of the Tory Party, 1640-1714.* Oxford, 1924.

Filmer, Sir Robert. *The Anarchy of a Limited or Mixed Monarchy.* 1648.

Finer, Herman. *The Theory and Practice of Modern Government.* 2 vols. London, 1932.

Fiske, John. *Essays, Historical and Literary.* 2 vols. New York, 1902.

Fletcher, F. T. H. *Montesquieu and English Politics, 1750-1800.* London, 1939.

Forbes, Harriette M. *New England Diaries, 1602-1800.* Topsfield, Mass., 1923.

Ford, W. C. *Bibliography of the Massachusetts House Journals, 1715-1776.* Boston, 1910.

Ford, W. C. and Matthews, Albert. *Bibliography of the Laws of the Massachusetts Bay, 1641-1776.* Boston, 1910.

French, Jonathan. *A sermon preached before His Excellency Samuel Adams, esq. governor . . . May 25, 1796.* Boston, 1796.

Friedrich, Carl J. "Separation of Powers," *Encyclopedia of the Social Sciences*, XIII. New York, 1934.

Frothingham, Louis Adams. *A Brief History of the Constitution and Government of Massachusetts.* Cambridge, Mass., 1916.

Galloway, Joseph. *Historical and Political Reflections on the Rise and Progress of the American Rebellion.* London, 1780.

Gates, Floy P. *James Otis and Jonathan Swift.* Reprint from *New England Quarterly*, 1932.

Gellhorn, Walter. *Administrative Law, Cases and Comments.* Chicago, 1940.

Gettell, R. G. *History of American Political Thought.* New York, 1928.

Bibliography 197

Goodell, Abner C. *List of Attorneys-General and Solicitors-General of Massachusetts from Andros to the Revolution. Proceedings, etc.* Boston, 1896.

Goodnow, Frank J. *Principles of the Administrative Law of the United States.* New York, 1905.

Gordon, Thomas. *The Character of an Independent Whig.* London, 1719.

Gordon, William. *History of the Rise, Progress, and Establishment of the Independence of the United States of America.* 4 vols., 2nd ed. New York, London, 1794.

———. *Sermon, before House of Representatives, July 19, 1775.* Watertown, Mass., 1775.

——— *Sermons.* Boston, 1775.

Great Britain. *The Statutes at Large.* Vol. IV, from the Tenth Year of the Reign of King William III, to the End of the Reign of Queen Anne; Vol. VI, from the Ninth Year of the Reign of King George the Second, to the Twenty-fifth Year of the Reign of King George the Second. London, 1786.

———. *State Tracts: Being a Collection of Several Treatises Relating to the Government.* London, 1689.

———. *State Tracts: From the Year 1660, to 1689.* London, 1692.

———. *A Collection of State Tracts, Published on Occasion of the Late Revolution in 1688 and during the Reign of King William III.* London, 1705.

———. *A Collection of State Tracts, Published during the Reign of King William III.* Vols. II and III. London, 1706 and 1707.

———. *A Collection of Scarce and Valuable Tracts . . . of the Late Lord Sommers.* Vols. I-III. London, 1748, 1750, 1751.

Green, Frederick. "Separation of Governmental Powers." XXIX *Yale Law Journal* (1920), 369-93.

Greene, Evarts B. *The Provincial Governor in the English Colonies of North America.* New York, 1898.

Grinnell, Frank W. "The Government of Massachusetts Prior to the Federal Constitution." X *Massachusetts Law Quarterly* (Nov., 1924), 175.

Grose, Clyde Leclare. *Select Bibliography of British History, 1660-1760.* Chicago, 1939.

Harvey, Ray Forrest. *Jean Jacques Burlamaqui: A Liberal Tradition in American Constitutionalism.* Chapel Hill, N. C., 1937.

Hastings, Wm. G. "Montesquieu and Anglo-American Institutions." XIII *Illinois Law Review* (1918-19).

Hawley, Joseph. *Criticism of the Constitution of Massachusetts.* Northampton, Mass., 1917.

Holdsworth, Sir Wm. S. "The Conventions of the Eighteenth-Century Constitution." XVII *Iowa Law Review* (1932), 161-180.

———. *History of English Law.* 12 vols. Vol. I, London, 1922; Vols. II-XII, Boston, 1923-38.

———. "The House of Lords, 1689-1783." XLV *The Law Quarterly Review*, 307-342. London, 1929.

Hopkins, Stephen. *The Rights of the Colonies Examined. Records of the Colony of Rhode Island,* VI. Providence, 1765.

Hosmer, J. K. *Life of Thomas Hutchinson.* Boston and New York, 1896.

———. *Samuel Adams.* Boston and New York, 1885, 1899.

Hutchinson, Thomas. *History of the Colony of Massachusetts Bay.* 3 vols. Boston, 1764 and London, 1768.

An Impartial Inquiry into the Reasonableness and Necessity of a Bill for Reducing and Limiting the Number of Places in the House of Commons. 1739.

Inquiry into the Influence of the Crown over Parliament. 1780.

Kimball, Everett. *The Public Life of Joseph Dudley.* London, 1911.

La Bigne de Villeneuve, Marcel de. *La fin du Principe de Séparation des Pouvoirs.* Rennes, 1933.

Laprade, Wm. T. *Public Opinion and Politics in Eighteenth-Century England.* New York, 1936.

Labaree, L. W. *Royal Instructions to British colonial governors, 1670-1776.* 2 vols. New York and London, 1935.

Locke, John. *Two Treatises of Government.* London, 1698.
Lowell, John. *Judge Lowell and the Massachusetts Declaration of Rights.* Boston, 1874.
Mason, Albert. "A Short History of the Supreme Judicial Court of Massachusetts." II *Massachusetts Law Quarterly,* No. 2 (Nov., 1916).
Massachusetts. *Acts and Laws of the Province of Massachusetts Bay, 1692-1742.* Boston, 1742 (with this are bound *Session Laws: 1742-59* and *Charter Granted by Kg. Wm. & Queen Mary to the Province of Massachusetts Bay.* Boston, 1742).
———. *Acts and Laws of the Commonwealth of Massachusetts, 1780-1781.* Boston, 1890.
———. *The Acts and Resolves of the Province of Massachusetts Bay.* 21 vols. Boston, 1869-1922.
———. *Journal of the Convention for Framing a Constitution of Government for the State of Massachusetts Bay, Sept. 1, 1779 to June 16, 1780.* Boston, 1832.
———. *Journal of the Debates and Proceedings in the Convention of Delegates Chosen to Revise the Constitution of Massachusetts, 1820.* Boston, 1853.
———. *Journals of the House of Representatives of Massachusetts,* 1715-42. Ed. by W. C. Ford. Boston, 1919.
———. *Journals of the Honourable House of Representatives of His Majesty's Province of the Massachusetts Bay.* Massachusetts State Archives.
———. *A Manual for the Constitutional Convention, 1917.* Boston, 1917.
———. *Records of the Governor and Company of the Massachusetts-Bay, in New England.* Ed. by Nathaniel B. Shurtleff. Boston, 1853-54.
Matthews, Albert. *Documents Relating to the Last Meetings of the Massachusetts Royal Council. Publications of the Colonial Soc. of Mass.* Boston, 1937.
———. *Massachusetts Royal Commissions. Publications of the Colonial Soc. of Mass.* Boston, 1915.
Mauduit, Jasper. *Agent in London.* Ed. by W. C. Ford. *Mass. Hist. Soc. Coll.* Boston, 1918.

Mechem, Floyd R. *A Treatise on the Law of Public Office and Officers.* Chicago, 1890.
Merriam, C. E. *A History of American Political Theories.* New York, 1928.
Minot, George R. *Continuation of the History of the Province of Massachusetts-Bay, from the year 1748 (to 1765).* 2 vols. Boston, 1798-1803.
Montesquieu, Chas. de Secondat, Baron de la Brède. *Spirit of the Laws.* 2 vols. Translated from the French by Thos. Nugent. London, 1748.
Morey, Wm. C. "The Genesis of a Written Constitution," *Annals* of the American Academy of Political and Social Science, April, 1891.
―――. "The First State Constitutions," *Annals* of the American Academy of Political and Social Science, IV. Philadelphia, 1893.
Morison, Samuel E. "Struggle over the Adoption of the Constitution of 1780," *Proceedings* of the Massachusetts Historical Society 1916-17, Vol. L. Boston, 1917.
Namier, L. B. *The Structure of Politics at the Accession of George III.* 2 vols. London, 1929.
New-England Historical and Genealogical Register, XXVIII. Boston, 1874.
Oliver, Andrew. *Letters of Governor Hutchinson and Lieutenant Governor Oliver, and Remarks, 1768-1774.* London, 1774.
Oliver, Peter. *The Puritan Commonwealth.* Boston, 1856.
―――. *The Origin and Progress of the American Rebellion.*
Osgood, Herbert L. *The American Colonies in the Eighteenth Century.* 4 vols. New York, 1924.
Otis, James. *Brief Remarks on the Defence of the Halifax Libel, on the British-American Colonies.* Boston, 1765.
―――. *Considerations on Behalf of the Colonists, in a Letter to a Noble Lord.* London, 1765.
―――. *The Rights of the British Colonies Asserted and Proved.* Boston, 1764.
―――. *Some Political Writings of James Otis, Collected with an Introduction by Charles E. Mullett.* University of Missouri Studies, IV, Pt. I, No. 3. Columbia, 1929.

———. *A Vindication of the British Colonies.* Boston and London, 1769.

———. *A Vindication of the Conduct of the House of Representatives of Massachusetts Bay.* Boston, 1762.

Paley, William. *The Principles of Moral and Political Philosophy.* London, 1785.

Palfrey, John G. *History of New England.* 5 vols. Boston, 1890.

Parsons, Theophilus. *Essays.* Boston, 1856.

———. *Memoir of Theophilus Parsons, Chief Justice.* Boston, 1859.

———. *Result of the Convention of Delegates Holden at Ipswich in the County of Essex.* Newburyport, 1778.

Petyt, William. *Jus Parliamentarium.* London, 1739.

Poore, Benjamin P. *Federal and State Constitutions, Colonial Charters, and Other Organic Laws of the U. S.* 2 vols. Washington, 1878.

Porritt, Edward, and Porritt, Annie Greene. *The Unreformed House of Commons.* 2 vols. Cambridge, 1909.

Pownall, Thomas. *The Administration of the Colonies,* 2nd edit. London, 1765.

Price, Richard. *Observations on the Nature of Civil Liberty.* London, 1776.

Quincy, Josiah, Jr. *Reports of Cases Argued and Adjudged in the Superior Court of Judicature of the Province of Massachusetts Bay between 1761 and 1772.* Boston, 1865.

Rapin-Thoyras, Paul de. *The History of England, as well ecclesiastical as civil.* 15 vols. London, 1726-31.

Read, Conyers, ed. *The Constitution Reconsidered.* New York, 1938.

Report of Record Commissioners of Boston, Vol. XVI. Boston Town Records. Boston, 1886.

Sawtelle, Wm. O. *Sir Francis Bernard and His Grant of Mount Desert.* Reprinted from *Publications of the Colonial Soc. of Mass.,* XXIV, 199-249. Cambridge, 1922.

Schuyler, Robt. L. *The Constitution of the United States.* New York, 1923.

Sharp, W. R. "The Classical American Doctrine of 'the Separation of Powers.'" II *U. of Chicago Law Review* (1935), 436.
Shute, Daniel. *A sermon preached before His Excellency Francis Bernard, Esq., Governor—May 25th, 1768.* Boston, 1768.
Spencer, Henry R. *Constitutional Conflict in Provincial Massachusetts.* Columbus, Ohio, 1905.
Spurlin, Paul M. *Montesquieu in America, 1760-1801.* University, La., 1940.
Stevens, C. Ellis. *Sources of the Constitution of the United States Considered in Relation to Colonial and English History.* New York, 1894.
Stillman, Samuel. *A Sermon Preached before the Honorable Council, and the Honorable House of Representatives, May 26, 1779.* Boston, 1779.
Story, Joseph. *Commentaries on the Constitution of the United States.* Boston, 1905.
Taylor, Hannis. *The Origin and Growth of the English Constitution.* 2 vols. Boston and New York, 1889.
Thacher, Oxenbridge. *Considerations on the Election of Counsellors, Humbly Offered to the Electors.* Boston, 1761.
———. *Considerations on Lowering the Value of Gold Coins, Within the Province of the Massachusetts Bay.* Boston.
———. *Letter to Benjamin Prat, 1762.* Mass. Hist. Soc. *Proceedings*, 1st Series, XX. Boston, 1884.
Thomson, Mark A. *A Constitutional History of England, 1642-1801.* London, 1938.
Thorpe, Francis N. *The Constitutional History of the United States.* 3 vols. Chicago, 1901.
Tudor, William. *The Life of James Otis.* Boston, 1823.
Turberville, A. S. *The House of Lords in the XVIIIthe Century.* Oxford, 1927.
———. *The House of Lords in the Reign of William III.* Oxford, 1913.
Warren-Adams. *Letters.* Mass. Hist. Soc. *Coll.*, Vols. LXXII and LXXIII. Boston, 1917, 1925.
Warren, Charles. "John Adams and American Constitutions," George Washington University *Bulletin*, Vol. XXVI, No. 1.
Washburn, Emory. *Sketches of the Judicial History of Massachusetts from 1630 to the Revolution in 1775.* Boston, 1840.

Bibliography

Webster, Wm. C. "A Comparative Study of the State Constitutions of the American Revolution," *Annals* American Academy of Political and Social Science, IX. Philadelphia, 1897.

Wells, Wm. V. *Life and Public Services of Samuel Adams.* 3 vols. Boston, 1865.

Whitmore, Wm. H. *The Massachusetts Civil List for the Colonial and Provincial Periods, 1630-1774.* Albany, 1870.

Whitney, Peter. *American Independence Vindicated. A Sermon delivered September 12, 1776.* Boston, 1777.

Winthrop, R. C. "Life and Services of James Bowdoin." Address delivered before the Maine Historical Society, at Bowdoin College, Sept. 5, 1849. Boston, 1876.

Wright, Benjamin F., Jr. "The Origins of the Separation of Powers in America." *Economica*, XIII (May, 1933).

Worcester Town Records (from 1753 to 1783). Worcester Society of Antiquity *Collections*, IV. Worcester, Mass., 1882.

INDEX

Act of Settlement, provision disqualifying any person who has an office, place of profit, or pension from the Crown, for the House of Commons, 72 n.

Acts of Trade, connivance to avoid in Massachusetts, 37; one-third of forfeitures to go to governor, 38

Adams, John, advocate of republican government, 139; appointed Chief Justice of the Superior Court of Judicature, 114; comment on plural office-holding by Hutchinson and his connections, 179; committee obligations in the Continental Congress, 115; counter-proposal against office-holding by members of the Continental Congress, 116; delegate to the Continental Congress, 114; deliberates on question of resigning the Chief Justiceship of the Superior Court, 117; derives concept of "a government of laws and not of men" from political theorists, 139; judicial appointments under the revolutionary government of Massachusetts, 114; leaves for France in November, 1779, 141; member of the Revolutionary Council, 114; no part in amending draft constitution on subject of separation of departments, 141; office of Chief Justice of the Superior Court held for him until 1777, 115; one of sub-committee of three to whom Committee of Thirty delegated preparation of draft of a constitution, 138; president of the board of war, 115; quotes Harrington on "a government of laws and not of men," 139; resignation from the Revolutionary Council, 1776, 116; resigns from office of Chief Justice of the Superior Court in 1777, 115; theory of human nature as "self-engrossing" led to need for separation of departments, 140; "whispering" campaign against his plural office-holding, 115

Adams, Samuel, Boston leaders in control of General Court in 1769, 96; comment on plural office-holding by Thomas Hutchinson and his connections, 180; defeated in Council elections of 1776, 114; delegate to the Continental Congress, 112; elected clerk of the House of Representatives in 1766, 81; explains use of a "select" Council in Massachusetts, 188; holds office of Secretary until the inauguration of the state government, 114; judicial appointments under the Revolutionary government of Massachusetts, 112-13; opinion of members of House asked on combining office of Secretary with a seat in the Council, 113; opposes Hutchinson on sound currency issue, 28; prevented execution of attachment against his estate, 28-29; Secretary to the Revolutionary government of Massachusetts, 113; views on plural office-holding when he is holder of several offices, 113

Administration, decentralized methods of in Province, 35

[205]

"Alociapt," pseudonym of writer opposing plural office-holding, 133-34

Articles of Confederation, acceptance considered by Provincial Congress, 126; comment proposes Senate with provision against plural office-holding, 127; delegates to Congress prohibited from holding any paid office under the United States, 126

Avery, John, 114

Barnstable, Town of, objection that exclusion of judges from the legislature inadequate in the Constitution, 162

Barre, Town of, objection to delegates to Congress occupying seats in the legislature, 161-62

Belcher, Andrew, 94

Bellingham, Town of, suggests substitute for Article II of Chapter VI of Constitution, 161

Berkshire County, resolution of towns that new Constitution be drawn up by a Convention, 121-22

Bernard, Sir Francis, account of his reconciliation with the Otises by Thomas Hutchinson, 183; addresses to the two houses of the General Court compared to those of the Stuarts, 84; administration called the "weakest and most arbitrary," by Otis, 56; advocates appointive upper legislative house, 100; advocates royal control of Council for maintenance of King's authority, 98; advocates title for members of legislative upper house, 100; appointed governor of the province of Massachusetts-Bay, 25; appointments approved by "select" Council attacked as unconstitutional, 97; appoints Colonel James Otis as Chief Justice of the Court of Common Pleas of Barnstable County, 68; appoints Colonel James Otis as Judge of Probate of Barnstable County, 68; approves Nathaniel Sparhawk for the Council in 1767, 93; attempts at conciliation of opposition, 51; builds up political support by distribution of commissions in House of Representatives, 71; comments on harmony in British Empire in 1760, 26; comments on harmony in administration in 1762, 54; controversy with merchants over enforcement of customs laws, 38; controversy with Surveyor-General over forfeitures, 38; delays Hutchinson's acceptance of province agency, 69; deplores annual election of Council, 82; despairs of loyal Council after elections of 1769, 96; dismissal of certain militia officers who were members of the House of Representatives, 86; dismisses Artemas Ward as militia officer, 86; efforts to compromise in election of councillors in 1766, 82; extra-legal meetings of Council members questioned, 97-98; failure of efforts to execute the Stamp Act, 76; finds two houses of assembly combined against administration, 91; merchants planning representations against him to mother country, 52; negative of James Otis as Speaker of the House of Representatives in 1766, 81; negatives councillors chosen in place of judges and Crown officers in 1766, 82; negatives eleven elected to the Council in 1769, 95; negatives five elected to Council in 1767, 93; negatives six elected to the Council in 1768, 94; offers to compromise with leaders of House in election of Council, 92; opinion that the people have too much weight in the government, 98; opposition undermined in spring of 1763, 66; policy to disengage himself from party politics, 51; popular disfavor for advising submission to the Stamp Act, 75; postpones General Court on conflict with session of Superior Court of Judicature, 104, 105; press opposed to his administration in 1766, 78; "privy Council" appointive by King advocated, 99; "privy Council" overlapping legislative upper house in membership advocated, 99; receives grant of Mount Desert from the Province, 53; recommendation that he take advice of the General Court as the great council of the province, 55; reconciliation with Otises, 67; refuses to fill empty seats in the Council left by defeat of judges and Crown officers in 1766, 86; regards annual election of Council as "fatal Ingredient," 98; reply of House of Representatives on election of Council in 1766, 184 et seq.; reply by two houses of General Court on election of Council in 1766, 85, 86; reports that he threatened negative of councillors elected in opposition in 1766, 81; reprimanded by House for encroachment upon their right of originating taxes, 55; second address to two houses of the General Court in 1766 seeks palliation of effect of election of Council, 84; seeks compromise in election of Council in 1768, 94; seeks instructions from Secretary of State on right of Lieutenant-Governor to seat in Council, 89; "select" Council in 1769, 96; submits plans for reform of Council to Ministry, 98; threats against because of his attempts to enforce the Stamp Act, 76; upbraids two houses of the General Court for attack upon government in election of Council, 83; uses pressure to secure election of his friend, Richard Jackson, as province agent, 70; warned against taking advice of a small clique, 55; writes that Province divided into parties nearly equal on his arrival, 51

Beverly, Town of, manner of expressing its opinion on the Constitution of 1778, 128

Blackstone, William, *Commentaries* quoted on independence of three branches of the legislature, 107

Bollan, William, 40, 49

Boston, Town of, advocates "Placebill" for Massachusetts like that of English disqualifying Act of 1705, 71; danger of plural office-holding one reason for opposing constitution-making by the Assembly, 124; instructions to representatives against placemen in the General Court in 1764, 71; instructions to representatives to oppose constitution-making by the Assembly, 124; instructions to representatives in 1766 against holding of incompatible offices, 80; instructions to representatives in 1776 recommend adequate salaries for members of General Court, 118; instructions to representatives in 1776 recommend "self-denying" ordinance on office-holding by members, 118; instructions to representatives in 1776 recommend that powers of government be independent and separate "as nearly as possible," 118; instructions to representatives in 1776, asking for a self-denying ordinance, 189; members control General Court in 1766, 76; members control General Court in 1769, 96; necessity for "self-denying" ordinance in making of new constitution, 129; opposed to office-holding by members of the General Court, 125; opposed to accumulation of offices in instruction to representatives, 124; opposition to constitution-making by the Assembly, 119; people incensed against Andrew Oliver, Stamp Act agent, 75; representatives not given leading part in drawing up new constitution, 125; states objections to Constitution of 1778 that it does not prevent monopoly of offices, and does not insure independence of legislative and executive branches of government, 131

Bourne, Sylvanus, 53

Bowdoin, James, becomes leader of the Council, 90; negatived by Bernard in Council election of 1769, 95; opposition to administration ascribed to controversy between Temple and Bernard, 29

Bowers, Jerathmeel, 95

Braintree, Town of, suggests exclusion of delegates to Congress from seat in House, Senate, or Council, 161

Brattle, William, 95

Bribery and Corruption, conviction disqualifies for a seat in the Legislature, or for any office of trust and importance, 149

Bristol, Town of, rejects the Constitution of 1778 because no provision was made for approval by articles, 128

"Cato Censorinus," 122

Chandler, John, 35, 94

Charter (Province), no provision giving Lieutenant-Governor right to sit as member or to preside except in absence of Governor, 88

Checks upon powers of government, preserve "adjustment" of powers, 43

Choate, John, 35

Clark, Rev. Jonas, 165

"Clitus," 122

Commissary-General, elective by the General Court, 35 n.

Commissioner, empowered by the General Court to deliberate on supplies for the French and to lay an account of proceedings before the General Court, 172; to attend conference with delegates from other states on supplies for French, elected by General Court, 172

Commissioner of Impost and Excise, elective by the General Court, 35 n.

Committee on Exclusion, Report to Constitutional Convention of list of officers proposed to be excluded from the General Court, 190

Concord, Town of, concept of a constitution as a set of fundamental principles, 121; objections to constitution-making by the legislature, 120

Congress of the Confederation of the United States, delegates elected and instructed by the two houses of the General Court jointly, 172

Constitution of Massachusetts. *See* Constitution of 1780; Constitution of 1778.

Constitution of 1778, delegates to Continental Congress may not hold certain state offices, 127; Art. IV provides for a separation in officeholding, 127; inadequate provisions for separation of departments one reason for rejection, 135; no opinion expressed by one hundred and twenty towns, 128; no provision for acceptance by separate articles, 128; objection by some towns to Art. XIX, providing for election of certain officers by General Court, 128; provision for election by the General Court of certain officers, appointment of others, 128; provisions for a separation of departments found inadequate by "Alociapt," 133-34; provisions for a separation of departments found inadequate by Rev. William Gordon, 132; provisions for a separation of departments found inadequate by *The Essex Result*, 131; rejected by Bristol because no provision was made for approval by articles, 128; rejected by estimated five-sixths of 12,000 persons voting on it, 129; towns return opinions on, article by article, 128

Constitution of 1780, article rejected providing for vacating seat of any member of Senate or House chosen as delegate to Congress, unless re-election is had, 150; Art. XXX and Art. II of Chap. VI probably acceptable to the voters, 157; Art. XXX as passed by the Convention contains neither the word "separation" nor "department," 143; Art.

XXX of the Declaration of Rights passed on February 10, 1780, 143; Art. XXX omits words "separate from" contained in draft article on separation of departments (Art. XXXI), 143; Art. II of Chap. VI accepted on March 2, 1780, 146; Art. II of Chap. VI comes up on January 29, 1780, and is recommitted, 144; Art. II of Chap. VI designates officers excluded from a seat in the Council, 149; Art. II of Chap. VI designates officers excluded from a seat in the General Court, 148; Art. II of Chap. VI designates offices of which not more than two to be held by one person, 148; Art. II of Chap. VI makes certain offices exclusive of each other, 148; Art. II of Chap. VI prohibits plural office-holding by heads of state, 146; article vacating seat of any member of Senate or House chosen as delegate to Congress adopted subsequently as Amendment VIII, 150 n.; attains separation of departments by limitation of plural office-holding, 174; Bellingham suggests substitute for Art. II of Chap. VI, that no person hold more than one state office at one time, 161; Braintree suggests exclusion of delegates to Congress from either house or the Council, 161; bribery and corruption a disqualification for a seat in the General Court, or for any office of trust or importance, 149; change in organization of Council result of experience of Massachusetts and of other colonies, 151; changes in organization of government practically all result of experience under the province charter, 152; exception to prohibition against plural office-holding that Judges of the Supreme Judicial Court may hold office of Justice of the Peace, 147; explained in "Address of the Convention to their Constituents," 155;

framers not all impractical theorists, 167; General Court acts as a high court of appeal after its adoption, 168; General Court exercises legislative, judicial, and executive powers after adoption, 168; governments grow up out of experience the view of Judge John Lowell, 167 n.; Groton recommends absolute veto for the governor to prevent domination of executive and judicial departments by the legislative, 159; history of separation of departments shows correlation of Art. XXX and Art. II of Chap. VI, 144; history of separation of departments shows that it consisted of separation in office-holding, 143; John Adams has no part in amending draft constitution on subject of separation of departments, 141; independence of departments of government a primary concern of framers, 153; Lincoln, Middleborough, Sandisfield and Wilbraham object to governor's veto on ground that contrary to the separation of departments, 159-60; new provision for executive Council chosen from Senate annually by joint vote of both houses, 152; Norton votes that additional exclusions of judicial officers from the General Court required by Art. II of Chap. VI, 162-63; objections to Constitution by Barnstable that exclusion of judicial officers from the legislature inadequate, 162; objection of Barre to permitting delegates to Congress to sit in legislature, 161-62; objection of Grafton that exclusion of judges from the legislature inadequate, 162; objection of Northborough that exclusion of judges from General Court inadequate, 162; objections of towns that ministers of the gospel should be excluded from the General Court, 163; objections of towns that provisions for a separation of departments did not go far enough, 157; objections to Constitution in returns of towns, 157; power of suspending the laws to be exercised only by the legislature, 149; prohibition against legislative conviction of treason or felony, 150; provision for Council one of outstanding changes in organization, 151; provisions on separation of departments satisfactory to majority of towns, 163; purpose of Art. XXX was to avoid the inconveniences of plural office-holding, 164; purpose of governor's veto stated to be to maintain the balance of the three departments of government, 156; purpose stated of separation of departments "that it might be a government of laws and not of men" probably work of John Adams, 139; regulation of plural office-holding practically uncalled for after adoption of, 174; rejected by Rehoboth with objection that separation in office-holding inadequate, 162; Report of Committee of provision allowing member of the House to accept a not incompatible civil office provided re-election is had, 150; returns of towns show approval of call for Convention to frame new Constitution, 136; Senate elective by voters to constitute upper house of the legislature, 152; separate chapter for list of officers excluded from seat in the General Court voted on February 25, 1780, 146; separation of departments not on basis of three types of power, 151; Shrewsbury suggests amendment of Art. II of Chap. VI prohibiting feemen a seat in the house, and limiting commissions, 161; separation of departments in Constitution to be achieved by separation in office-holding, 163-64; separation of departments in practice in less extreme form than Art. XXX indicates, 167; separation of departments understood by some to slow up processes of government, 167; towns asked if they approve of calling a Convention to draft new Constitution, 136; towns make no suggestion in returns that separation in office-holding of Art. II of Chap. VI goes too far, 161; veto of governor not a great deviation from previous practice, 152; veto of governor in Report of the Committee of Thirty probably the work of John Adams, 152-53; Wells recommends that governor be given an absolute veto, 159; West Springfield votes that additional exclusions from the legislature required by Art. XXX, 162; Wrentham recommends that Art. XXX be amended to agree with separation of departments provided for in Constitution, 159. *See also* Constitutional Convention.

Constitutional Convention, "Address of the Convention to their Constituents" gives reasons for separation of departments, 155; "Address of the Convention to their Constituents" uses "Powers" in sense of "departments," 155; adjourns from time to time until end of January, 1780, 141; Art. I of Chap. II, Sec. 1 (providing that governor to have a negative to preserve independence of the executive and judicial departments) dropped, 142-43; article on exclusion of officers from a seat in the General Court accepted on March 2, 1780, 146; Art. XXXI of Report of Committee of Thirty combined with second paragraph in preamble of second chapter, 142; Art. XXXI of Report of Committee of Thirty provides for independence of judiciary, 137; articles on separation of departments considered in January, 1780, 141; brief debate on separation of departments in November, 1779, 141; committee of one appointed to bring in an article providing for re-election of members of

General Court appointed to incompatible offices, 145; committee on exclusion and incompatibility of offices reports, 144; exclusion from General Court of each officer on list reported by committee considered separately by Convention, 145; framers advocate checks among departments to secure liberty, 153; framers base qualified veto of the governor upon their own experience, 153; instructions to committee to which Art. II of Chap. VI recommitted to report article on plural office-holding, 144; John Adams no part in amending draft constitution on subject of separation of departments, 141; Journal of the Convention contains few passages on adoption of Art. XXX, 141; Journal shows no analysis or definition of three different kinds of power, 154; members publish "Address of the Convention to their Constituents," 155; message to towns states that subject of separation of departments not yet taken up, 141; motion expunging Art. XXXI of Report of Committee of Thirty and offering substitute article passed on February 10, 1780, 142; motion that words "separate from and" be omitted from Art. XXXI of Report of Committee of Thirty, 142; omissions and additions made to list of officers excluded from General Court in report of the committee, 145; power of suspending the laws to be exercised only by the legislature, 149; Preamble to the Frame of Government in Report of Committee of Thirty provides for separation of departments, 138; preparation of draft of a constitution delegated by Committee of Thirty to sub-committee of three, 138; principle of a separation of departments required by instructions of some towns to delegates, 136; prohibition of legislative conviction of treason or felony, 150; provision requiring re-election of any member of the General Court chosen as delegate to Congress considered, 146; publishes message to towns urging better attendance in January, 1780, 141; purpose of framers in excluding office-holders from legislature to keep departments separate, 156; purpose of governor's veto stated to be to maintain the balance among the three departments, 156; relationship between Art. II of Chap. VI and Art. XXX of the Declaration of Rights scarcely evident from Journal, 142; report of committee excludes long list of officers from General Court, 144; report of committee of provision allowing member of the House to accept civil office, provided re-election is had, 150; report of committee on exclusion of office-holders from the General Court does not list Governor and Lieutenant-Governor, 144; report on "Incompatibility of Offices" dealing with chief offices of state, accepted on March 1, 1780, 146; separate chapter for list of officers excluded from seat in General Court voted on February 25, 1780, 146; separation shown in Journal is one in office-holding, not of abstract powers, 154; severity of winter of 1779-80 results in scanty attendance, 141; some towns give instructions to delegates, 136; union of office of Justice of the Supreme Judicial Court and that of Justice of the Peace allowed only after repeated consideration, 147; votes down provision in Report of the Committee of Thirty for absolute veto of governor, 153; word "department" added after word "Legislative" in first sentence of Art. XXX, 143. *See also* Constitution of 1780.

Continental Congress, committee obligations of John Adams, 115; counter-proposal of John Adams against office-holding by members under either old or new governments, 116; Maryland delegates instructed to move for a "self-denying" ordinance, 115; motion for "self-denying" ordinance, 116; recommendations to conform to charter in revolutionary government followed in Massachusetts, 109; recommends that authority under Crown be suppressed in 1776, 119; refers to grievance of appointive Council in 1775, 109

Council of Magistrates (Colony), 12; general power to act in "vacancy" of General Court, 12; in colony period, 11. *See also* General Court items.

Council (Province), advisory powers, 13; allowance for members in 1761 and 1762, 33; appointments postponed until after adjournment of General Court, 97; approval of Samuel Dexter by Governor Bernard in 1768, 94; attendance upon by judges when courts sitting at same time impossible, 42; complaints of governors to England on methods of selection, 20; consists of sixteen members in 1769, 96; consists of twenty-two members in 1768, 94; control in popular party in 1769, 96; control in the popular party during years 1766 to 1774, 110; defeat of Andrew Belcher in 1768, 94; defeat of Israel Williams, 92; defeat of John Chandler in 1768, 94; defeat of "Tories" in 1769, 95; determination of Lieutenant-Governor's right to seat in Council left to Council by Secretary of State, 90; election by two houses of General Court, 16; exclusion of judicial and executive officers from continued, 91; executive business transacted after adjournment of General Court, 96; executive sessions presided over by governor, 17; Governor Bernard offers to compromise with leaders of House in election of, 92; governor forbidden to preside over legislative sessions, 17; governor's negative in election ineffective, 16-17, 91; incompatibility of a seat with judicial office, 42, 180; influence of governor over, 17, 19; judicial power of, 13; Justices Lynde and Leonard resign their seats prior to elections of 1766, 81; leadership in hands of James Bowdoin, 90; Lieutenant-Governor no right to sit as member or preside by charter or laws, 88; "mandamus" members required to renounce commissions from Crown, 108; members appointed to judicial office, 18; members hold executive offices in counties, 35; members meet and transact business without governor, 98; members of named, 35; members to be men of property by instruction to governor, 16; negative of eleven popular members by Governor Bernard in 1769, 95; negative of governor in election opposed by agents, 16; negative of six candidates by Governor Bernard in 1768, 94; nomination of members, 17; nonconcurrence in resolution of the House of Representatives that courts of justice should function without use of stamps, 77; number of members who constituted "mandamus," 108; opinion of James Otis that no right on part of the Lieutenant-Governor to a seat in Council or to the presidency, 187; pamphlet of Thacher on union of powers in hands of members, 41; plans for reform of by Governors Bernard and Hutchinson, 98 *et seq.*; plural office-holding by members attacked in 1761, 41; power to remove judges, 19; practical inexpediency of combining membership with judicial office, 103; provision for appointive Council ("mandamus") of thirty-six members, 108; reason for exclusion of judicial and Crown officers in election of 1766, 85; resolution on right of Hutchinson to preside, 87,

Index 213

187; "select" Council explained by Samuel Adams, 188; "select" Council used by Governor Bernard in 1769, 96; separation into legislative council and council of state advocated by Thomas Pownall, 102; separation of legislative and executive functions advocated by Governors Bernard and Hutchinson, 100; several capacities of, 13; service of members in colony government, 15; subject to pressure from governor and House of Representatives, 20; subordination in legislation, 14; support of governor, 15; title for members proposed by Governor Bernard, 100

Council (Revolutionary), "Alociapt" recommends that no executive officer should be chosen to Council, 133-34; each member commonly given a judicial appointment, 112; exercised powers of governor as well as those of Council, 109; five office-holders in addition to John Adams resign in 1776, 116; holding of plural offices by popular election distinguished by Hawley from holding by gift of the Crown, 113; members all receive additional appointments, 112; members elected on July 21, 1775, 109; Samuel Adams, John Hancock and Robert Treat Paine fail of re-election in 1776, 116

Council (State), Art. II of Chap. VI designates officers excluded from a seat, 149; election by the General Court from the Senate should have furnished indirect control over executive, 176; election from members of Senate falls into disuse, 176; Governor with Council empowered by General Court to pass upon all matters pending before previous Council, 171; Governor and Council do not need augmented powers in recess of General Court by resolve of the General Court, 171; provision for one of the outstanding changes in organization of government, 151-52; to consist of councillors chosen from upper house annually by joint vote of both houses, 151

County Courts, under colony charter, 11

Court of Assistants (Colony), under colony charter, 11

Courts of General Sessions of the Peace, draw up estimates for county budget and apportion among towns, 171

Cushing, John, 35
Cushing, Thomas, 112

Danforth, Samuel, 35
Dexter, Samuel, 94
Dudley, Town of, instructs delegate to Constitutional Convention against office-holding by members of the Assembly, 137

Election Sermon, preached by Rev. Jonas Clark warning against a "government of men," 165
Essex Result, The, advocates division of Council into small privy Council and legislative upper house, 132; advocates independence and balance of departments of government, 132

Flucker, Thomas, 95
Freeman, Samuel, 117
French, Rev. Jonathan, 166

General Court (Colony), "cheife civill power of the common wealth," 12. *See also* Court of Assistants (Colony); Governor (Colony).
General Court (Province), administration supporters prefer not to attend, 77; allowance for members in 1762, 33; bill passed by both houses to prevent issue of writs of assistance, 49; bill to exclude justices of the Superior Court from a seat in either house of, 50; bill to exclude judges and executive officers from the Coun-

cil voted down, 77; changes in election of representatives in 1766, 81; chooses Richard Jackson, friend of Governor Bernard and Secretary to Lord Grenville, as province agent, 71-72; committee on grievances appointed in 1766, 77; committee to inquire into tenure and fixed salary for justices of the Superior Court of Judicature, 49; control in Boston leaders in 1766, 76; in 1769, 96; Council consists of twenty-two members in 1768, 94; of sixteen members in 1769, 96; disallowance of Acts by Privy Council, 12; dismissal of friends of James Otis in spring of 1763, 67; dismissal of militia officers who were members of the House of Representatives by Governor Bernard, 86; elections of 1766 explained by House of Representatives to the Earl of Hillsborough, 93; elects Thomas Hutchinson agent of province February, 1764, 68; failure of efforts to enforce Stamp Act through, 76; Governor Bernard offers to compromise with leaders of House in election of Council, 92; governor's negative on Acts under Charter of 1691, 12; harmony promoted by news of Peace of Paris, 1763, 66; instructions of Boston to representatives, *see* Boston; instructions of Worcester to representatives, *see* Worcester; intimidation used against "supporters of government," 91; legislative powers of, 14; limitation of number of members in House of Representatives advocated by Hutchinson, 101; list of thirty-two representatives published with recommendation for purge, 78; nineteen of list defeated, 78; loyal address of the two houses in spring of 1763, 66; military and customs officers sit in the House of Representatives, 72; model instructions for a representative suggested, 79; negative of eleven elected to the Council in 1769, 95; number of office-holders in House of Representatives in 1764, 73; objection by House of Representatives to Lieutenant-Governor's sitting in Council without election, 88; opinion of House in regard to Lieutenant-Governor's seat in Council, 89; popular party outnumbers administration after elections of 1766, 91; pressure by people of Boston on members to prevent election of Andrew Oliver to Council, 75; refuses to allow Hutchinson time to obtain leave as Lieutenant-Governor in order to act as province agent, 69; report drawn up by Secretary Oliver on usage in regard to Lieutenant-Governor's seat in Council, 89; representatives for Boston vote against Hutchinson for province agent, 68; resignation of seat by James Otis, 1763, 67; resolution of Council on right of Thomas Hutchinson to preside in Council, 87; resolution of House that Lieutenant-Governor no right to seat in Council unless Governor absent, 89; resolution that courts of justice should function without stamps passed by the House of Representatives, 77; resolution voted down by the Council, 77; opinion of Justices of Superior Court upon resolution, 77; right of Lieutenant-Governor to seat in Council left to decision of Council by Secretary of State, 90; three branches under Charter of 1691, 12; time of convening altered to avoid conflict with judicial courts, 103; two houses in unity on provincial policy, 91; writs for convening on October 5, 1774, cancelled by Governor, 108. *See also* Council (Province); Governor (Province).

General Court (Revolutionary), (Provincial Congress), assembles as revolutionary body on October 7, 1774, 109; bill against holding of incompatible offices brought in and read, 111; Boston opposed to office-holding by members of, 125; constitution-making by opposed by "Clitus," "The Observer," and "Cato Censorinus," 122; dismisses Rev. William Gordon as chaplain because of his criticism, 133; experience under not reassuring as to lack of necessity for separation of departments, 177; follows recommendations of Continental Congress in revolutionary changes in government, 109; issues call for a Convention to frame a new Constitution, 136; majority of towns accept proposal for drawing up new Constitution, 119; members accused of dividing civil and military offices among themselves and their friends, 118; plural office-holding by members, 110; proceeds to draw up new Constitution, although some members not so empowered, 125; proposes to draw up new Constitution for Massachusetts, 119; questions put to towns on calling Convention to frame new Constitution, 136; Resolve asking consent of towns to their framing a new Constitution, 119; Resolve that towns should instruct members to frame new Constitution, 124; Resolve that towns consider Constitution when completed, 124; some towns resist proposal of Constitution-making by Assembly, 119; Stoughton instructs its representative not to accept any office without the approval of his constituents, 134. *See also* Council (Revolutionary); House of Representatives (Revolutionary).

General Court (State), appoints judges of Supreme Judicial Court to adjust and liquidate principal and interest due upon depreciation notes, 170; Art. II of Chap. VI designates officers excluded from a seat, 148; authorizes justices of the Supreme Judicial Court to grant a new trial to a felon in their discretion, 169;

awards "suit of cloathes" to each of two employees of the government in response to their petition, 173; character as "the chiefe civill power of the common wealth" after adoption of the Constitution, 168; commissioner on supplies for the French empowered to deliberate and to lay an account of proceedings before the General Court, 172; delegates to Congress elected and instructed by two houses jointly, 172; directs executive officers to give immediate attendance to inform regarding conduct of their offices, 173; directs executive officers to take certain action, 172; directs Inferior Court of Common Pleas of Lincoln County to continue a contract action, where "equitable intervention" required, 169; directs justices of the Supreme Judicial Court to deliver opinion in writing on meaning of term "money-bills" in the Constitution and to determine value of bills of public credit, 170; directs sheriff to apprehend suspected Loyalist and to commit to the county jail, with instructions for his custody, 170; directs Treasurer to exchange twenty dollars, defaced and unfit for circulation, to issue execution against collectors, and to recall execution against a town delinquent in military enlistments, 173; election of Council from members of the Senate falls into disuse, 176; election of Council from members of Senate should have furnished indirect control over executive, 176; elects commissioner from Massachusetts to attend a conference with delegates from other states, on supplies for French, 172; empowers Governor and Council to pass upon matters pending before previous Council, 171; empowers Governor with advice of Council to take measures in recess of Court for defense of eastern parts, account of expenditures to be laid before the General Court, 171; exclusion of judges by Constitution not complete, 176; exclusion of "placemen" by new Constitution recommended, 127; executive action under control of, 171; exercises legislative, judicial, and executive powers after the adoption of the Constitution, 168; exercises powers of a high court of appeal after adoption of the Constitution, 168; Governor and Lieutenant-Governor not among the officers excluded from, 175; Governor and Lieutenant-Governor not excluded by Art. XXX, 175; grants a continuance in all actions scheduled for certain session of an inferior court, 168; grants leave to appeal from an inferior court to a higher court, 169; grants "rehearing" of an action which had already proceeded to judgment in an inferior court, 169; issues orders for administration of estates, 170; Lieutenant-Governor elected by, 176; notifies selectmen of towns to appear before General Court, to give reasons for tax delinquency, 173; opinion that further exclusion of judges from desirable, 176; permits "reopening" of case decided more than three years before by purchase of a "writ of review," 169; Petersham objects in return on Constitution of 1780 to power of impeachment conferred on General Court, 158; popular election of Governor together with tradition of independence prevented development of a "Cabinet" system in Massachusetts, 175; removes an action from one district of the Maritime Court to another, 169; requests Governor to inform officer in charge of eastern parts, that measures being taken for their defence, 172; requests Governor to inform other states of policies adopted by the General Court, 172; requests Governor "with Advice of Council" to lay certain persons under restrictions, 173; resolve that powers of the Governor and Council need not be augmented in the recess of the Court, 171; resolve that two out-patients of the State Hospital no longer under direction of the physician in charge, 173; supervises administration of justice in the state, 170; suspends privilege of the writ of habeas corpus, 169; ultimate responsibility for conduct of government, 174; upper house to consist of Senate elected by voters, 152

Gerrish, Joseph, 95

Gordon, Rev. William, advocates adequate salaries and single places to avoid error of plural office-holding, 126; analyzes provisions of the Virginia Constitution, 126; criticizes certain representatives for having taken part in framing Constitution of 1778, 133; criticizes the Revolutionary Assembly for having assumed constituent powers, 132; discusses provisions of South Carolina, New Jersey and Virginia Constitutions, 126; dismissed as chaplain by the General Court for his criticism, 133; finds provisions of Constitution of 1778 providing for separation in office-holding inadequate, 132; recommends Virginia's provision on separation of departments, 126

"Government of Men," in Massachusetts during colony period, 11

Governor (Colony), *Primus inter pares* under colony charter, 11

Governor (Province), appointed by Crown under charter of 1691, 11; case of Gray v. Paxton brought to reduce his share in forfeitures, 39; considered to be absent by revolutionary government, 109; distributes judicial and executive commissions among members of the House of

Index

Representatives, 20; instructed to assist in enforcing Acts of Trade, 37; negative on election of councilors ineffective, 91; patronage used to gain support in House of Representatives, 20; profits from forfeitures under Acts of Trade, 38; right to forfeitures under Acts of Parliament, 38; veto in election Council, 12, 16; veto over Acts of Assembly, 12. *See also* Bernard, Sir Francis; Hutchinson, Thomas.

Governor (State), Council not to have augmented powers in recess of General Court by resolve of the General Court, 171; Council empowered by General Court to take measures in recess of Court for defence of eastern parts, account to be laid before General Court, 171; empowered by General Court with Council to pass upon all matters pending before previous Council, 171; exclusions from General Court by provisions of Art. II of Chap. VI do not include, 175; his Council in Constitution of 1780 to be elected from Senate, 176; request of General Court to inform officer in charge of eastern parts, that measures being taken for their defence, 172; not excluded from the General Court by Art. XXX, 175; popular election under Constitution of 1780, vii, 175; popular election of prevents development of a "Cabinet" system in Massachusetts, 175; purpose of veto to maintain balance of departments of Government, in "Address of the Convention to their Constituents," 156; requested by the General Court to inform other states of policies adopted by the General Court, 172; requested by General Court to lay certain persons under restrictions "with Advice of Council," 173; veto might be over-ridden by two-thirds both houses of General Court, 152

Grafton, Town of, objection that exclusion of judges from the legislature inadequate in Constitution, 162

Gray, Harrison, member of the Council (Province), 35; Treasurer and Receiver-General (Province), 35

Great Britain, fundamental maxim stated by James Otis that powers must be kept separate, 47; House of Commons, exclusion of common law judges from a protection to liberty, 43; House of Commons, practice of disqualifying and requiring re-election of members who accept office recommended for Massachusetts by Otis, 58; House of Lords, chancellors and chief justices of King's Bench and Common Pleas created peers, given seat, 61; House of Lords, practice of allowing seats to judges held not necessarily consistent with separation of powers by "T.Q.," 62; independent tendencies in American colonies might be counteracted by use of patronage, 22; loss of colonies in America attributed to lack of control through patronage, 22, 23; observation of Otis that oligarchy may develop in British form of government, 48; opinion of James Otis on "mixed monarchy" of its Constitution, 182; opinion of James Otis that the most perfect form of government, 47; Revolution of 1688, results in "adjustment" of powers of government, 43; theory that "a mixed monarchy" composed of three orders repeated by James Otis, 47

Greenleaf, Benjamin, 95

Groton, Town of, recommends absolute veto for Governor to prevent domination of executive and judicial departments by the legislature, 159

Hancock, John, Delegate, to the Continental Congress, 116; fails of re-election to the Revolutionary

218 Index

Council in 1776, 116; negatived in Council election of 1769, 95

Harrington, James, quoted by John Adams on "a government of laws and not of men," 139

Hawley, Major Joseph, attacks right of Hutchinson to sit in Council by virtue of his office of Lieutenant-Governor, 87; declines election to the Council in 1769, 95; distinguishes holding plural offices from Crown and by election of the people, 113

Henshaw, Joshua, 95

House of Representatives (Province), explanation of their action in election of the Council in 1766 to the Earl of Hillsborough, 93, 187; Governor Bernard offers to compromise with leaders in election of Council, 92; instruct province agents to oppose appointive Council, 107; letter to agent de Berdt on right of Lieutenant-Governor to seat in Council, 89; limitation of number of members recommended by Hutchinson, 101; militia officers who are representatives dismissed by Governor, 86; reply to Governor Bernard on election of Council of 1766, 185; reply to Governor Bernard on election of Council in 1766 finds redressal of grievance of plural offices, 84, 85; reply to Governor Bernard on election of Council written by Samuel Adams and James Otis, 83; resolution that Lieutenant-Governor no right to seat in Council unless Governor absent, 89; second reply to Governor Bernard after election of Council in 1766 asserts charter right of free election, 85; separation in office-holding essential to independence of, 177; warns the Earl of Hillsborough against misrepresentation of the province, 93

House of Representatives (Revolutionary), certain members called "disinterested patriots," 117; military commissions held by members, 117; number of members estimated at 130 by Hutchinson, 101; publishes letter in Journal on undue influence derived from plural office-holding by Hutchinson, 90

Hubbard, Thomas, 35

Hutchinson, Foster, 34

Hutchinson, Thomas, account of reconciliation between Governor Bernard and the Otises, 183; accused by Colonel James Otis of holding up his appointment, 67; advocates a "fixed invariable" monetary standard, 47; appointed as Chief Justice of the Superior Court, 31; articles on currency answered by James Otis, 47; charged with treachery for drawing conciliatory address on the subject of the Stamp Act, 75; claims seat in Council by virtue of his office of Lieutenant-Governor, 87; commander of fort on Castle Island, 32; comment by John Adams on plural office-holding by him and his connections, 179; comment by Samuel Adams on plural office-holding by him and his connections, 180; complains of too great popular share in power of government, 100; customary grant of additional £40 to Chief Justice refused to him, 49; efforts of popular party to drop from the Council in 1765, 75; elected agent for Massachusetts, February, 1764, 68; election to the Council prevented by interference of James Otis, 92; first election to Council in 1749, 27; friends and relatives placed in the offices, 32; house and personal property destroyed by a mob, 76; instrumental in preparing petition against the Sugar Act, 70; Judge of Probate of Suffolk County, 28, 32; incurs popular hostility by action in case of writs of assistance, 40; letter of House on his undue influence derived from plural office-holding, 90; Lieutenant-Governor of the Province, 25, 28; loses seat in Council in 1766, 82; opinion of James Otis that no right on part of Lieutenant-Governor to a seat in Council or to the presidency, 87, 187; opposition to him in General Court apparent in 1759, 28; opinion of James Otis that illegal for him to hold offices of Chief Justice and Judge of Probate at same time, 58; originator of sound currency bill, 28; part taken in appointment of Chief Justice, 58; proposes Council less under control of House of Representatives, 100; rebuked by Thacher for expression of opinion on monetary standard while Chief Justice of the Superior Court, 47; recommends legislative council triennially elected, 101; recommends limitation of number of members in House of Representatives, 101; recommends privy council annually appointed by governor, 101; report on fees and salaries of justices of the Superior Court of Judicature, 179; reports apparent reconciliation between Otises and Governor Bernard, 52; resigns office of Judge of Probate as result of pressure, 76; resolution of Council on his right to preside, 87, 187; secures copy of writ of assistance as it issued from the exchequer, 40; selectman for town of Boston, 27; several offices held in 1760, 32; total remuneration from various public offices, 34; writes that he is discouraged by inimical attitude of Otis, 57

Incompatibility of offices, of United States office with any state office in a model constitution, 123; by Constitution of 1778, 127; defined by Constitution of 1780, 148-49; by common law, 10; in Articles of Confederation, 126

Inferior Courts, large number of judges members of General Court, 104; sessions altered to avoid conflict with General Court, 104

"J," pseudonym (John Worthington, of Springfield?), 60 n.
Jackson, Richard, 70
Judges, in House of Lords to advise on law only, 43; of common law courts excluded from House of Commons, 43; should be aloof from party politics, 43; tenure under province charter, 19; Thacher's recommendation that they should be released from political pursuits, 45
Judicial office, incompatible with seat of councillor by Thacher's theory, 41; Thacher's theory that incompatible with legislative seat, 45

Lathrop, Rev. John Shipping, 166
Lenox, Town of, states objection to appointing power of Senate and plural office-holding in return on Constitution of 1778, 130
Lexington, Town of, objections to the Constitution of 1778, provision for separation of departments inadequate, 129; reasons for objecting to constitution-making by the Assembly, 120
Lieutenant-Governor (Province), considered to be absent by revolutionary government, 109; excluded from seat in Council under three previous governors, 89; no right to sit or preside in Council except in absence of governor, 88; opinions as to his right to sit as member of the Council, 89
Lieutenant-Governor (State), elected by General Court, 176; exclusions from General Court by provisions of Art. II of Chap. VI do not include, 175; not excluded from the General Court by Art. XXX, 175
Lincoln, Town of, objection to the governor's veto as contrary to the separation of departments, 160

Locke, John, theory of revolution cited in connection with appointive Council, 107; theory of revolution justified by James Otis in 1764, 107
Lowell, Judge John, 167 n.
"L.Q.," pseudonym in *Boston Gazette*, May 16, 1763 (probably Oxenbridge Thacher), 66
Lynde, Benjamin, 34

Maryland, letter of John Adams to delegate on subject of office-holding by members of the Continental Congress, 116
Massachusetts-Bay (Colony), government under colony charter, 14
Massachusetts (Province), Act for the better regulating the Government of, 1774, 108; Act passed conflicting with Act of Parliament dissolving "Land Bank," 29; address drawn up by General Court in spring of 1763, 66; agents instructed to oppose appointive Council, 107; Charter of 1691, 14; Charter of 1691 (Revolutionized), government under continued until October 25, 1780; constitutional conflict, 14; factions developed over issue of currency, 27; failure of control through distribution of patronage, 23; "Land-Bank" dissolved by Act of Parliament, 28; "Land-Bank" formed for expansion of currency, 28; opinion of Otis that oligarchy exists in government, 48; origin of political parties traced to defense of colony charter, 27; people influenced by New York address against the Stamp Act, 74; people influenced by Virginia Resolves against the Stamp Act, 75; petition against Sugar Act not phrased in terms of "Rights," 70; popular and prerogative parties, 27; vacancy on Superior Court bench in 1760, 25; William Bollan, province agent, dismissed, 49
Massachusetts (Revolutionary), constitutions of South Carolina, Virginia, New Jersey, Pennsylvania read in 1776, 125; exclusion of "placemen" from the General Court in Constitution recommended, 127
Massachusetts (State), a model constitution for by "Phileleutherus," 123
Merchants, planning representations against Governor Bernard to mother country, 52
Metcalf, John, 164
Middleborough, Town of, suggests amendment providing the separation of departments required by Art. XXX by taking away Governor's veto, 160-61
Montesquieu, Charles de Secondat (Baron de la Brède), advocates absolute veto upon legislation in hands of executive, 153; basis for theory of separation of powers, 4; definition of liberty quoted in *Boston Gazette*, April 13, 1763, 59; his principle of a separation of powers debated between Massachusetts contemporaries, 60; his principle of a separation of the powers interpreted by Oxenbridge Thacher, 43; his principle of a separation of powers interpreted to require a separation in holding of majority of offices in each department, 61; his principle of a separation of powers *not* a complete separation to Massachusetts contemporaries, 60; his principle of separation of powers referred to in *Boston Gazette*, May 16, 1763, 66; his *Spirit of the Laws* quoted by James Otis, 48; independence of departments a primary aim of his theory, 153; theory derived from earlier writers, 5; theory directed against French monarchy, 5; theory that tyranny the result of union of powers applied by James Otis, 47
Mount Desert, granted to Governor Bernard by the Province in 1762, 52

New Jersey, State Constitution read in Massachusetts in 1776, 125

Index

New York, address of colony against the Stamp Act influential in Massachusetts, 74

Northborough, Town of, objection that exclusion of judges from legislature inadequate in Constitution, 162

Norton, Town of, refuses to assent to constitution-making by the Assembly, 119-20; vote that Art. II, Chap. VI, required additional exclusions of judicial officers from the General Court, 162

"Observer, The," pseudonym of writer opposing constitution-making by the Assembly, 122

Offices, county and local received by "inheritance," 32 n.

Offices of government, loss of liberty if centered in hands of a few persons, 44; plurality in holding detrimental to civil interest as well as to ecclesiastical, 46; plurality in holding discussed prior to election, May, 1761, 46

Oligarchy, centered in the House of Lords in the eighteenth century, 37; control of government by, 36

Oliver, Andrew, draws up report on usage in regard to Lieutenant-Governor's seat in the Council, 89; efforts of popular party to drop from the Council in 1765, 75; his son the representative from Salem, 34; Judge of Inferior Court of Common Pleas of Essex County, 34; loses seat in Council in 1766, 82; member of the Council (Province), 34; Secretary of Province, 34; Stamp Act agent in Massachusetts, 75

Oliver, Peter, brother of Andrew Oliver, 34; Justice of Superior Court of Judicature, 34; loses seat in Council in 1766, 82; member of the Council (Province), 34

Otis, Colonel James, accuses Thomas Hutchinson of holding up his appointment, 67; allowed to "settle" Barnstable County to his liking, 52; apparent reconciliation with Governor Bernard reported by Hutchinson, 52; appointed Chief Justice of Court of Common Pleas of Barnstable County in 1764, 53, 68; appointed Judge of Probate for Barnstable County in 1764, 53, 68; a supporter of the administration, 30; declines office of Speaker of the House in 1762, 53; elected to Council in 1762, 53; judicial appointments under the Revolutionary government, 112; member of the Revolutionary Council, 112; negatived by Governor Bernard for a seat in the Council in 1766, 82; in 1769, 95; prominent lawyer in Barnstable County, 25; sacrifice his offices preferred to election Hutchinson to Council, 94; solicitation for offices in Barnstable County from Governor Bernard, 67

Otis, James, account of his part in appointment of Chief Justice, 58; Acting Advocate-General in Court of Admiralty, 25; a leader of opposition to the administration in 1761, 41; answers Hutchinson's articles on currency, 47; apparent reconciliation with Governor Bernard noted by Hutchinson, 52; applies Montesquieu's theory that tyranny the result of a union of powers, 47; argument in case of writs of assistance, 40; attacks right of Hutchinson to sit in Council by virtue of his office as Lieutenant-Governor, 87; blames Hutchinson for divisions in political life of province, 56; boasts that judges and Crown officers will be dropped from the Council in 1766, 81; Boston leaders in control of General Court in 1769, 96; calls administration of Governor Bernard the "weakest and most arbitrary," 56; comment on English practice of plural office-holding, 183; comment on plural office-holding of Thomas Hutchinson, 183; compares General Court to British Parliament as great council, 55; election as representative of Boston in General Court practically unanimous, May, 1761, 41; friends dismissed by General Court, 1763, 67; states basic maxim in British form of government that powers must be separate, 47; elected Speaker of the House of Representatives, 81; negatived as Speaker by Governor Bernard, 81; instigates reprimand of Governor Bernard by House on subject of taxation, 55; interferes to prevent election of Hutchinson to the Council, 92; irreconcilable in opposition to election of Hutchinson to Council, 92; justifies Locke's theory of revolution in his *Rights of the British Colonies Asserted and Proved*, 107; letter shows no reconciliation with administration, 57; makes threats of inflaming province if father not appointed to Superior Court, 30; member of committee drawing up bill to exclude justices of the Superior Court from either house of assembly, 50; opinion on "mixed monarchy" established by British Constitution, 182; opinion that British government the most perfect form of government, 47; opinion that illegal for Hutchinson to hold commissions of Chief Justice and Judge of Probate at same time, 58; opinion that no right on part of Lieutenant-Governor to seat in Council or to the presidency, 187; opposed to oligarchy in British form of government, 48; popular hero as result of case of writs of assistance, 41; position on taxation of colonies by Act of Parliament in letter of instructions to agent, June 13, 1764, 70; previous position on taxation of colonies by Parliament opposed to that in petition against Sugar Act, 70; proposed account of grant of Mount Desert to Governor Bernard did not appear, 54; publishes *Rights of the British Colonies Asserted and Proved*, 1764, 70; publishes *Vindication of the Conduct of the House of Representatives* in fall of 1762, 55; threatens members of House with defeat at election for support of administration, 91; quotes from Montesquieu's *Spirit of the Laws*, 48; recommends that any representative who should accept office should be disqualified or stand for re-election, 58; repeats theory that Great Britain "a mixed monarchy," 47; resignation from office of Acting Advocate-General, 31, 38 n.; resignation of his seat in the General Court, 67; said to have supported grant of Mount Desert to Governor Bernard, 52; threats in connection with Superior Court vacancy explained, 30-31; votes against Hutchinson as province agent, February, 1764, 69

Otis, Joseph, 53

Paine, Robert Treat, delegate to the Continental Congress, 112; fails of re-election to the Revolutionary Council in 1776, 116; judicial appointments under the Revolutionary government, 112; member of the Revolutionary Council, 112

Paine, Timothy, 95
Pargellis, Stanley, 6
Paxton, Charles, 25
Pemberton, Thomas, 163
Pennsylvania, State Constitution read in Massachusetts in 1776, 125
Petersham, Town of, connection between Art. XXX of Constitution and Art. on Exclusion and Incompatibility of Offices stated in return, 157; objection in return on Constitution of 1780 to power of impeachment conferred on General Court, 158

"Phileleutherus," publishes a model constitution for Massachusetts, 123

Index

"Philo-Politiae," pseudonym of writer from Barnstable in *Boston Evening-Post*, 68

Place Act of 1372, excluding sheriffs from the House of Commons, 73; of 1695, excluding tax collectors from the House of Commons, 73; of 1701, excluding customs officers and commissioners from the House of Commons, 73; of 1705, excluding designated officers from the House of Commons, and requiring re-election to offices which did not disqualify, 72 n., 73; of 1742, disqualifying certain commissioners, and inferior office-holders from sitting in the House of Commons, 72, 73

"Place bills," looked upon in Massachusetts as disclaiming executive influence in House of Commons, 72

Plurality in office-holding, criticized by "Alociapt" in connection with Constitution of 1778, 134 n.; discussion of tendency to develop into tyranny by Oxenbridge Thacher, 181; fear that it may lead to destruction liberties of the province, 60; general rule prohibiting holding more than one office or place in state government set out in a model constitution, 123; instances of by Massachusetts leaders, 188; necessity for it had long ceased to exist, 59; objection to by "Mentor," as tending to produce an aristocracy, 134; opposed as resulting in *too much* power in officers of state, 59; proposal that senators of the United States should hold no other place, except that of justice of the peace, 127; regulation practically uncalled for after adoption of the Constitution of 1780, 174; results in detriment to public business at critical time, 118; under Revolutionary government discussed in press, 117

Plymouth, Town of, states objection to appointing power of Governor and Senate as leading to monopoly of offices in return on Constitution of 1778, 130

Powers of government, Thacher's theory that judges in Massachusetts had "whole" executive power, 44; Thacher's theory that judges in Massachusetts did not exercise "whole" legislative power, 44; tyranny results if one branch of powers dominates other branches, 43; united if personnel holding legislative and executive offices identical, according to Thacher, 44; whole legislative and executive powers not united in Massachusetts, according to Thacher, 44

Pownall, Thomas, 102

Price, Richard, 140, 189

Provincial Assembly (Provincial Congress). *See* General Court (Revolutionary).

Public Works, construction and repair in province period, 36

Rehoboth, Town of, objection in rejecting the Constitution of 1780 that separation in office-holding inadequate, 162

Rochester, Town of, objection to Constitution of 1778 that no person should hold more than one office at same time, 130

Ropes, Nathaniel, 95

Russell, Chambers, 35

Russell, James, 35

"S. A.," pseudonym in *Boston Evening-Post*, May 23, 1763, 66

Sanders, Thomas, 95

Sandisfield, Town of, instructs delegate to Constitutional Convention on separation in office-holding, 136-37; objection that Justices of the Peace should be excluded from the legislature according to Art. XXX, 160; objection to the governor's veto as contrary to Art. XXX, 160

Secretary of State, leaves determination of Lieutenant-Governor's right to seat in Council to decision of Council, 90

Selectmen of Towns, notified to appear before General Court, to give reasons for tax delinquency, 173

Senate (State), upper house of legislature, elective by voters, 152

"Separation" of Departments, achieved by English "Place" Acts, 11; advocated by "Mentor" as method of preventing growth of an aristocracy, 134; advocated by Richard Price in his "Observations on the Nature of Civil Liberty," 140; advocated by the *Essex Result*, 131-32; "Alociapt" finds provisions for in Constitution of 1778 inadequate, 134 n.; argument that *complete* separation not required by Montesquieu's principle, by "J," 61; articles in newspapers for voters in 1766, 79; articles on before the Constitutional Convention, January, 1780, 141; attained by limitation in plural office-holding in Constitution of 1780, 174; Boston advocates that "Ballance" of Constitution be maintained, 72; chief executive office should not be united with that of councillor, according to "T.Q.," 63; concept in 18th Century, 44; consisting in separation of offices forms article in model constitution, 123; debate on by Constitutional Convention, 141; draft of a constitution in Report of Committee of Thirty includes, 137-38; election of Council in 1766 explained on basis of, 93; establishment of independent judiciary universally approved, 176; exclusion of judges from the General Court by provisions of the Constitution not complete, 176; experience in Massachusetts and in England produces in less extreme form than Art. XXX indicates, 167; experience under the Provincial Congress not reassuring as to lack of necessity for, 177; furthered in England by Revolution of 1688, 10; General Court exercises legislative, judicial, and executive powers after adoption of the Constitution, 168; Groton recommends absolute veto for the governor to prevent domination of executive and judicial departments by the legislature, 159; harmony among independent departments of government prayed for by Rev. John Shipping Lathrop, 166; *influence* of one department over another the danger to liberty according to "T.Q.," 64; in U. S. Constitution, 3; in State constitutions, 3; justices of the peace should be excluded from the General Court when their influence appears dangerous, in "T.Q.'s" theory, 65; liberty endangered by single member of judiciary in the legislative body according to "T.Q.," 65; liberty gone, according to "T.Q.," if prince should share in legislation by power of *resolving*, 63; Lincoln, Middleborough, Sandisfield, and Wilbraham object to governor's veto on ground that contrary to the separation of departments, 159-60; meaning set out in "Address of the Convention to their Constituents," 155; necessity for demonstrated under revolutionary Assembly, 1774-1780, 110; interpretation that King has sole executive power, and share in legislative by "J," 62; King said to have share in legislation by power of rejecting, but not of resolving by "T.Q.," 62; no analysis or definition of three different kinds of power to be found in Journal of the Constitutional Convention, 154; not an end in itself, 178; objection of towns to provisions in Constitution of 1780 generally that they did not go far enough, 157; objections of towns that separation provided in Constitution inadequate, 161 *et seq.*; opinions of Massachusetts towns on provisions for in Constitution of 1778, 129 et seq.; opinions of some towns that Constitution of 1778 did not go far enough, 129 et seq.; "powers" used in the sense of departments in "Address of the Convention to their Constituents," 155; prayed over by Rev. Jonathan French, 166; problem in 1780 and at present time one of *how much* separation, 178; problem one of separation in office-holding in eighteenth century, 44; provision allowing member of the House to accept civil office, provided re-election is had, considered after the adoption of Art. XXX, 150; provisions in Act of Settlement, 10; provisions in Constitution of 1778 found inadequate by Rev. William Gordon, 132; provisions of Constitution of 1780 satisfactory to majority of towns, 163; purpose of Art. XXX was to avoid the inconveniences of plural office-holding, 163-64; purpose of framers in excluding office-holders from the legislature to keep departments separate, 156; purpose of framers to maintain departments in state of balance according to "Address of the Convention to their Constituents," 155; purpose of governor's veto to maintain balance of three departments, 156; purpose of principle in Massachusetts, 23; purpose in Constitution of 1780, 9; recommended that Massachusetts provision should follow Articles of Confederation on, 127; report of Committee on Exclusion to the Constitutional Convention of a list of officers proposed to be excluded from the General Court, 190; Report of Committee of Thirty of Constitutional Convention probably work of John Adams, 138; separation in office-holding essential to independence of House of Representatives, 177; separation in office-holding necessary to independence of action of departments, 177; theory a protection against oligarchy, 10; theory said to be produced by "indigenous experience," 6; theory of Thacher that separation would depend upon importance of offices concerned, 184; understood by some to impede processes of government at times, 167; Virginia Constitution includes first provision for, 125; Wrentham recommends that Art. XXX be amended to agree with separation of departments actually provided for in Constitution, 159

Separation of Powers, modern writers on impracticability, 7; problem one of separation in office-holding in eighteenth century, 44

Shrewsbury, Town of, suggests amendment of Art. II of Chap. VI prohibiting feemen a seat in the House, and limiting commissions, 161

South Carolina, state constitution read in Massachusetts in 1776, 125

Sparhawk, Colonel Nathaniel, 82

Stamp Act, members of House of Representatives who showed approval of recommended for purge, 78; New York address against brought into Boston, 74

Stoughton, Town of, instruction to delegate to Constitutional Convention for a separation of departments, 137; instructs representatives not to accept any office without the approval of his constituents, 134; reasons for refusal to assent to constitution-making by the Assembly, 121

Sugar Act, evasion of in Massachusetts, 37; representations against hampered by Bernard's postponement of meeting of General Court, 69

Sullivan, Judge James, 150

Superior Court of Judicature, appointment of John Adams as Chief Justice, 114; bill to exclude justices from a seat in either house of assembly, 50; committee to inquire into question of fixed salary for justices, 50; committee to inquire into tenure of justices, 49-50; Justices Lynde and Leonard resign seats in Council prior to elections of 1766, 81; opinion upon resolution of House of Representatives that courts of justice should function without use of stamps, 77; practical inexpediency of a justice discharging duties of a councillor, 103; report of committee on tenure and salaries of justices, 50; resignation of John Adams as Chief Justice, 115; salaries and fees of justices, 33; salaries of justices reduced in 1762, 49; schedule altered in 1765 to fit in with sessions of General Court, 105; sessions altered to avoid conflict with sessions of General Court, 103; Thomas Hutchinson's report on fees and salaries of judges of, 179

Supreme Judicial Court, General Court permits reopening of case decided more than three years before by purchase of "writ of review" from clerk, 169; judges appointed by General Court to adjust and liquidate principal and interest due upon depreciation notes given to army, 170; judges authorized by General Court to grant new trial to convicted felon in their discretion, 169; judges directed by General Court to deliver opinions in writing on meaning of term "money-bills" in the Constitution, 170; judges directed by General Court to determine value of bills of public credit, 170

Suspension of the laws, power to be exercised only by the legislature, 149

Thacher, Oxenbridge, aim of his theory on separation the independence of departments, 45; a leader of opposition to the administration in 1761, 41; argument as counsel against writs of assistance in 1761, 29; argument in case of writs of assistance, 40; as "T.Q." answered by "J." in *Boston Evening-Post*, May 23, 1763, 60; author of "Considerations on the Election of Councellors," 41; comment on silencing of opposition to administration, 54; credited with defeat of Hutchinson as candidate for province agency, 69; discussion of incompatibility of judicial office and a seat in the Council, 180; interpretation of Montesquieu's principle of a separation of powers, 43; opinion that "whole" legislative and executive powers not united in Massachusetts, 44; opposition to the Massachusetts petition against the Sugar Act unavailing, 70; pamphlet "Considerations on the Election of Councellors" reprinted, 46; pamphlet "Considerations on the Election of Councellors" quoted by "S.A." in *Boston Evening-Post*, May 23, 1763, 66; pamphlet "Considerations on the Election of Councellors" referred to, 106; probably "T.Q." writing in *Boston Gazette*, April 18, 1763, 59; probably "L.Q." in *Boston Gazette*, May 16, 1763, 66; rebukes Thomas Hutchinson, Chief Justice of the Superior Court, for expression opinion on monetary standards, 47; recommendation that judges be released from political pursuits, 45; theory that judicial office and legislative seat incompatible, 45; theory that tyranny the result of union of offices of government, 44; theory that necessity of separation would depend upon importance of offices concerned, 184

"T.Q.," pseudonym, probably Oxenbridge Thacher, 59

Treasurer (Province), elected by the General Court, 35-36

Treasurer (State), directed by General Court to issue execution against collectors, 173

Trowbridge, Edmund, 35, 82

Index 227

United States, delegates to the Congress of the Confederation elected, 172

Upton, Town of, one reason given for rejection Constitution of 1778 that the departments of government should be more distinct, 129

Virginia, provision for separation of departments in Constitution takes form of separation in office-holding, 125; resolves against the Stamp Act influential in Massachusetts, 75; State Constitution read in Massachusetts in 1776, 125; State Constitution the first to include provision for a separation of departments, 125

Ward, Artemas, 95
Warren, James, 117
Wells, Town of, recommends that governor be given absolute veto in return on Constitution, 159
Westminster, Town of, states objection to monopoly of offices in return on Constitution of 1778, 130
West Springfield, Town of, votes that additional exclusions from the General Court required by Art. XXX, 162
Weymouth, Town of, suggests that members of the Board of War be excluded from the legislature, 163
Whitney, Rev. Peter, 121
Wilbraham, Town of, objection to governor's veto that contrary to the separation of departments and Art. XXX, 159
Williams, Israel, 35, 92

Worcester County, proposal of towns that new Constitution be framed by a Convention, 122
Worcester, Town of, instructions to representatives against plural office-holding, 184; instructions to representatives favor measure requiring re-election of members of House of Representatives accepting office, 80; instructions to representatives in 1775 on example of British Parliament in plural office-holding, 110-11; instructions to representatives in 1775 on subject of plural office-holding, 110; instructions to representatives in 1775 on "self-denying" ordinance, 188; instructions to representatives in 1775 state that legislators should not appoint themselves to executive office, 111; instructions to representatives in 1775 suggest disqualifying Act following English practice, 111
Worthington, John, 60, 95
Wrentham, Town of, recommends amendment of Art. XXX to agree with actual separation of departments achieved in the Constitution, 159
Writs of Assistance, arguments of Otis and Thacher in case, 40; bill to prevent issue of negatived by governor, 49; bill to prevent issue of passed by both Houses of Assembly, 49; case to determine legality of, 39; case continued in February, 1761, until next term, 40; granted by Superior Court, 40; hostility to, 40; importance of case in effect on public opinion, 40; issued from Superior Court from 1755, 39; manner of bringing case on, 39; merchants defeated in case of, 41; Superior Court, judgment in favor of, 40

www.ingramcontent.com/pod-product-compliance
Lightning Source LLC
Chambersburg PA
CBHW021122300426
44113CB00006B/260